What readers are saying about
Heaven ... Your Real Home—

Not merely in spite of but actually *because* of her own suffering, Joni is able to give to us her keen vision of heaven's joy.

Elisabeth Elliot

Joni Eareckson has a unique gift for stating the profoundest wisdom in the vividest and most warmhearted way, and in *Heaven ... Your Real Home* she excels herself. Theologically, spiritually, and humanly, her modeling from her wheelchair of healthy hope for the Christian's homeland is pure gold, as powerful as it is poignant. Don't miss it!

J. I. Packer,
Sangwoo Youtong Chee Professor of Theology

What a wise and warm and wonderful book! It will build up many people's faith and hope and love for God and Heaven.

Dr. Peter Kreeft,
Professor of Philosophy, Boston College

As long as I've known Joni, her heart has been set on heaven. She pores over the biblical promises with an expectant heart. Her conversation, her songs, and her messages reflect a heavenly preoccupation. Now Joni has collected her thoughts on heaven in this moving book, filled with contagious expectation, rich biblical insight, and the warm glow of heaven itself. Joni, always a gifted artist, paints such a vivid picture of heaven that you'll get the sense she has lived half her life there.

Dr. John MacArthur,
Grace Community Church

My friend Joni Eareckson Tada is one of God's choice servants of today.

Chuck Colson, Prison Fellowship

Drawing from her work with the disabled, Joni has given us some of the most poignant images of heaven: a place where she will be on her feet dancing, a place where her mentally challenged friends will receive at last completed minds. Now, in *Heaven*, she gives a full treatment to one of the most important, yet sadly overlooked, doctrines of Christian faith.

Philip Yancey,
author of *Where Is God When It Hurts*
and *The Jesus I Never Knew*

Heaven

YOUR REAL HOME

JONI EARECKSON TADA

GRASON

Minneapolis, MN

This special edition is published with the permission of
Zondervan Publishing House, Grand Rapids, MI.

Heaven
Copyright © 1995 by Joni Eareckson Tada

Requests for information should be addressed to:

ZondervanPublishingHouse
Grand Rapids, Michigan 49530

Library of Congress Cataloging-in-Publication Data

Tada, Joni Eareckson.
     Heaven : your real home / Joni Eareckson Tada.
        p.   cm.
     Includes bibliographical references.
     ISBN: 0-89066-278-9
     1. Heaven—Christianity. 2. Spiritual life—Christianity. I Title.
BT846.2.t33   1995
236'.24—dc20   95-12441
                                                  CIP

This edition printed on acid-free paper and meets the American National Standards Institute Z39.48
standard.

International Trade Paper Edition ISBN 0-310-20411-9

Edited by John Sloan
Interior design by Sherri L. Hoffman

Printed in the United States of America

96 97 98 99 00 01 02 /❖ DH/ 10 9 8 7 6 5 4 3 2

For Al Sanders—
This world is not his home,
he's just a-passin' through—

and for Margaret,
who makes his journey
as smooth as possible.

Contents

Acknowledgments

It's odd to express appreciation to a wheelchair, but I do. Almost thirty years of quadriplegia, and almost as many studying God's Word, have deepened my gratitude to God for these bolts and bars. The chair has shown me the way Home by heart.

Great writers and thinkers have helped guide my heart toward heaven. Over the years I have scoured bookshelves for every essay, sermon, or commentary written by C. S. Lewis and Jonathan Edwards, from Bishop J. C. Ryle to contemporaries like Peter Kreeft and John MacArthur. Of course, when I want to reflect on a more poetic view of heaven, I always brush the dust off old favorites like George MacDonald and Madame Jeanne Guyon. I acknowledge here those marvelous philosophers and theologians, many whose fingerprints you will detect on the following pages.

I also express gratitude to a few others . . . Scott Bolinder of Zondervan who has been saying for years, "We'd love to hear what you have to say about heaven." And John Sloan, my editor, who graciously gave me a free hand and a wide berth to write what is on my heart. Also, Bob Hudson for examining my paragraphs with a magnifying glass. John Lucas, art director at Zondervan, and James Sewell, my art instructor who provided guidance as I worked on the rendering for the cover. And thanks to my friends at Wolgemuth & Hyatt for helping to make it all happen.

I thank Judy Butler and Francie Lorey for graciously serving as my "hands" on this project. And Steve Estes for reviewing the manuscript to keep me on the scriptural straight and narrow. I offer special thanks to the women who come to my home on different days to get me up, dressed, sitting in my wheelchair and ready to face the tasks at hand: Irene Lopez and Carolyn Simons, Patti Guth and Francie Lorey, Donna Condon, Judy Butler and Karen Crum. These friends make a heavenly investment every time they patch my pressure sores, scrub my teeth, or give me bran-and-orange-juice. Of course, I can't miss saying "thank you" to my husband, Ken, who tolerated more than his share of Mexican take-out platters while I worked late on the manuscript.

Lastly, I'm so grateful that the Lord Jesus moved on the hearts of so many prayer warriors who faithfully interceded. Bunny Warlen, Mary Lance Sisk, Jean Kenoyer, Pam Rosewell Moore, and my Wednesday night prayer group at church. Also, the JAF Ministries staff who gather together every morning before work to pray.

One more thing. I thank you for taking the time to join me on this journey toward heavenly glories above. And who knows. Perhaps before you finish reading, you'll discover you know the way Home by heart too.

Though I spend my mortal lifetime in this chair,
I refuse to waste it living in despair.
And though others may receive
Gifts of healing, I believe
That He has given me a gift beyond compare. . . .

For heaven is nearer to me,
And at times it is all I can see.
Sweet music I hear
Coming down to my ear;
And I know that it's playing for me.

For I am Christ the Savior's own bride,
And redeemed I shall stand by His side.
He will say, "Shall we dance?"
And our endless romance
Will be worth all the tears I have cried.

I rejoice with him whose pain my Savior heals.
And I weep with him who still his anguish feels.
But earthly joys and earthly tears,
Are confined to earthly years,
And a greater good the Word of God reveals.

In this life we have a cross that we must bear;
A tiny part of Jesus' death that we can share.
And one day we'll lay it down,
For He has promised us a crown,
To which our suffering can never be compared.

—"Joni's Waltz" by Nancy Honeytree

Chapter 1

What's So Great About Heaven?

*I*t was a dark and windy night.

Before returning to the warmth of the house, I huddled against the cold air to listen to my neighbor's whistling pine trees and gaze at the thin slice of moon smiling on the horizon. My eyes scanned the canopy of stars above to locate the constellation Ursa Major—I knew the Big Dipper was part of it, but having only recently memorized it from a book, I had never seen the whole thing.

I searched and searched, and suddenly, there it was, the familiar arrangement of stars spread out grand and glorious across one-fourth of the sky. I had no idea it was so *big*. Nor had I realized how beautiful.

I shivered, feeling small and swallowed up underneath the starry dome that seemed to reverberate with a song. Yes, I could have sworn I heard a song. Was it the faint tune of a hymn in my heart? Was it the morning stars singing together? I don't know, but the song struck a chord in me, like a tuning fork resonating in my soul. The stars and music took my breath away, and before the cold drove me indoors, my heart broke with joy, and I whispered toward the sky, "Jesus, I'm coming home; I belong up there."

I wheeled out of that moment, through the garage door, and into the kitchen. The fluorescent light made me squint as I nudged the door shut. I breathed in the aroma of dinner cooking. The house was warm and softly lit, the television was droning in the living room, and my husband, Ken, was in the hallway talking to a friend on the phone.

For a long minute, I sat in the kitchen, letting the warmth caress my icy cheeks. Outside I had touched a moment of great happiness and wisdom, but I knew I was incapable of holding onto that heavenly moment. Few are skilled at holding themselves in a state of listening to heaven's music. Ordinary things—like kitchen pots clattering, telephones ringing, and TV commercials about frozen food and dishwashing detergent—drown out the song. It is too delicate to compete against mundane things. The music and the moment fades, and we become our ordinary selves, leaving the child outside, and shelving our fascination with the moon, the stars, and the night wind. We consign heavenly thoughts to some other time.

Yet we live in the powerful memory of those moments.

Whether we are adults or children, our best memories are usually the sort which, like a tuning fork, strike that resonant chord in our souls. It's a song we never quite forget and recognize immediately whenever we catch its echo. We recognize it because it is so full of heartbreaking beauty. Like deep calling to deep, it is stamped with His imprint; and since we bear His image, the memory is sealed in that deepest, most profound part of us. Such moments cast soundings and plumb the real depths of who we are. And what we hear is a heavenly echo.

We may hear the haunting echo under a night sky or even in a symphony, a poem, or catch it in a painting. In fact, it is singers, writers, and painters who most often try to capture the echo, this heavenly music that compels us to sing, write, or paint something truly beautiful.

I know because I'm an artist. I have to confess, though, I've never succeeded in painting a picture of heaven. People have asked me why, and I haven't come up with a good answer, except to say that heaven defies the blank canvas of the artist. The best I can offer are scenes of breathtaking mountains or clouds that halfway reflect something of heaven's majesty. I'm never quite able to achieve the effect.

And neither is earth. Actual mountains and clouds are exalting, but even the most beautiful displays of earth's glory—towering thunderheads above a wheat field or the view of the Grand Canyon from the south rim— are only rough sketches of heaven. Earth's best is only a dim reflection, a preliminary rendering of the glory that will one day be revealed.

Trouble is, we rarely let that fact sink in. That is, until we are stopped short by one of those brilliant nights when the air is clear like crystal and the black sky studded with a million stars. It takes such a moment to make us pause, watch our breath make little clouds in the night air, and think, "What is your life? You are a mist that appears for a little while and then vanishes" (James 4:14).

Then we rush indoors to catch the six o'clock news or referee an argument between our kids. The heavenly moment is lost and we think, *Life doesn't seem like a mist that quickly vanishes.*

We really don't believe it's all going to end, do we? If God hadn't told us differently, we'd all think this parade of life would go on forever.

But it will end. This life is not forever, nor is it the best life that will ever be. The fact is that believers *are* headed for heaven. It is reality. And what we do here on earth has a direct bearing on how we will live there. Heaven may be as near as next year, or next week; so it makes good sense to spend some time here on earth thinking candid thoughts about that marvelous future reserved for us.

I love thinking and reading about heaven. But I've noticed as I've flipped through the pages of Scripture—our best resource about heaven—that its language is cryptic. You almost have to crack heaven's hieroglyphics before any of it makes sense.

What's more, I've gotten lost in the chronological chaos, wondering how Jesus' return to earth connects with the millennium, the rapture, the judgment, and the bowls, scrolls, and trumpets in the book of Revelation. How can we pursue heaven through so much confusion or consider our future "marvelous" if we keep stumbling over word pictures of crowns and thrones?

These things only seem to be deterrents. They are actually incentives. The symbols Scripture uses of palms, crowns, streets of gold, and seas of glass are just that—symbols. They never quite satisfy our curiosity about heaven, and they're not meant to. They are only shadowy images of the real thing, as well as guides and signposts that point us in the right direction to show us the way home.

That's what the following pages are. Guides and signposts to point you to heaven, the real home of our heart and spirit. I want to tap on your heart, open up a map, and show you the way home. The thoughts contained here are for those whose hearts break for heavenly joy, or at least would like to have their hearts break for heaven. It's even for those who don't have the faintest idea about heavenly joy but are haunted with curiosity.

True, heaven may defy the printed page of the author, but words and even paintings, like the one I did to go at the front of this book, can sometimes strike a resonant chord, helping us hear that ancient and heavenly song which the morning stars sang together. Rather than let that song retire in the presence of mundane things like scratchy AM radios and grinding dishwashers, I hope the following pages will help you tune into heaven's melody.

Like stealing a tiny sip of stew before dinner, it's meant to be a foretaste of what to expect when you get to the banquet table.

It's meant to point you to the sky and help you see something far, far beyond the constellation of Ursa Major.

Let's not get too settled in, too satisfied with the good things down here on earth. They are only the tinkling sounds of the orchestra warming up. The real song is about to break into a heavenly symphony, and its prelude is only a few moments away.

A First Hint of Heaven

The first time I heard that haunting heavenly song, so ancient and so new, was in the summer of 1957. My family and I had packed up, piled into our old Buick, and were heading west through the country roads of Kansas. Daddy pulled the car over onto the gravel shoulder to stop by a roadside ditch so my sister could go to the bathroom. I jumped out of the sweltering backseat and wandered beside a barbed wire fence along the road. It was a chance to dry the sweat off my back, as well as to explore.

I stopped and picked up a piece of gravel, examined it, and then heaved the stone beyond the fence far out into the biggest, widest, longest field I had ever seen. It was an ocean of wheat, waves of golden grain rippling in the wind, all broad and beautiful against a brilliant blue sky. I stood and stared. A warm breeze tossed my hair. A butterfly flittered. Except for the hissing sound of summertime bugs, all was quiet, incredibly quiet.

Or was it?

I can't remember if the song came from the sky or the field, or if it was just the sound of crickets. I tried hard to listen, but instead of actually hearing notes, I felt ... space. A wide-opened space filling my heart, as if the entire wheat field could fit into my seven-year-old soul. I rolled my head back to look up at a hawk circling overhead. The bird, sky, sun, and field were lifting me in some heavenly orchestration, lightening my heart with honesty and clarity like an American folk hymn in a major key, pure, upright, and vertical. I had never felt—or was it, heard?—such a thing. Yet as soon as I tried to grasp the haunting echo, it vanished.

I was only seven, but standing there by the barbed wire fence of a Kansas wheat field, I knew my heart had been broken by God. No, I didn't actually know Him at the time, but I wasn't so young that I couldn't sense the occasional stirrings of His Spirit. I kept staring while humming an old Sunday school favorite: "This world is not my home, I'm just a-passin' through." For me, the moment was heavenly.

Daddy honked the horn and I ran back. Our family drove away with a slightly changed little girl in the backseat.

I can recount handfuls of similar moments when my heart seemed to be a beat ahead of my body and very much in rhythm with the Spirit. One such moment was a few years after the 1967 diving accident in which I became paralyzed. I was just beginning to get my spiritual act together with Jesus, having been pressed up against a wall that caused me seriously to consider His lordship in my life. Those were times I spent long evenings with my friend, Steve Estes, by the fireplace as he pored over his open Bible.

He was guiding me through the Word of God to help me learn about heaven. Immediately, he had my attention. Everybody wants to go to heaven. We are all curious to know where it is, how it looks, who's there, and what they wear and do. I'm no exception.

I was fascinated to discover that one day I would no longer be paralyzed but have a new glorified body. Immediately I began imagining all the wonderful things I would do with resurrected hands and legs. Swim a couple of laps. Peel a few oranges. Sprint across fields and splash into waves, scale a few rocks and skip through meadows. Such thoughts enraptured me, and sitting there, in a wheelchair and unable to move, I began to sense a longing, a rising echo of that heavenly song about to stretch wide open my heart's capacity for joy. I could tell my heart was, once again, ready to break for joy.

Sensing my wonder with it all, Steve pointed me to a passage in Revelation chapter 21. I couldn't wait to read all about this future God was reserving for us. I picked it up with the first verse:

"'Then I saw a new heaven and a new earth ...'"

"Okay, I'll buy that. This old planet is in bad need of repair."

"'...for the first heaven and the first earth had passed away ...'"

"Wait a minute, you mean everything about this earth will disappear and pass away? But there are lots of things I like. Chili dogs with cheese. The NBA playoffs. Bridal Veil Falls at Yosemite National Park."

"'...and there was no longer any sea.'"

"What! No sea? But I love the ocean. The waves. The wind. The smell of salt in the air. What about splashing in the breakers? What about digging my toes in the sand? To me, heaven *has* to have oceans in it."

"'I saw the Holy City, the new Jerusalem, coming down out of heaven from God, prepared as a bride beautifully dressed for her husband.'"

"No seas? No sand dunes? No Great Barrier Reef? No fields of wheat or sequoia trees? That does it! I hate cities, even if they are holy. Who wants sixteen-story housing projects in the center of heaven? Some people may like perfect urban planning, but not me, brother."

My friend closed his Bible. He sensed my disappointment. He knew that as quickly as the wonder of heaven had risen in my heart, it had disappeared. This was *nothing* like the sensation of gazing out over that Kansas field as a kid. Something was terribly wrong, either with me or with the Bible's descriptions of heavenly glories above.

Sound familiar?

Be honest. Be like any red-blooded, right-thinking Christian with both feet planted firmly on earth. Haven't there been times when word pictures of heaven from the Bible fall flat and boring next to the breathtaking sight and thunderous roar of Niagara Falls? Or scanning the serene Colorado plains from the pinnacle of Pikes Peak? Or swaying with the motion of acres of rippling waves of golden grain? Do you sense that sometimes the musical notes of God's creation almost eclipse Ezekiel's footnotes describing things in heaven as wheels that intersect other wheels as well as move in four directions? "Their rims were high and awesome, and all four rims were full of eyes all around" (Ezekiel 1:18). *Whhaat?*

Reading about heaven in Scripture can almost sound like bad copy in a Triple A tour book:

> *A large set of pearl-studded gates will welcome you to heaven, but be careful of slippery roads that are paved with gold. Don't bother look-*

ing for interesting local cuisine as there is no need to eat while in heaven, neither will you need to look for lodging since comfortable beds, crisp sheets, and downy pillows have no purpose.

Topping the list of scenic points is a sea of glass. However, local conditions preclude sunsets, sunrises, or full moons. Do not miss the spectacular New Jerusalem, a striking city of the future, employing award-winning architectural design. Marvel at its twelve foundations. Stand amazed before its twelve gates, each made of a gigantic, single pearl. For sheer spectacle, the New Jerusalem eclipses even the Emerald City of Oz.

"This is upsetting. I don't understand," I said to Steve.

For encouragement, he flipped to Jesus' words in John 14:1–4, "'Do not let your hearts be troubled. Trust in God; trust also in me. In my Father's house are many rooms; if it were not so, I would have told you. I am going there to prepare a place for you. And if I go and prepare a place for you, I will come back and take you to be with me that you also may be where I am. You know the way to the place where I am going.'"

My friend tried to excite my imagination, explaining that if Jesus is presently preparing heaven, it must be out-of-sight. It only required seven days for Him to create the earth; and, hey, He's had almost two thousand years to work on my room in His mansion.

A clever maneuver, but it dive-bombed. I could only think of the times I had become bored with the most beautiful hotel rooms in less than a week. He tried again, explaining that all this stuff about mansions and rooms was probably allegorical, anyway. I gave him a puzzled look, wondering how that idea improved on the previous.

You can understand why, at least in the beginning, I preferred thinking about heaven from the edge of a cliff overlooking a stormy ocean rather than from the edge of Revelation chapter 21.

Why Do Heaven's Symbols Sound So Negative?

I don't mean to poke fun, but like you, I'm struck that heaven is often described in terms of "no this" and "no that." No more sea. No more night. No more time. No more moon or sun. And what about food, marriage, sex, art, and great books? Do Ezekiel and the writer of Revelation assume that all the other benefits in heaven should outweigh the "no this" and "no that"? Sitting in a wheelchair for decades has loaded me with a lifetime of glorious memories, everything from feeling my fingers on the cool ivory keys of a piano to the euphoria of diving through the breakers at high tide. Such memories flood every nerve and fiber of my being and, thus, my imagination. It's awful to think that the best stuff of which memories are made will have no place in heaven. You could say the same.

"However," Steve challenged, "'as it is written: No eye has seen, no ear has heard, no mind has conceived what God has prepared for those who love him....' Your imagination can't begin to picture all that God has in store."

"Well then," I fumed, "God can't expect us to get very excited about heaven. If I've got to stomp underfoot all the wonderful things I enjoy about earth just so heaven can come off looking better, then count me out."

It was lost on me how so much of heaven's happiness could be described in negative terms. Why did God seem to talk about heaven in terms of what it will *not* be, rather than what it will be?

That's not all. I was also struck that the positive descriptions about what heaven *is* seem clumsy and ungraceful. Rainbow thrones? Streets of gold? Pearly gates? A glittering city 1,400 miles in length and as wide and high as it is long with walls 200 feet thick and made of jasper? It more closely resembled Minnesota's monolithic Mall of America. I was embarrassed to admit it, but even the descriptions about everlasting peace and eternal felicity seemed boring.

My friend sighed and gave one more stab at it. "Joni, you know the Bible well enough to realize it won't steer you wrong. So rather than put us off, shouldn't such descriptions ignite our hearts? Aren't you just a little relieved that heaven can't be reduced to terms we can manage?"

I looked at him blankly.

"Doesn't it console you to think that its marvels defy description?" He paused a long minute then added, "Simply put, there are no words for heaven." Now it was his turn to look at me blankly.

What he was saying was, as someone put it, darkness to my intellect but sunshine to my heart. He was right. I wanted those streets of gold and pearly gates to ignite my heart, not throw ice water on it. My heart wanted heaven to be the tuning fork God strikes. I wanted the deepest part of me to vibrate with that ancient yet familiar longing, that desire for something that would fill and overflow my soul.

I smiled. Then we both smiled. We knew God had not brought us this far only to disappoint me with mere negatives. I was not about to be daunted. There must be positives. The Bible was a book to be trusted, so there *must* be more behind the rainbow throne than met the eye. All this stuff about golden cities and seas of glass had to be clues in some amazing mystery. And if Psalm 25:14 was correct, if "the Lord confides in those who fear him," then it's a mystery that God intends to stimulate me to seek, to rouse and stir my interest until I grasp what heaven is about.

I felt recharged. I decided to tell Steve about that long ago and far-away summer afternoon by the wheat field in Kansas. "I was only a little girl, but heaven seemed so close to me then, so real," I sighed. I described the joy and the wonder, the feeling of space and the sound of music. I then told him I wanted heaven to feel like that ... I wanted a kind of map back to that wheat field.

"But your longings about heaven have to hang on something," my friend warned. "You can't ignore streets of gold and rainbow thrones just because they don't thrill you at first glance. They're the images God gave us—the symbols Scripture invites us to ponder. They're not deterrents to your faith, they're incentives."

I knew he was right on this point too. If I skirted the glittering celestial city with walls 200 feet thick and made of jasper—just because I didn't like the idea of urban planning in heaven—I'd have nothing to hang my faith on but my imagination. And that could be dangerous, if not a little New Age-ish.

"Joni, don't mistake signs in the Bible for the reality they only represent. It's like this: Suppose we're driving down the road and see a green highway sign that reads, 'Chicago: 50 miles.' In no way would we mistake that road sign for Chicago, right?"

"Right."

"We both understand it's pointing us fifty miles down the road to a reality far, far beyond a five-by-eight-foot green sign with white lettering."

This was easy to track.

"In the same way, don't walk up to a wall 1,400 miles high made of sparkling jewels and stop there. Don't get down on all fours to examine whether the gold streets are 18-karat as opposed to 24-karat. These things are only pointing to a mind-boggling reality far beyond mere symbols."

Slowly the light dawned. The problem lay not with the Bible's descriptions of heavenly glories, but with the way I was looking at those symbols.

Steve charged ahead. "Since you seem less than enthusiastic about the New Jerusalem, consider this: Its walls are said to be the same height, width, and length. The city is a perfect cube of 1,400 mile proportions. What do you think that means?"

"That heaven's ugly," I replied.

"Aha! Watch it or you'll smack your face on a Chicago road sign," he laughed. "If you stop with only the symbol, you're right, it's not a pretty sight. But symbols point away from themselves to something else."

We turned to the Old Testament description of King Solomon constructing the Holy of Holies in the ancient temple in Jerusalem, the room where the ark of the covenant rested. First Kings 6:20 reads, "The inner sanctuary was twenty cubits long, twenty wide and twenty high."

"You see," he said, "the proportions are identical, only heaven is said to be about a quarter of a million times larger. Since the book of Revelation insists that no temple is found in heaven, the idea is probably that Paradise is all temple. Just as God's dazzling presence filled the Holy of Holies, so it will fill that Holy City. Only more intensely."

"Hmmm . . . that's something to think about," I mused.

"Exactly! You have to think. When you take time to ponder Scripture, your faith has something to hold onto. Something that's factual and true. Your faith has something to feed on, something from which your dreams about heaven can take root."

I didn't realize it at the time, but Steve Estes had just shown me how to read the map, how to understand the legend and symbols that would show me the way home to heaven. For when it comes to heaven, there is no limit to what the Lord will confide to those whose faith is rooted in Scripture.

Seeing Heaven Through Eyes of Faith

The Bible provides the symbols. But it is faith that makes the hieroglyphics of heaven come alive. And heaven *has* to come alive! After all, you're a citizen of the kingdom of heaven and according to Philippians

3:20, you're supposed to be eagerly awaiting it. Heaven is your journey's end, your life's goal, your purpose for going on. If heaven is the home of your spirit, the rest for your soul, the repository of every spiritual investment on earth, then it must grip your heart. And your heart must grip heaven by faith.

Heaven has been, and always shall be, a matter of faith. "Now faith is being sure of what we hope for and certain of what we do not see" (Hebrews 11:1). Stop and pick that verse apart. Faith means believing in realities that go beyond sense and sight. It is being sure of something you hope for, that is, sure about unfulfilled things in the future. And it's being certain of something you can't see, that is, being aware of unseen divine realities all around you. To put it another way, faith not only makes you sure that heavenly streets of gold really exist, but it helps you see something beyond the earthly streets of asphalt that exist in the here and now.

Now, it takes no more than a mustard seed-sized grain of faith to be sure of unfulfilled things in the future. It takes no great faith to be aware of unseen divine realities all around us. If you are aware of realities you can't see, and if you're certain there are many more realities yet to be fulfilled, you are halfway to solving the mystery!

Let's try it out on a few word pictures in the book of Ezekiel.

The prophet is sitting by a river bank when suddenly—in a flash—he squints at the heavens opening above him. "I looked, and I saw ... an immense cloud with flashing lightning and surrounded by brilliant light. The center of the fire looked like glowing metal, and in the fire was what looked like four living creatures ... their faces looked like this...." Then Ezekiel goes on to describe four heads with eyes, ears, noses, and mouths of oxen and men, lions and eagles. I think.

My heart goes out to Ezekiel. He was just minding his own business by the river when, without warning, God pressed his eyes smack-flat against the brilliance of heaven, a brilliance that the ordinary faithful see from a distance, and then, only through a glass darkly. The prophet strained to find words to describe what he witnessed, but after hunting through his dictionary for adequate nouns and adjectives to draw a picture of heaven, he had to fall back on language that was old and familiar. Thus, the strange pictures of beasts with weird faces and wheels that science fiction writers would dream up.

Ezekiel courageously plunged ahead and put it into writing. God revealed to him something supernatural—a whole bunch of unseen divine realities—but God didn't give the prophet a thesaurus of supernatural words. So Ezekiel had to rely on the language of resemblance. The center of the fire looked *like* this ... and the faces looked *like* that. In fact, the nearer Ezekiel approaches the burning throne, the less sure his words.

You can almost hear Ezekiel stutter and stammer starting with verse 26 of chapter 1:

> Above the expanse over their heads was what looked like a throne of sapphire, and high above on the throne was a figure like that of a man. I saw that from what appeared to be his waist up he looked like glowing metal, as if full of fire, and that from there down he looked like fire; and brilliant light surrounded him. Like the appearance of a rainbow in the clouds on a rainy day, so was the radiance around him. This was the appearance of the likeness of the glory of the Lord.

Did you count all the "looked likes" and "like that ofs" and "what appeared to bes" and "as ifs"? Poor guy. The throne wasn't anything like King David's; the piece of furniture Ezekiel observed was more like "the appearance of a throne." And the Lord who was sitting on it? He could only be described as "the likeness of the appearance of a man."[1]

The same is true for the apostle John scrambling to write down his heavenly vision as he sits on the beach on the island of Patmos. Thus, the apostle's best effort to describe what looks like rivers of glass, streets of gold, and gates of pearl.

My point? Were Ezekiel and John sure of what they hoped for? Of course. Were they certain of things they had never seen? You bet. They witnessed far into the future something yet to be fulfilled, and when the Lord pulled back the curtain so they could actually see the unseen realities, they trusted Him to bring it to pass. Their faith about heaven may have been hazy in days gone by, but once their eyes were opened, realities with a small *r* became Realities with a capital *R*.

Now it's true they had a slight advantage. When they saw heaven, it was a little like standing in front of an arc light without sunglasses on. They couldn't miss it. They saw with their eyeballs what they had been hoping for all their lives. But before you envy them, remember that "hope that is seen is no hope at all. Who hopes for what he already has?" (Romans 8:24–25).

Ezekiel and John saw their hope. We cannot. And this is why the heavenly song is still an echo. It's a yearning, unfulfilled. A longing that is still an ache. But that's not such a bad thing. We may strain and squint to see heaven through a glass darkly, but when we, the ordinary faithful, catch a glimpse, we may be in a more blessed state than even that of a prophet. How so? Jesus commends the faith of people like you and me in John 20:29 when He elevates us, saying, "Blessed are those *who have not seen* and yet have believed."

Jesus says there is a special kind of blessedness, a unique happiness reserved for people like you and me who dig through earth's dirt to decipher heaven's hieroglyphics. When it comes to heaven, if you can move beyond the symbols and be sure of what you hope for, as well as certain that what you do not see is *there,* then you are edging close to the fellowship of prophets and apostles. For although a rainbow throne was emblazoned on their eyes, you can glimpse what the throne symbolizes, and you can see what's beyond, albeit through a glass darkly.

Why Heaven Is Hard to Understand

There is something else we can learn from Ezekiel and John. As weird and strange as the word pictures are, they convey one thing for certain: The whole scene in heaven is very real. There's nothing wispy or vaporous about the exact measurements of a twelve-layered foundation of precious stones.

It's real, but entirely alien to anything people have heard of on earth.

God has good reasons for describing it this way. You see, if Ezekiel or John or even we were able to break down the infinitely high wall that separates "everything that is spiritual" from "everything that is not spiritual," if we were able to scale that wall with the ropes and grappling irons of human understanding, then, good grief, our faith wouldn't mean very much.

God designed both heaven and humans so that a cloud of mystery would prevent you and me from fully grasping heaven with language and logic. The apostle Paul, like Ezekiel and John, saw heaven with his own eyes; but unlike them, he was not only unable to describe the sights, he wasn't permitted! The mystery is *supposed* to remain intact. We cannot fashion heaven solely out of the Lincoln Logs of our logic. Even if we could, we would merely be illuminating the sun with a flashlight. We are only allowed to break through the glass darkly by faith.

I'm thankful heaven is grander than human language. And as for those "clunky" sights in that Triple A tour book, faith removes the clunkiness. Trying to grasp heaven without faith is like trying to admire the outside of a huge great cathedral with grand windows. Standing outside, you see an impressive but imposing structure. The building is striking, but has no real glory. But if you go inside the cathedral—which is a little like looking at heaven through eyes of faith—you are breathless as you stand washed in glorious colors from the light that streams through the window.[2]

Faith takes us beyond the imposing and impressive language of golden cities and thrones, and reveals the better, brighter glory inside the walls of the New Jerusalem. Faith takes the descriptions of 24-karat asphalt and big pearls swinging on hinges and makes us certain that what we hope for is far, far better than here.

How much better?

Look Beyond the Negatives

Remember how I soured on all the "no this" and "no that" descriptions in heaven? No food, no marriage, no moon, no need for good books? *Faith reminds us that every negative is only the reverse side of a fulfilling.* A fulfilling of all that God intended our humanity to be. True, we may enjoy a good charcoal-broiled steak or a night of romance with our husband or wife under a full moon, but faith tells us these things are inklings of better tastes and enraptured delights yet to come. They won't be negated, no; rather, the whisper of what they are on earth will find complete fulfillment in heaven.

Don't assume that if there is no marriage in heaven, we shall be forced to embark on an eternal abstinence. Don't chew on the idea that with no charcoal grills in heaven, we shall be compelled to take nourishment in gray tasteless pills.

Use your eyes of faith. Think of it in terms of "future divine fulfillments." See that every negative is just a reverse side of a fulfilling. Because what is no longer needed for biological purposes, such as procreation or digestion, may serve a far higher, more beautiful function.

This is one of those realities that goes beyond sense or sight. Consider where it says, "Blessed is the man that endureth temptation: for when he is tried, he shall receive the crown of life ... " (James 1:12 KJV). From a verse like this we can infer that when we curb our appetites on earth and refuse to let lust and gluttony ruin wonderful things like marriage or food, our victories gain glory and splendor in heaven. If we controlled our hormones on earth, then fidelity in marriage will serve us in eternity as a triumphant weapon with which we defeated temptation. All this will bring greater glory to God.

I broached this subject of "controlling hormones" on another one of those pleasant evenings around the fireplace with Steve. It was the big question everybody wonders about heaven sooner or later. I was only a teenager and embarrassed to use the word *sex,* so I casually remarked, "What's this stuff about 'no marriage in heaven' supposed to mean?"

He seemed to read my mind, and smiling, he said, "Joni, things like procreation and digestion are physical functions necessary for our life here on earth. When it comes to heaven, I don't think we'll become genderless or never sink our glorified teeth into a juicy peach. It's just that heaven promises something far, far better. Far better than even the pleasure people enjoy in marriage."

I looked at him with skepticism. "I'm not married, but that's pretty hard to imagine."

"No, it's not hard to imagine, it's impossible. Absolutely impossible. We have no idea what God is preparing. But look at this verse in Psalm 16:11," he said as he flipped back to the Old Testament. "'You will fill me with joy in your presence, with eternal pleasures at your right hand.' Faith tells us that the pleasures and the privileges people enjoy in marriage are only hints and whispers of greater delights yet to come."

I gave him a doubtful grin. I decided, though, he was right. My questions about intimacy and food would have to be shoved to the back burner for the time being. I would have to cultivate faith that every negative is only the reverse side of a fulfilling. A fulfilling of all that God intended our humanity to be.

Not only will there be no need for procreation and digestion, there will not—I repeat will not—be a sun or a moon in heaven. Revelation 21:23 says, "The city does not need the sun or the moon to shine on it."

But don't grieve. Heaven won't be less than the wonder you experience over a glorious sunrise or a glowing moonlit night, "for the glory of God gives it light, and the Lamb is its lamp." Even light will have its future divine fulfillment, for it will be a better light, "not as a candle flame that is put out, but as a candle flame which becomes invisible because someone has pulled up the blind, thrown open the shutters, and let in the blaze of the risen Son."[3]

Faith tells us not to grieve. We will not lose in heaven. We will gain. The Lord who has planted the seed of future divine fulfillments in almost every good thing on earth will carry it on to completion until the day He arrives and makes crystal clear all the unseen divine realities. God won't throw any good thing away. "The old field of space, time, matter, and the senses is to be weeded, dug, and sown for a new crop."[4]

See Into the Positives

May I pose a question that will explain something else about all those negatives in heaven? Do you know why a photographer uses a negative to take your photo? He uses it to show us a positive image. It's the same principle when I paint at my easel. Sometimes I choose not to outline a shape, such as a leaf, with a brush, but rather I paint the sky all around the leaf, which then defines its shape. It's called "negative space" painting, and it's a way—some would say a better way—of giving definition to the shapes of leaves against a sky. The artist helps you see by painting what you don't see.

The principle is the same when it comes to heaven: *The negatives are used in order to show us the positive.* On earth, we know all too well what the negatives are: suffering, pain, and death. Show us their opposites, the positive side, and we shall have the best possible idea of the perfect state. For instance, there may be no moon, no marriage, and no need to eat in heaven, as suggested in Revelation 21, but there are also some pretty *good* negatives we can relate to and curiously, they're all listed in Revelation 21 too.

No more sorrow.

No more crying.

No more pain.

No more curse.

And, praise God, no more death.

Selah. Pause. Think of that.

We'd all admit that the sum of human misery on earth vastly out-weighs the sum of human happiness. Job said, "Man born of woman is of few days and full of trouble" (14:1). David the psalmist expresses this in Psalm 55:6, 8: "Oh, that I had the wings of a dove! I would fly away and be at rest.... I would hurry to my place of shelter, far from the tempest and storm."

I'm with Job and David: Get me outta here!

Have you ever felt that way? I can't tell you how much sorrow I've held at bay over the years. Tears could come easily if I allowed myself to think of all the pleasures of movement and sensation I've missed. Diving into a pool and feeling my arms and legs slice through the water. Plucking guitar strings with my fingers. Jogging till my muscles burn. Cracking steam-broiled Maryland crabs with a mallet. Throwing back the covers in the morning and hopping out of bed. Running my hands across my husband's chest and *feeling* it. To think that one day we shall hear these words uttered that haven't been spoken since Adam was thrust out of Eden: "There shall be no more sorrow."

Faith to Find Your Way Home

Do you see it? Are your eyes of faith focusing better? Or rather, can you hear it? The faint echoes of some distant heavenly song? It's whisper-ing that heaven will not be an *unmaking* of all the good things we know, but a new and vastly improved version. Heaven will also be an *undoing* of all the bad things we know as God wipes away every tear and closes the curtain on pain and disappointment.

In fact, I'm going to correct something I wrote earlier. Remember the comment made during one of those fireplace discussions, "There are no words for heaven"? It should be, "Heaven is too specific, too real for lan-guage."[5] If we've learned anything from the prophet Ezekiel and the apos-tle John, it's that heaven is real. It's not a state or a condition, but a place. A place with streets, gates, walls, and rivers. We are wrong in thinking heaven is wispy, thin, and vaporous. It is earth that is like withering grass, not heaven.

What it takes to know the place Jesus has gone ahead to prepare, is faith. Faith in what God has to say about heaven from His Word. For when

God chose to talk about heaven, He did so using the nouns and verbs, syntax and grammar of the Bible. And although He mainly expounded on heaven in highly symbolic books like Ezekiel and Revelation, these symbols are meant to be motivation for our minds and fodder for our faith....

Faith that focuses not *on* the scriptural symbols, but *inside* and *beyond* them.

Faith that develops the skill of holding onto that heavenly moment.

Faith that shows you the way home.

This kind of faith will bring heaven forward into vivid reality. It will bring into vital contact with your heart the things that people call invisible and distant. It will involve your heart and your eyes. If the apostle Paul were here, he would repeat Ephesians 1:18: "I pray also that the eyes of your heart may be enlightened in order that you may know the hope to which he has called you, the riches of his glorious inheritance in the saints."

Step back for a moment, focus your eyes of faith, and then walk with me into a world you've heard about from your youth but have never seen: heaven. What will we be like there? What will we do? Where is this place called heaven and why is it called "home"? Look with me through a glass darkly, and you just might discover that Home is closer—and more real—than you ever thought.

Part 1

What Will Heaven Be Like?

Chapter 2

Who Are We in Heaven?

———

I've been thinking about my heavenly home for years. Naturally, you can understand why: My earthly body doesn't work. That's one reason I dream about heaven all the time.

I can't say my dreams are Technicolor versions of pearly gates and streets of gold; rather, they're more like rough sketches or dim reflections, as when my "eyes ... see the king in his beauty and view a land that stretches afar" (Isaiah 33:17). Like the rolling vista of a Kansas wheat field ...

...Except for one extraordinary heaven dream I had one night in a hotel in Stavanger, Norway. My quiet time that week centered on Revelation 21:21 where it says, "the great street of the city was of pure gold, like transparent glass." It didn't make sense. Gold is not transparent; and it's nothing like glass because you can't see through it. It was another one of those heavenly images gone gawky. I shrugged my shoulders and closed my Bible.

That night, as the cold Norwegian wind rattled my bedroom window, I snuggled down and slipped into the most amazing dream. I saw myself standing in a bright yellow bathing suit at the edge of a pool. This was astonishing since I rarely dream about being on my feet. Usually I can't see or feel my body from the shoulders down; my torso and legs are always hazy and unfinished, like the half-completed edges of a painting. But not in this dream.

I stretched my arms above my head, arched my back, and gracefully dove into the water. When I came up and slicked my hair with my hands, I was stunned to see them glow, all rose-red wet and honey-ivory, bathed in life, beauty, and well-being. I pressed my palms to my nose. They smelled wild and sweet. Some might have mistaken me for an angel, but I never felt more human, more a woman. I cocked my head and admired my out-stretched arms and then looked around. This is hard to describe, but the water and air were brilliant, ablaze in light, like pure gold, as transparent as glass.

Each breath was piercing to my lungs, but with a sweet sting that made me want to breathe deeper. I looked down to see the pool water shimmering like diamonds. You know how we say "the water sparkles"? In my dream it was doing exactly that. The air was sparkling too. Every-thing was flashing, clear, and golden.

I saw a friend sitting poolside, relaxing in a chair under a white cabana and watching me. Oddly, he looked awash in light too. He seemed more real, more a man than ever before. He was my old friend but a thou-sand times more himself, and when our eyes met, youth infused my heart. I wondered if he felt the same. I smiled, waved, and then began swimming, smoothly parting the water with long, powerful strokes. The ripples felt cool and slick, more like satin than water. After a while, my friend dove in. He touched my shoulder and it burned, but in a painless way. There was no need to talk; our smiles said that we were friends for the first time again. We swam together stroke-for-stroke. And the longer we swam, the stronger we grew. Not weaker, but stronger.

It was the most remarkable dream I've ever had. When I woke up, I had no doubt it was a dream about heaven. I was convinced "pure gold like transparent glass" existed. It wasn't a gawky image. I saw it with the eyes of my heart.

New Bodies

One day the dream will come true.

One day, if I should die before Jesus returns, my soul will be reunited with my body. Pause and dream with me....

One day no more bulging middles or balding tops. No varicose veins or crow's-feet. No more cellulite or support hose. Forget the thunder thighs and highway hips. Just a quick leapfrog over the tombstone and it's the body you've always dreamed of. Fit and trim, smooth and sleek.

It makes me want to break up into giggles right now! Little wonder "we eagerly await a Savior from [heaven], the Lord Jesus Christ, who, by the power that enables him to bring everything under his control, will transform our lowly bodies so that they will be like his glorious body" (Philippians 3:20–21).

Our lowly bodies ... will be like His glorious body. Astounding. Like Jesus in His resurrected body, we will have hands and arms, feet and legs. We won't be spirit beings, floating around like angels who have no bodies.

A promise like this, though, almost raises more questions than answers. Does a glorified body translate into glorified digestive systems? What about sleeping? What if we prefer our teeth a little crooked rather than perfect and straight? Will we look the same? And if we do, will we recognize each other? Will my husband be "Ken Tada" and my mother, "Margaret Johanna Eareckson"? Will I wear a bright yellow bathing suit in heaven if I want to and take a swim with a friend if I wish?

Another thing. What about people who died in the ocean centuries before; whose bodies long ago became fish food? Or people who were blown to smithereens in bomb blasts; or pioneers who perished on the prairies, whose bodies dissolved into dust that was scattered to the four winds? Will God vacuum up the winds, collect and sort everyone's body particles, and divvy out the correct DNA?

These questions became real to me in the summer of 1990 when my ninety-year-old father passed away. He had led a cowboy roughrider life, trading with Indians, riding fast horses, and scaling the highest peaks of the Rockies. So it was not unusual that summer for my family and Ken and me to drive to the top of Pikes Peak to scatter my father's ashes.

We found a private place near the edge of a cliff. Thousands of feet beneath us spread a green valley patchworked in sun and cloud shadows. The icy wind whipped our hair and we held onto our wool hats. An eagle hang glided above our heads. Ken opened *The Book of Common Prayer* and read: "Forasmuch as it hath pleased Almighty God, in his wise providence, to take out of this world the soul of our beloved father, John Eareckson, we therefore commit his body to the ground; earth to earth, ashes to ashes, dust to dust; awaiting the Resurrection at the appearing of our Lord Jesus Christ; at whose second coming ... the earth and the sea shall give up their dead; and the corruptible bodies of those who sleep in him shall be changed, and made like unto his own glorious body ... "[1]

Ken closed the book and read a final verse from Romans 8:11, which assured us that "if the Spirit of him that raised up Jesus from the dead dwells in you, he that raised up Christ from the dead shall also quicken your mortal bodies by his Spirit that dwelleth in you." With that, my mother stepped closer to the edge, took her husband's ashes in her hand, and threw them to the wind. I watched with wet eyes as a gust carried my father's ashes up and beyond the clouds.

Ashes to ashes and dust to dust.

Later that afternoon, we talked about how God would resurrect our dad's body. We didn't get into details, but our faith assured us that somehow it would happen. That night in bed, I wondered *how* will it happen? Billions and billions of people have lived on earth and have probably shared the same dust and ashes. For all I know, my father's ashes settled on some field in that green valley, providing fertilizer to feed the next generation. It seems silly, but how will John Eareckson's molecules remain distinct from the rest?

Others have wondered the same. The apostle Paul framed their thoughts in 1 Corinthians 15:35 when he said, "But someone may ask, 'How are the dead raised? With what kind of body will they come?'"

Paul then cuts those big scary questions down to size when he says, "How foolish!" In other words, "Guys, get real. Open your eyes." And starting with verse 36, he sketches a few lessons from nature, "What you sow does not come to life unless it dies. When you sow, you do not plant the body that will be, but just a seed, perhaps of wheat or of something else. But God gives it a body as he has determined, and to each kind of seed he gives its own body."

How Are the Dead Raised?

Have you ever seen those nature specials on public television? The ones where they put the camera up against a glass to show a dry, old lima bean in the soil? Through time-lapse photography, you watch it shrivel, turn brown, and die. Then, miraculously, the dead shell of that little bean splits open and a tiny lima leg-like root sprouts out. The old bean is shoved aside against the dirt as the little green plant swells. The lima plant came to life because the old bean died.

Not even a Ph.D. in Botany can explain how life comes out of death, even in something so simple as a seed. But one thing is for sure: it's a lima bean plant. Not a bush of roses or a bunch of bananas. There's no mistaking it for anything other than what it is. It has absolute identity. Positively, plain as day, a lima bean plant. It may come out of the earth different than when it went in, but it's the same.

So it is with the resurrection body. We'll have absolute identification with our body that died. I will be able to positively recognize my dad as John Eareckson. The "daddy" I meet in heaven will be my dad; he won't be neutered in my eyes, stripped of all the trappings that made him my father. He may come forth from the earth different than when he was buried, but he won't be mistaken for anyone else.

And what about his dust and ashes scattered to the winds? How many of my father's molecules are required to be reassembled before he can be raised? Very little, I suspect. I once read that if all the DNA were collected from the five billion or so persons now inhabiting the earth, it would approximate the size of two five-grain aspirin tablets. The "who" you are and the "who" I am is not that big. It's actually very small.[2]

Besides, how much of that old lima bean was the "seed" out of which life miraculously came forth? The best botanists in the world can't answer that one. No one knows how much of that seed is required or even how life can spring from a dead seed. It's one of God's miracles of nature.

So it will be with the resurrection. God will not have to use every part of your body in order to resurrect it. Anyway, you do not possess today any particle of your body that you had a few years ago. We learn in Biology 101 that human cells are being replaced every three and one-half years. The flesh and blood that make up "you" today is not the same flesh and blood you had in your teens. Yet, somehow, the particular person that you are carries on.

Obviously, God is not as hung up as we are on DNA. Jesus gives a simple biology lesson in John 12:24: "I tell you the truth, unless a kernel of wheat falls to the ground and dies, it remains only a single seed. But if it dies, it produces many seeds." It is no more difficult to believe in the resurrection than it is to believe in the harvest.

What Kind of Body?

What about the second question, "With what kind of body will they come?" True to the apostle Paul and his lessons from nature, all we have to do is open our eyes and look around. "You do not plant the body that will be, but just a seed. . . . If there is a natural body, there is a spiritual body. . . . And just as we have borne the likeness of the earthly man [Adam], so shall we bear the likeness of the man from heaven [Jesus]" (1 Corinthians 15:38, 44, 49).

You do not plant the body that will be. I learned this lesson on one of those blustery November afternoons when I tend to get thoughtful and meditative. I glanced outside my window and spied a fat, furry squirrel doing his autumn ritual of collecting acorns. I watched him sniff each one, inspecting them in his paws, then stuffing his cheeks with the tastiest nuts. Others he dropped on the ground.

The acorns he discarded rolled around in the stiff breeze. I knew most of them would blow away. Others would remain on the dirt to dry in the chilly air. And a few, just a few, would take root under the soil. They would be the ones next season to sprout forth green shoots of new life. These were the acorns destined to be trees.

I shook my head in amazement. If you were to tell that tiny acorn that one day he would be as tall as a building with heavy branches and thick, green leaves, a tree so great it would house many squirrels, that nut would say you were crazy. A gigantic oak tree bears absolutely no resemblance to an acorn. The two, although related, seem as different as night and day. Somehow, somewhere within that acorn is the promise and pattern of the tree it will become.

Somehow, somewhere within you is the pattern of the heavenly person you will become, and if you want to catch a glimpse of how glorious and full of splendor your body will be, just do a comparison. Compare a hairy peach pit with the tree it becomes, loaded with fragrant blossoms and sweet fruit. They are totally different, yet the same. Compare a caterpillar with a butterfly. A wet, musty flower bulb with an aromatic hyacinth. A hairy coconut with a graceful palm tree.

It's no wonder you and I get stymied thinking about our resurrection bodies; whether or not our teeth will be straight or our digestive systems intact. First Corinthians 15:42–44 only touches on it: "The body that is sown is perishable, it is raised imperishable; it is sown in dishonor, it is raised in glory; it is sown in weakness, it is raised in power; it is sown a natural body, it is raised a spiritual body." *It* is sown . . . *it* is raised. We may not be able to describe the changes, but we know it's the same *"it."* You and what you will one day be are one and the same—yet different.

Trying to understand what our bodies will be like in heaven is much like expecting an acorn to understand his destiny of roots, bark, branches, and leaves. Or asking a caterpillar to appreciate flying. Or a peach pit to fathom being fragrant. Or a coconut to grasp what it means to sway in the ocean breeze. Our eternal bodies will be so grand, so glorious, that we can only catch a fleeting glimpse of the splendor to come. C. S. Lewis marveled: "It is a serious thing to live in a society of possible gods and goddesses."[3]

Lima beans. Kernels of wheat. Peach pits. Acorns and oak trees. Examples in nature are what the Bible invites us to use since "what we will be has not yet been made known" (1 John 3:2). One of the best ways to understand the resurrection is to take a field trip after the apostle Paul's lesson in nature: Go find an acorn on the ground, look up into the billowy skirts of the tree from which it fell, and then praise God that "so it will be with the resurrection of the dead."

Can you now see why I enjoy dreaming about heaven?

Somewhere in my broken, paralyzed body is the seed of what I shall become. The paralysis makes what I am to become all the more grand when you contrast atrophied, useless legs against splendorous resurrected legs. I'm convinced if there are mirrors in heaven (and why not?), the image I'll see will be unmistakably "Joni," although a much better, brighter "Joni." So much so, that it's not worth comparing. There's no way I can comprehend it all because I'm just an "acorn" when it comes to understanding heaven. But I'll tell you this: Whatever my little acorn shape becomes, in all its power and honor, I'm ready for it.

I'm ready to have this lowly body transformed. That means I won't merely be revived from the dead, like Lazarus when he came out of his tomb. People who return from the dead—whether from the tomb or off the operating table—aren't, like Christ, able then to appear and disappear, walk through walls, or transport themselves through time and space with a single thought.

No, I will bear the likeness of Jesus, the man from heaven. Like His, mine will be an actual, literal body perfectly suited for earth *and* heaven. Whether flinging a Frisbee or flying past Ursa Major. Scaling walls or walking through them. Speaking with friends or conversing with angels. Whether trout fishing in the Crystal Sea or going for seconds at the Wedding Supper, at all times and in all places we shall be perfectly fitted for our environment, whether it be the new heavens or new earth.

A New Heart

Please don't assume that all I ever do is dream about springing out of this chair, stretching glorified fingers and toes, and pole-vaulting over the pearly gates. However much I relish the idea of leaving this wheelchair behind, that is still, for me, not the best part of heaven.

I can put up with legs and arms that don't obey. For me, hands that refuse to pick up things no matter how much my mind commands them to move are a fact of life. I can cope with this.

However, there's something with which I can't cope. In fact, the older I get and the closer to heaven I draw, the less I'm able to adjust to it. I am sick and tired of combating my flesh; that is, "the law of sin at work within my members" that just won't do as I command. "When I want to do good, evil is right there with me. For in my inner being I delight in God's law; but I see another law at work in the members of my body, waging war against the law of my mind and making me a prisoner of the law of sin at work within my members. What a wretched man I am!" (Romans 7:21–24).

That's why the best part of heaven will be a completely purified heart.

I'm reminded of this every time I recite those beautiful words in the General Confession from *The Book of Common Prayer* that say,

> Almighty and most merciful Father; we have erred and strayed from thy ways like lost sheep. We have followed too much the devices and desires of our own hearts. We have offended against thy holy laws. We have left undone those things which we ought to have done; and we have done those things which we ought not to have done; and there is no health in us ... miserable offenders.[4]

I love those words. And I hate those words. I'm weary of constant confession. I despise sinning. It pains me to keep erring and straying, to do things that I shouldn't do, to always fall face-flat in the dirt, grieving that I miserably offend the God I love. My heart is soiled and stained, and that drives me to the Lord on my knees (at least, metaphorically). What's odd is, the closer I draw to Jesus, the more intense the heat of the battle.

Never do I feel more on the frontline of this battle than when I offer praise to God. Right in the middle of adoring Him in prayer or singing a praise hymn, my heart will start wandering off into some wicked thought. I have to grab my heart by the aorta and jerk it in line time and again!

"Who will rescue me from this body of death? Thanks be to God—through Jesus Christ our Lord!" (Romans 7: 24–25). One day Jesus will come back to complete the salvation He began when I first believed. One day He will release me from the presence and influence of evil. That's why the bad news of Romans chapter 7 is followed by the good news of Romans chapter 8: "We ourselves, who have the firstfruits of the Spirit, groan inwardly as we wait eagerly for our adoption as sons, the redemption of our bodies" (Romans 8:23).

Right here is the highest and most exalted reason that "flesh and blood cannot inherit the kingdom of God" (1 Corinthians 15:50). Entrance to heaven requires a redeemed body. The body must be rid of the law of sin at work in its members. At this present time, the spirit is willing but the flesh is weak. The day is coming, however, when instead of being a hindrance to the spirit, the body will be the perfect vessel for the expression of my glorified mind, will, and emotions. Right now, we wear our souls on the inside. But one day we will be "clothed in righteousness" as we wear our souls on the outside, brilliant and glorious.[5]

I can't wait to be clothed in righteousness. Without a trace of sin. True, it will be wonderful to stand, stretch, and reach to the sky, but it will be more wonderful to offer praise that is pure. I won't be crippled by distractions. Disabled by insincerity. I won't be handicapped by a ho-hum halfheartedness. My heart will join with yours and bubble over with effervescent adoration. We will finally be able to fellowship fully with the Father and the Son.

For me, this will be the best part of heaven.

A New Mind

I look forward to heaven because I've got a lot invested there. A new body. A new heart free of sin. But I have some other friends who have just as much, if not more, invested.

I encountered these friends in a Sunday school class not long ago where I shared my testimony. They were young adults with mental handicaps, some from Down syndrome, others with autism or various brain injuries. It was pretty tough getting their attention. A few were looking out the window, others were drumming their fingers on their desks, and some were ambling around the back of the room. The teacher clapped her hands and directed the class's attention my way.

One or two of them leaned on their elbows and studied me in my wheelchair with casual curiosity. I caught their interest when I flailed my useless arms and told them that the guys that run Six Flags Over Magic Mountain wouldn't let me ride the giant water slide. They felt bad. Some booed. Then I told them that one day, when I get my new body, I'd not only master the water slide, but also snow ski the Cornice at Mammoth Mountain or run the New York City marathon if I wanted to (a few of them laughed when I told them I really didn't want to).

"It's going to be great having a new body." I smiled at the men and women who were now looking with intense interest. The guys in the back found their seats, and the others quit throwing spitballs and drumming pencils on their desks. Everybody wanted to hear about heaven.

"They say that the gates of heaven are made from a single pearl," I said with wide eyes.

"Na-a-ahh!" a teenager with Down syndrome said in unison with a couple of his buddies. They giggled and covered their mouths. "No pearl that big!" he scoffed.

"Oh yes there is," I teased. "And can you guess how big the oyster will be who makes that pearl?" By this time, half the class was spreading wide there arms, trying to size up how large of an oyster was needed to produce a pearl the size of a gate.

I had their attention. I challenged them to come up with other neat things I'd do with a new body. They thought it would be great for me to walk into McDonald's and stand in line. I'd be able to unwrap a Snicker's bar. I could flush a toilet (that got more giggles). One girl wanted to know if I'd still have my plastic arms in heaven. I looked at her a little funny because there's nothing plastic about my arms; but I grinned, shrugged my shoulders, and said wistfully, "No, no more plastic in heaven. I'll have a real body and I'll be able to do all kinds of things, even go swimming if I want."

My comment drew a new level of empathy. One girl came up, patted my arm, and said, "Be careful next time, okay?"

"Okay," I promised. The class wanted to talk more about heaven. They invented all sorts of wild and wonderful heavenly activities. Riding giraffes. Going on a picnic with Jesus. Petting sharks. Earning lots of money. Shaking hands with Kareem Abdul-Jabaar. I reminded them that was only possible if Mr. Jabaar knew Jesus. It was then suggested that someone should pray for the L.A. Lakers.

As their enthusiasm mounted, I finally blurted, "Hey guys, I may have a new body, but one day, you will have ... new ... *minds!*" The entire class jumped to their feet and wildly applauded. Amidst whistles and cheers, I went on to say, "You will be able to think better than your teacher, here. And you will show your sister how to do her homework, even the hard stuff like math and things. You will think high-powered, super-charged thoughts and know just about everything there is to know. Your brain will burn rubber! Most of all, you and Jesus will be together, and you'll have lots of things to talk about."

By the time Sunday school was over, the class was well on their way to setting their hearts and minds on heavenly glories above. They were looking out the window to see if Jesus was coming back, clapping their hands, and jumping up and down. I thought I had taught them a lesson about heaven, but they had taught me what it meant to "have the mind of Christ."

A new mind!

First Corinthians 13:12 describes it this way: "Now we see but a poor reflection as in a mirror; then we shall see face to face. Now I know in part; then I shall know fully, even as I am fully known." We will have the mind of Christ. No need to worry about feeling dumb or not knowing the answers. "We will know as we are known," and our present knowledge shall increase beyond belief. What's more, the shine of our best thoughts and memories will be made more resplendent as they are magnified through our new mind.

But what about the sad thoughts left over from earth? Isaiah 65:17 says, "Behold, I will create new heavens and a new earth. The former things will not be remembered, nor will they come to mind. But be glad and rejoice forever in what I will create." This, at first, looks like a snafu. Didn't we just read that we will fully know *all* things? Are bad things excluded?

Our ignorance or imperfect thoughts and memories won't be erased so much as eclipsed, like the stars are mitigated by the rising of the sun.

Something so dazzling is going to happen in the world's finale that its light will obscure every dark memory. We won't forget so much as have no need nor desire to remember. Bad things will not, as Isaiah observes, come to mind, for they will be blocked out by the brilliance of the knowledge of God.

Only good things will come to mind. Our thought processes will no longer connive; we won't devise nasty words or scheme wicked plans. We won't battle against idle daydreams or lustful fantasies. Rather, our thoughts will be gloriously elevated for "when he appears, *we shall be like him,* for we shall see him as he is" (1 John 3:2).

Think of perfect obedience to the Ten Commandments. Having no other gods before the Lord? Easy, we will be one with Him. I don't know about you, but I would love to tiptoe alongside the ranks of the seraphim and harmonize as they constantly proclaim day and night, "Holy, holy, holy is the Lord God Almighty."

Jealousy? You and I will have nothing but admiration for whomever is selected to sit on the right and left hand of Christ.

Keeping the Sabbath? We will have entered God's seventh and final day, the Sabbath-rest of peace and joy for eternity.

Adultery? I will love everyone as perfectly as Christ loves, and I will never be grieved with the thought that I am slighted by those I love or that their love is not fully and fondly returned. I will find in every person that facet of the Lord's loveliness that only he or she can uniquely reflect—I'm going to be in love with a mountain of people, both men and women!

Coveting? We will be joint-heirs with Christ. We'll have everything.

Bearing false witness? The father of lies will be dead. The flesh will no longer entice us to lie. Only truth will spring from our heart.

Misusing the name of the Lord? Only praise will be on our lips.

Never a hurtful thought.

Oh, happy day, we shall have the mind of Christ!

And with the mind of Christ we shall "know fully." Not halfway, but fully. While we were on earth, we only sort-of-knew or partially understood the "all things that God kept working together for our good" and the good of others, especially in the midst of painful trials. Most of the time, we scratched our heads and wondered how the matted mesh of threads in Romans 8:28 could possibly be woven together for our good. On earth, the underside of the tapestry was tangled and unclear; but in heaven, we will stand amazed to see the topside of the tapestry and how God beautifully embroidered each circumstance into a pattern for our good and His glory.

This will be one of those fringe benefits not essential for our eternal happiness, but simply nice to know. The parents of the little girl paralyzed in a drunk driving accident will understand. They will see how her accident touched the lives of friends and neighbors, sending out repercussions far and wide. They will see how God used the prayers of people halfway across the country; and how those prayers reached relatives and friends of relatives, rippling out farther than they ever dreamed. They will see how God's grace cradled their daughter, forging her little character with nobility and courage. They will see that nothing—absolutely nothing—was wasted and that every tear counted and every cry was heard. "Record my lament; list my tears on your scroll—are they not in your record?" (Psalm 56:8).

My sister, Linda, will understand why God took her five-year-old daughter, Kelly, through brain cancer. My friend, Diane, will see how her multiple sclerosis safeguarded her from falling into spiritual indifference. My coworker, Greg, will realize the measure of mercy God poured out to him after his divorce. You will marvel at the time you scolded yourself for making a wrong left-hand turn at a traffic signal, a wrong turn by which you narrowly missed a terrible accident—an accident that never happened.

We will lift our hands and glorify God when we see how He used the hundred dollars we sacrificed at the missions conference to reach many hundreds in Brazil. We'll see how many times He engineered the right places and the right moments so that we'd meet just the right people—and the happy marriages and friendships which resulted.

We will understand how everything fit. Everything counted. Nothing was wasted. "The Lord works out everything for his own ends—even the wicked for a day of disaster" (Proverbs 16:4). Every jot and tittle of life will give supreme glory to our all-wise and all-powerful God.

Perfection of Body and Soul

Perfection of body and soul can, to some, sound boring.

I have two friends, John and Mike, with whom perfection just doesn't click. They are wonderful brothers in Christ, but they are the robust sort who would rather tackle the work of the kingdom on earth and not get sidetracked with future things. They'll do their God-appointed job here and let heaven take care of itself. Anyway, their picture of heaven is static—a never ending do-nothingness in which there are no more things to achieve or goals to accomplish. For them, heaven is literally the end. The idea of a "never-ending relationship at the feet of Jesus," though comforting, doesn't get them charged.

Perfection? Nah, they savor the spice of a good argument now and then. "Who wants a friend, or even a wife, who always agrees with you?" they say.

These guys would rather help pave the streets of gold with titanium monster trucks, back loaders, and steamrollers. They'll take kayaking on the River of Life any day, and would rather take Joseph and Daniel fly-fishing than sit around and listen to them explain dream therapy.

I'm not about to fault these friends of mine. Frankly, I hope they take me fly-fishing as well. They're just being left-brained. They're into logic and explanations and—watch it—clunky earthly symbols. Perfection of body and soul has nothing to do with casting the perfect fly or playing the perfect round of golf. (Although I remember the time an eighth-grader once told me he couldn't understand how anyone would ever score in a heavenly game of basketball if the offense was as perfect as the defense, to which I replied, "Well, if there are going to be different levels of gift-edness and skill in heaven—and I think there will be—you'll just have to find a few saints to play with whose perfect lay-up isn't as classy as yours!")

But even with that eighth-grader, we've got to watch it. We can't construct heaven with the Lincoln Logs of our logic. We can't forget that what we imagine turns clunky when we rely on earthly images.

To appreciate the perfection of our bodies and souls, we have to begin to get our hearts and minds somewhat in tune for heaven. Heaven is a prepared place for prepared people. Otherwise, heaven is a turnoff.

It's like this. I love listening to Mozart. That's because Mozart was a master at composing perfect music. I'm told that he arranged his notes flawlessly in every bar of every page and even employed certain numerical progressions that reflect absolute order and symmetry in tone and balance. Mathematicians study this composer. He's perfect.

Now if I were to play his *Magic Flute* for a couple of homeboys from my husband's high school, they'd guffaw and turn up the volume on their boom box. Hip-hop and death-rap is more their speed. But it's a far, far cry from perfect music. You have to spend a lot of time listening to perfect music before you can appreciate it.

My point? You have to spend time doing the "be ye perfect as I am perfect" thing here on earth before you can enjoy the idea of heavenly perfection. To John and Mike this, at first, may chill rather than awaken their desire for heaven. But whether left-brained or right-brained, whether macho or meditative, each of us must never avert our eyes from those elements of heaven that seem puzzling or repellent; for it is precisely the puzzlement of perfection that conceals what we do not yet know and yet need to know.

"Duh ... what was that?" I can hear my macho friends now.

The closer we draw to the Lord Jesus and the more we set our hearts and minds on heavenly glories above, the better prepared we shall be for heaven's perfection. Fellowship won't mean sitting at the feet of Jesus and fighting back boredom while everyone else is enraptured. No. Fellowship will be the best of what earthly friendship merely hinted at.

I would like to tell John and Mike, "Hey, don't forget, Christ knows better than you what it means to be human. He sailed on the seas, hiked mountains, and slept under the stars by a rushing brook. He realizes what gets your heart pumping. Remember, He made you. You won't stop being human. Rather, you'll enjoy the full richness of all that your humanity was designed to be. You, with all your propensity for chumming it up around the campfire, will be a better ... you!"

And a better you is a perfect you.

Perfect People in Perfect Fellowship

Heaven's Wedding Supper of the Lamb will be the perfect party. The Father has been sending out invitations and people have been RSVP-ing through the ages. Jesus has gone ahead to hang the streamers, prepare the feast, and make our mansion ready. And like any party, what will make it sweet is the fellowship.

Fellowship with our glorious Savior and with our friends and family.

There are countless people I'm waiting to see. Queen Esther, Daniel, Jonah, and, of course, Mary and Martha. What's amazing is that I'll immediately recognize these people and all the other redeemed whom I never met on earth. If the disciples were able to recognize Elijah and Moses standing next to Jesus on the Mount of Transfiguration—saints they had never laid eyes on—then the same is true for us. I can't wait to meet them all!

However, one person I'm particularly eager to see in heaven is Steve Estes, my friend whom I mentioned in chapter 1. He's a small-town pastor of a country church in Pennsylvania. And next to my husband, he's my dearest friend. Ken is the first to understand and accept my affection for Steve. After all, Ken realizes that in the sixties the Lord used this young man to lift me out of my suicidal despair. Steve understood nothing about wheelchairs, but he loved Christ with a passion, and he wanted me—his depressed neighbor fresh out of the hospital—to find help and hope in God's Word. So we made an arrangement: I would provide plenty of RC Cola and he would come to my house on Friday nights with his Bible to help me painstakingly piece together the puzzle of my suffering. Yes, I found the help and hope he talked about. And the rest is history.

That was a long time ago, and even though we only visit occasionally over the phone, our friendship remains strong and secure. Still, whenever I miss "the good ol' days" or wish I could see him more often, these longings are tempered by one amazing thought: We shall be forever friends.

Our friendship is no coincidence. God has something eternal in mind for me and Steve. How do I know? In Acts 17:26 it says, "From one man he made every nation of men, that they should inhabit the whole earth; and *he determined the times set for them and the exact places where they should live.*"

Did you catch that? Of all the billions of possibilities, of all the millions of people with whom I could be friends, the Lord chose Steve for me. A few more miles between our houses, or a few more years between our ages, and chances are, we would never have encountered each other. But for Christians, as C. S. Lewis says, there are no such chances. "Christ who said to the disciples, 'You have not chosen me, but I have chosen you,' can truly say to every group of Christian friends, 'You have not chosen one another but I have chosen you for each other.'"[6]

This has powerful implications for eternity. Friendship initiated on earth barely has time to get started; we only scratch its surface in the few short years we reside on earth. Its greater and richer dimension will unfold in heaven. God has a plan for Steve and me in eternity and together we will play an intimate role in carrying out that special plan. I will love him as I never thought possible on earth. Wow, if I think my husband, and Steve, and others that I hold dear bring me joy in the here and now, just think what's in store for us in heaven!

How it will pan out is yet to be seen, but this I know: All the earthly things we enjoy with our friends here will find their more exalted expression in heaven. I'll never forget one night when, sitting by the fireside, Steve opened his Bible and took me through a study on heaven. My heart burned as bright as the coals in the fireplace as I caught glimpses of heavenly joy, especially the excitement of a new glorified heart, mind, and body. It was a moment both human and divine. In fact, our joy was so great we raced outside on the front lawn to sing and howl at the midnight moon. We just had to *do* something human to express our divine joy. And minus the howling at the moon, I'm assured heaven will be much like that. It'll be a place where we *do* things with our friends for the sheer joy of being together and blessed by God.

Heavenly fellowship with friends won't be some ethereal do-nothingness where we yawn, sit around on clouds, and ogle at angels. Because heaven is the home of redeemed humans, it will be thoroughly "human" in its structure and activities. As one writer said: "Its joys and occupations must all be rational, moral, emotional, voluntary and active. There must be the exercise of all the faculties, the gratification of all tastes, the expression of all talents, the realization of all ideals ... the intellectual curiosity, the aesthetic instincts, the holy affections, the social affinities, the inexhaustible resources of strength and power native to the human soul, must *all* find in heaven exercise and satisfaction."[7]

Oh, the things we shall do! You and your friends will rule the world and judge the angels. Together, friends will eat the fruit of the tree of life and be pillars in the temple of God. Together, we shall receive the morning star and be crowned with life, righteousness, and glory. Most of all, together we shall fall on our faces at the foot of the throne and worship our Savior forever.

Note how many times I've used the word "together." Heaven is by no means a hangout for mavericks roaming the universe and doing their own thing. It's a place of sweet togetherness and maybe that's why it says we all live in a city, the New Jerusalem. We won't be speckled here and there in rural cottages isolated from one another, but we'll live in harmony in a city. A *nice* city. A holy city!

Dreaming about this makes missing Steve—and many other dear friends—more bearable. It even makes my relationship with friends who have died and gone on to glory sweet and close.

The same is true for you. Read Acts 17:26 again and rejoice that it's no accident that you are living in this decade, in your part of the country, and in your town where you enjoy your best friends. These dear ones in your life are no coincidence. You could have been born in another time and another place, but God determined to "people" your life with these particular friends.

These special ones strike a resonant chord in your heart; there is something about them, some aspect of beauty or goodness that reminds you of God. I have an inkling that when you see the face of God in heaven, you will say, "Yes, I always knew You!" It was Him all along that you loved whenever you were with that treasured person. In friendship, God opens your eyes to the glories of Himself, and the greater the number of friends with whom you share deep and selfless love, the better and more clear the picture of God you will have.

What I'll Do When I Get to Heaven

I grew up in a little Reformed Episcopal Church where they preached the gospel, read the liturgy, sang hymns from the heart, and kneeled in prayer. Banners and candles, processionals and recessionals were a part of regular worship. Sunday morning worship was serious business, and I learned as a child what it meant to bend my knee before the Lord. Yes, kneeling felt hard on the knees, but what it did for my heart felt better.

I don't intend to make an issue of kneeling. God listens when His people pray standing, sitting, lying prone or prostrate. What's my point about kneeling? It's just that I wish I could do it. It's impossible for me to bow in worship.

Once at a convention, the speaker closed his message by asking everyone in the large room to push their chairs away from the tables and, if they were able, to kneel on the carpeted floor for prayer. I watched as everyone in the room—maybe five or six hundred people—hiked up their cuffs and got down on their knees. With everyone kneeling, I certainly stood out. And I couldn't stop the tears.

I wasn't crying out of pity or because I felt awkward or different. Tears were streaming because I was struck with the beauty of seeing so many people on bended knees before the Lord. It was a picture of heaven.

Sitting there, I was reminded that in heaven I will be free to jump up, dance, kick, and do aerobics. And although I'm sure Jesus will be delighted to watch me rise on tiptoe, there's something I plan to do that may please Him more. If possible, somewhere, sometime before the party gets going, sometime before the guests are called to the banquet table at the Wedding Feast of the Lamb, the first thing I plan to do on resurrected legs is to drop on grateful, glorified knees. I will quietly kneel at the feet of Jesus.

To *not* move will be my chance to demonstrate heartfelt thanks to the Lord for the grace He dispensed year after year when my legs and hands were limp and motionless. To not move will be my last chance to present a sacrifice of praise—paralyzed praise.

And after a while, I shall spring to my feet, stretch my arms, and shout out to anyone within earshot of the whole universe, "Worthy is the Lamb who was slain to receive power and riches, wisdom and might, honor and glory and blessing!" I wonder if, at that point, my Episcopalian roots will have me clap my hand over my loud mouth. If so, at least for me, the party will have gone up a notch. It will be a dignified celebration of worship, eloquent and regal.

It's been decades since I've been able to kneel. Those long-ago Sunday mornings at our little church seem so far away. I didn't appreciate then the privilege of Psalm 95:6: "Come let us bow down and worship, let us kneel before the Lord our Maker."

I sure appreciate it now. And the day is drawing near when I'll be able to kneel again. I know it, I can feel it. Heaven is just around the corner. So, do me a favor: Do what so many of us who are paralyzed or too lame or old *can't* do. Flip open your Bible to Psalm 95:6; read it aloud and take its advice. And when you kneel in prayer, be grateful for knees that bend to the will of God. Be grateful you're destined for heaven, for a new heart, mind, and body.

Our risen heart, sin-free will be
pure passion poured
purely
Adore!
He will give us this heart free
to love for the first time again.
Our risen body, light, bright
clothed in right-
eousness, blessed with glowing flesh
that feels, really feels for the first time again.
But now we wait
wait
wait for our Risen Lord
who will reward we who weep
yet still seek Him above all
so ...
stand we tall together
for the first time ever
then fall, please, on grateful knees ...
Eternity is ours.

—Joni Tada

Chapter 3

What Will We
Do in Heaven?

I still can hardly believe it. I, with shriveled, bent fingers, atrophied
muscles, gnarled knees, and no feeling from the shoulders down, will
one day have a new body, light, bright, and clothed in righteousness—
powerful and dazzling.

Can you imagine the hope this gives someone spinal cord-injured like
me? Or someone who is cerebral palsied, brain-injured, or who has multiple sclerosis? Imagine the hope this gives someone who is manic depres-
sive. No other religion, no other philosophy promises new bodies, hearts,
and minds. Only in the Gospel of Christ do hurting people find such
incredible hope.

It's easy for me to "be joyful in hope," as it says in Romans 12:12, and
that's exactly what I've been doing for the past twenty-odd years. My
assurance of heaven is so alive that I've been making dates with friends to
do all sorts of fun things once we get our new bodies—like the following
conversation with a girl in a wheelchair I met at a conference.

"Since we've been sitting here talking about heaven," I said, "would
you like to make a date to get together up there?"

The girl, sitting twisted and humped over, gave me a funny look and
asked, "And do what?"

"What would you like to do?"

"Uh ... I'd like to be able to knit," she said hesitantly.

"Then let's make a date to meet in a cabin, pull up a couple rocking
chairs by the fireplace, and reach for our knitting needles, okay?"

My friend in the wheelchair scoffed, "You're just saying that. Heaven's not going to have cabins and rocking chairs. That stuff's only on earth."

I looked at her in all seriousness and said, "I believe heaven will. Heaven is by no means ambiguous. Isaiah 65:17 says that God is planning 'new heavens and a new earth.' Did you get that? Heaven has our planet in it. A new earth with earthy things in it. Nothing clunky ... no gawky images ...just warm and wonderful things that make earth ... *earth*."

"How can you be so sure of what the new earth will be like?"

"'Cause I don't think God is going to switch dictionaries on us and suddenly redefine what *earth* is. If there are streets, rivers, trees, and mountains in the new earth, like the Bible says there will be, then why not all the other good things? Why not ... rocking chairs?"

She sat looking at me with a wry smile and then her skepticism vanished. She started deliberating of which sweater pattern to use. She learned what most people discover after spending a few minutes talking to me. I take heaven seriously.

I take it as seriously as do children. One morning while I was waiting in an airport, I told my five-year-old friend, Matthew Fenlason, and his little brother, Stephen, to grab hold of the arm of my wheelchair and come with me to look for some kids with whom we could play. We found a couple of little boys sitting with their parents in the waiting area, and I asked if they would like to play a game with us. Within minutes, in the open area of the airport lounge, we started a game of Duck-Duck-Goose. When Matthew tagged me "goose," I raced in my wheelchair around the circle of children, but I couldn't catch him. Feeling badly that I wasn't able to get up and run, he whispered, "Don't worry, Joni, when we get to heaven your legs will work, and we'll be able to *really* play Duck-Duck-Goose."

He meant it. And so did I.

Rana Leavell and I plan to climb the mountains behind the Rose Bowl. Thad Mandsager and I, both quads, will ski the Sierras. My sisters Linda, Kathy, Jay, and I are going to play doubles tennis. Michael Lynch plans to teach me how to dance the *paso doble,* and my husband, Ken, has already said, "I don't mind who fills up your dance card in heaven ... but save the last one for me." I have a whole circle of Romanian orphans I want to take picnicking on the Hungarian plains, and I can't wait to put my friend Judy Butler on a really fast horse and go racing across Windsor Great Park.

Horses in heaven? Yes. I think animals are some of God's best and most avant-garde ideas; why would He throw out His greatest creative achievements? I'm not talking about my pet schnauzer, Scrappy, dying and going to heaven—Ecclesiastes 3:21 puts the brakes on that idea. I'm talking about new animals fit for a new order of things. Isaiah foresaw lions and lambs lying down together, as well as bears, cows, and cobras; and John foresaw the saints galloping on white horses. I have no idea where they will fit, but I'm certain they will populate part of the new heavens and new earth. Again, underline that word "earth." It just wouldn't be "earth" without animals. So, if you want to go horseback riding, meet Judy and me at the statue of the Copper Horse at the end of the bridle path in Windsor.

You can tell I don't take these appointments lightly. I'm convinced these things will actually happen. Goodness, I thought my friend under the white cabana next to the swimming pool was pleased to see me in a glorified state, just think of the pleasure we all will experience to see each other sin-free with glowing bodies all light and bright. It will be the answer to all our longings.

And not only our longings, but those of Jesus.

Rewards in Heaven

You are the fulfillment of Jesus' desire.

You can hear the yearning in Jesus' voice in John 17:24: "Father, I want those you have given me to be with me where I am, and to see my glory, the glory you have given me because you loved me before the creation of the world." My heart glows to think of His delight over our joy. I keep picturing His pleasure when He sees us dressed in white raiment for the Wedding Supper.

In fact, you give Him so much pleasure, that somewhere in the midst of the royal heavenly celebration—maybe right before the banquet or soon after—Jesus will rise, ascend His throne, and present rewards and crowns to all the guests. This is a *most* unusual celebration. For it is not the guests who come bearing gifts, but the Host. The Lord Jesus does all the gift giving.

And these rewards aren't your average party favors.

We shall be given crowns. 2 Timothy 4:8 reads like the invitation to a coronation: "Now there is in store for me the crown of righteousness, which the Lord, the righteous Judge, will award to me on that day—and not only to me, but also to all who have longed for his appearing."

Wow, God wants to award me a crown! Maybe some adults pooh-pooh the idea of rewards, but I don't. The child in me jumps up and down to think God might actually award me something. I remember when I took piano lessons as a kid and would squirm with delight on my bench whenever Mrs. Merson pasted gold crowns on my sheet music for a job well done. I wasn't so much overjoyed with my performance as I was in pleasing Mrs. Merson. My focus wasn't on what I did; it was on her approval. Sophisticated adults aren't into such whimsy, but children sure are.

Nothing is so obvious in a heavenly minded child of God as his undisguised pleasure in receiving a reward—a reward that reflects the approval of the Father. C. S. Lewis said, "To please God ... to be a real ingredient in the divine happiness ... to be loved by God, not merely pitied, but delighted in as an artist delights in his work or a father in a son—it seems impossible, a weight or burden of glory which our thoughts can hardly sustain. But so it is."[1]

So, for all the children whom Jesus said were best fit for the kingdom of heaven, get ready for God to show you not only His pleasure, but His approval.

What does a crown in heaven look like? Does it look like the Shah of Iran's with spotted ermine, studded with pearls and diamonds, or the kind Queen Victoria wore with a cross on top? Watch it, I have a sneaking suspicion we're edging close to earthly imagery again.

Psalm 149:4 gives a hint as to what kind of crown God means, "For the Lord takes delight in his people; he crowns the humble with salvation." Aha! God probably doesn't mean a literal crown, because salvation isn't something you put on your head. Heavenly crowns must represent something He does, something He gives, as when He crowns us with salvation. Anyway, this is more resplendent and illustrious than any old hunk of platinum with a lot of sparkly things in it.

There's also the *crown of life* in James 1:12, reserved for those who persevere under trials. This means God awards us with life eternal.

There's the *crown of rejoicing* in 1 Thessalonians 2:19, given to believers who introduce others to Christ. This means God awards us with joy that lasts forever.

The *incorruptible crown* in 1 Corinthians 9:25, presented to those who are found pure and blameless on the judgment day. Nothing God gives will ever perish, spoil, or fade.

And in 1 Peter 5:2–4, there's the *crown of glory,* reserved for Christian leaders who have guided others. God awards us glory that will never diminish, but only increase.

And my favorite, the *crown of righteousness* mentioned in 2 Timothy 4:8 for those who are itching to have Jesus come back. God will award us right-standing with Him that never changes.

Get ready for crowns!

The Judgment Seat of Christ

"For we must all appear before the judgment seat of Christ, that each one may receive what is due him for the things done while in the body, whether good or bad" (2 Corinthians 5:10).

Uh-oh, all of a sudden this doesn't sound like a coronation celebration. This sounds scary. Especially the "whether good or bad" part. Surely the party will turn sour once everyone sees all the bad things you did on earth. They'll wave you off and groan, "*Now* I know what he was really like all those years on earth. Boy, am I disappointed in him!"

I used to feel the same about heaven back in high school. I never could understand why Christians longed to go there. To me, heaven was a place where not only God would know all and see all, but my friends and family would too. Upon passing through the pearly gates, I saw myself standing under a marquee of a theater: NOW SHOWING, THE UNCENSORED VERSION OF *JONI*. I pictured myself walking down the aisle and passing people I respected, like my ninth-grade teacher, my hockey coach, and my Sunday school leader. On each aisle I spotted others like the handicapped boy in school I made fun of and the girl down the street I beat up in a fistfight. I pictured reaching the first row, sinking into a seat, and cringing as God then rolled the movie of my life for all to gawk at. Talk about guilt and judgment!

I'm inclined to believe that the real judgment seat of Christ will be quite different.

Just consider 1 Corinthians 4:5: "Therefore judge nothing before the appointed time; wait till the Lord comes. He will bring to light what is hidden in darkness and will expose the motives of men's hearts. At that time each will receive his praise from God."

Read that one more time. *Each will receive his praise from God.* When Christ ascends His throne and sits at the judgment seat, I don't believe He'll roll an uncut, uncensored version of your life. He won't wear the scowl of a rigid and inflexible judge who bangs the gavel and reads aloud your sins for the court record. No, that already happened at another judgment. The judgment at the cross. It was there the Father slammed down the gavel and pronounced His Son "Guilty!" as He became sin for us. It went on record in the courts of heaven and then the indictment was canceled with the words "Paid in Full," written not with red ink, but red blood. Anyway, "If you, O Lord, kept a record of sins, O Lord, who could stand? But with you there is forgiveness; therefore you are feared" (Psalm 130:3–4).

Your sins will not condemn you in heaven. Psalm 103:10–12 promises that: "He does not treat us as our sins deserve or repay us according to our iniquities. For as high as the heavens are above the earth, so great is his love for those who fear him; as far as the east is from the west, so far has he removed our transgressions from us." If you have placed your trust in Christ for having borne your transgressions on His cross, then you have nothing to fear. He did away with it. Erased it. Sin no longer has power to wound or to inflict remorse and regret.

The judgment seat of Christ is different. It's not a trial to determine whether you are guilty or innocent, it is more like a judging stand to ascertain your capacity to serve God.

The following analogy is probably too simple for a seminary student, but I like to picture a judge's stand at a housing contractor's convention where rewards are distributed to all the architects, builders, foremen, and construction crews. The judge examines the quality of each man's work. Each receives praise for what he has built and how he has built it. Praise, not condemnation. It's true that the praise doled out to some contestants will be greater than others, but each will receive his reward. And the prize? The judge will say, "Well done! You've accomplished much with these few buildings, now we will put you in charge of a big development." Thus, the architects and foremen are awarded larger and more elaborate contracts. And the builders get to roll up their sleeves and tackle the newest and best homes on the market. Each person walks away from the convention happy, heartened, and with an increased capacity to serve the industry.

It's a little like this for Christians. While we're on earth, we have a chance to "lay up treasures in heaven" and to send ahead, so to speak, building materials so that something of eternal worth can be constructed. That's why "each one should be careful how he builds. For no one can lay any foundation other than the one already laid, which is Jesus Christ. If any man builds on this foundation using gold, silver, costly stones, wood, hay, or straw—his work will be shown for what it is, because the Day will bring it to light. It will be revealed with fire, and the fire will test the quality of each man's work. If what he has built survives, he will receive his reward. If it is burned up, he will suffer loss; he himself will be saved, but only as one escaping through the flames" (1 Corinthians 3:10–15).

I'm constructing with an eye toward eternity, and so can you. Every day we have the opportunity to roll up our spiritual sleeves and apply our spiritual energies toward building something that lasts, in our lives and the lives of others. We are warned to be careful and choose as our building materials gold, silver, and costly stones; that is, service rendered out of a pure heart, a right motive, and an eye for God's glory. Or we can choose wood, hay, or straw; things done out of an impure motive and an eye to our own glory.

We will bring to the judgment seat of Christ all that we are and all that we've done. One look from the Lord will scrutinize the quality of what we've built, and selfish service will be consumed in a fiery flash. Although it's true that no child of God will be scolded, some will walk away scalded from the heat; their only reward will be their eternal salvation.

This is sobering. I can't help but see myself coming away a little singed on the edges. Don't get me wrong, I believe I will bask in God's approval for my service on earth, but pride and impure motives have probably sullied a lot of it. Burnt away will be those times I gave the gospel out of puffed-up pride. Up in flames will go any service I performed for "performance's sake." Reduced to charcoal will be manipulative behavior and lies-dressed-up-like-truth.

But hey, even if a lot of people survive the judgment seat by the skin of their teeth, keeping only their crown of salvation, that's plenty of cause for rejoicing. Look at all the people who trusted Christ on their deathbed with barely time to say yes to Jesus, let alone build anything for eternity. Think of being snatched from the jaws of hell seconds before one dies. Such joy would be hard to beat.

One look from the Lord will consume worthless service. But it will illuminate God-honoring service. Like gold and precious stones, pure service will easily survive the test. It is *this* for which we shall be commended. We will drop to our knees in front of the judgment seat with the words of our Master ringing in our hearts, "Well done, good and faithful servant! You have been faithful with a few things; I will put you in charge of many things. Come and share your master's happiness! . . . For everyone who has will be given more, and he will have an abundance" (Matthew 25:23, 29).

I'm dying to hear those words. Literally. I want to put to death every selfish motive and prideful pretense so that when the Lord's eyes scan my service, what I have built will stand the test. I want to be careful how I build, and realize that every smile, prayer, or ounce of muscle or money sacrificed is a golden girder, brick, or two-by-four. I want everything I do here to be an eternal investment, a way of building something bright and beautiful there. That's how much things down here count.

And no one will be left out. Each will receive his reward. Each of us will have a capacity to serve in heaven, we will have something to do.

Eternal Worship That Is Never Boring

I can just see my two macho friends, John and Mike, the ones who hated the idea of doing nothing in heaven, as they stare open-mouthed and wide-eyed after the judgment seat. While on earth, they always knew they were sons of God, but they also knew "what we will be has not yet been made known." But now, in heaven, they are sons of God in the fullest sense. What power, what privilege! And God has crowned them as proof.

I picture them grabbing each other, jumping up and down, and exclaiming, "Oh boy, now we get to *do* something! We get to serve!" They rub their hands together, roll up the sleeves on their white robes, and ask, "Okay, Lord, what are our jobs? Just point us in the direction, and we're ready to go!"

Jesus may then repeat His own words from John 4:23 and say, "Yet a time . . . has now come when the true worshipers will worship the Father in spirit and truth, for they are the kind of worshipers the Father seeks."

Our first assignment is praise. Our most important service to God in heaven is worship. Heaven is a place of eternal, loving worship. Our service will be to continually praise God without interruption.

"Huh?" I can just see my guy friends say.

And if God weren't able to read their thoughts, they might dare think, *This is great and I'm all for it, but isn't this going to get a little tedious after a while? Won't we run out of Scripture choruses and praise songs after a few millennia?*

Again, I used to feel the same about heaven. To me, anything changeless had a high boredom factor. Anything, even a great vacation at the beach, always had a hidden potential to be boring if it went on too long. I was always happy for good things to come to an end after a time.

But in heaven, praise will never become boring.

First, the only reason we find even the best things monotonous after a while is because of ... *a while.* In other words, because of the passage of time. Eternity is not changelessness (which is boring) because changelessness means that time passes while everything stays the same. It's not like that in heaven at all. Eternity is not many millennia. It's not even a billion millennia or a trillion. Time doesn't pass in heaven, it just *is.*

Next, I can hear my macho friends retort, "Yeah, but you can only be enthralled over truth, goodness, beauty, and the purity of heaven for so long. There's something stifling about arriving at perfection; we almost preferred the thrill of getting here rather than arriving. Heaven is so, so ... final!"

You could only say this if you conceive of truth, goodness, or even eternity and heaven as static and abstract. It's not. Truth and goodness, eternity and heaven—yes, God Himself—are not static, but dynamic. Not abstract, but concrete. More real than anything we have ever touched or tasted on earth. Remember, we are wrong in thinking heaven is wispy, thin, and vaporous. It is earth that is like withering grass, not heaven.

In C. S. Lewis's *The Great Divorce*, there is a dialogue between a confused ghost from hell and a heavenly spirit who is trying to teach him about the concreteness of eternity. The heavenly spirit begins ...

"Will you come with me to the mountains?"

"I should require some assurances ... an atmosphere of free inquiry ..."

"No ... no atmosphere of inquiry, for I will bring you to the land not of questions but of answers, and you shall see the face of God."

"Ah, but ... for me there is no such thing as a final answer ... you must feel yourself that there is something stifling about the idea of finality ... to travel hopefully is better than to arrive ... what is more soul-destroying than stagnation?"

"You think that, because hitherto you have experienced truth only with the abstract intellect. I will bring you where you can taste it like honey and be embraced by it as by a bridegroom. Your thirst shall be quenched."[2]

In heaven, praise won't be inert and abstract, like the impression you have when you hear a musty old hymn sung by a handful of stone-faced worshipers in a huge cathedral. Or like the feeling you get when singing a praise chorus for the hundredth time. Even the most beautiful Scripture choruses wear out after a while and you moan, "We've sung that a zillion times. Can't we sing something new?" Our heart really doesn't care if the song itself is new—some of the oldest hymns of the church are still fresh—but our heart cannot tolerate words or songs of praise that have dug ruts over the passage of time. If joy and satisfaction aren't in your worship, then you know you're missing the mark. You want to offer something fresh that hits home in the heart of God.

In heaven, praise will never be empty or short of its target. Worship won't be suspended between us at point A and God at point B. This kind of praise may be endured on earth, but it's hanging in the breeze when it comes to heaven.

Praise in heaven will have substance. We shall eat from the tree of life.

Taste hidden manna like honey.

Smell truth like a flower.

Wear righteousness like light.

Hold the morning star like a scepter.

Shine like the stars of the heavens.

Enter into the joy of the Lord.

There's nothing inert or abstract about those verbs. Everything in heaven will have more substance than we ever dreamed.

In eternal praise, the thrill of getting there will be more than matched by what we see, hold, taste, and wear when we arrive. For John and Mike, the thrill will include not only climbing the mountain, but enjoying the view from the top, and doing both at the same time. We shall travel hopefully and arrive, as it were, all at the same moment—we will no longer desire our God who is absent, but rejoice in our God who is present.

Why We Will Praise Him Forever

Next, our worship of God will never end. It's like the excitement I used to feel as a child when my father would read me a story. To me, the beginning was always the most fascinating part. It was fresh. That's because the beginning touches something timeless that no events in time can tarnish. Unfortunately, as the story progressed, my interest frittered away, along with my wonder.

Except for one fairy tale. In C. S. Lewis's *Last Battle*—the conclusion of *The Chronicles of Narnia* series—there wasn't the usual "and they lived happily ever after." Instead, on the last page, after scores of exhilarating adventures and journeys in all the previous books, C. S. Lewis wrote that now he had come to the beginning of the real story. All the previous chapters of adventures in Narnia had only been the cover and the title page. The real Chapter One was about to begin, a story no one on earth had ever read, which would go on forever and ever with each chapter better than the last.

As a child, I remember thinking, *You mean all that's happened up until now has only been the preface to the real story? All the good stuff was only foreshadowing a greater story!* The wonder was back. I was at the beginning again.

Most people wish it were like that in real life. Just as in a story, people labor through chapter after chapter of their lives, and the fascination and wonder they felt as a child fade as the years go by in a succession of events. We grow tired and weary, never able to grasp the dreams that enthralled us at the beginning. The state that we long for is never quite embodied. And so, our interest fritters away.

But for Christians, all the things that stir our interest about eternity *will be embodied.* We shall behold the Lamb. Savor purity. Touch truth. Be clothed in righteousness. Like a grand story, it will always be an enchanting beginning. Or better yet, the end *and* the beginning, as God is both Alpha and Omega, the First and the Last, the Beginning and the End.

Little wonder flesh and blood cannot inherit heaven. To be at both the beginning and the end, or to wear righteousness like a bright raiment, requires a complete metamorphosis. Like a caterpillar becoming a butterfly or a peach pit becoming a blossoming tree. Our earthly bodies would never be able to contain the joy or express the praise. Our fleshly hearts and minds could never hold it all. Heavenly worship would split the seams and break the human container. We're not talking shedding snakeskins here, we're talking radical transformation. We little caterpillars and peach pits need to go from death to life so that our glorified bodies and hearts are fit for the filling and overflowing of ecstatic praise. As Jesus declared, "I tell you the truth, unless a man is born again, he cannot see the kingdom of God" (John 3:3).

No, praise will not be something we will be assigned or commanded to do; it will be natural. Rather, a supernatural effervescent response of the born-again creature, new and fit for heaven. Professor E. L. Maskell puts it this way: "We do not praise God because it does us good, though no doubt it does. Nor do we praise Him because it does Him good, for in fact it does not. Praise is thus strictly ecstatic in the sense that it takes us wholly out of ourselves; it is purely and solely directed upon God. It takes our attention entirely off ourself and concentrates it entirely upon Him."[3]

I can't wait! I get so sick and tired of thinking about myself. I sometimes feel like the self-absorbed woman in the movie *Beaches* who says to her friend, "Enough talk about me ... let's talk about you. Tell me, what do *you* think about me?" Ever feel that way? Well, in heaven, self-forgetfulness will be second nature; thus, nothing will be tedious. Praise would only be boring if we were able to stop and look at ourselves to see how we were doing, how we were sounding or performing; but such self-consciousness will be foreign in heaven. The crowning glory for us will be in losing ourselves and yet finding ourselves in the Alpha and the Omega. This is pure praise. Total preoccupation with God.

Finally, because we will be one with Him, and full of light as He is, our bright, dazzling bodies can't help but be shot through with the glory of God. After all, "glory" is the reflection of God's essential being, whether holiness, justice, compassion, or mercy. Whenever He reveals Himself in any of these qualities on earth or in heaven, we say that He is "glorifying Himself." And in heaven, we, like diamonds, will give off prism-like praise as every facet of our being reflects His Shekinah glory. It will be impossible *not* to praise Him. Daniel 12:3 turns on the light switch when it says, "Those who are wise will shine like the brightness of the heavens, and those who lead many to righteousness, like the stars for ever and ever."

Remember my dream in which everything—the air, water, and my body—dazzled with light? I don't think my dream is that far off from the real heaven. Heaven will shine by the Lamb who is the Lamp. Light will so much *be* in heaven that "the moon will be abashed, the sun ashamed; for the Lord Almighty will reign on Mount Zion and in Jerusalem, and before its elders, *gloriously*" (Isaiah 24:23). God's glory and His light go hand in hand. Heaven is a place full of glory, light, and praise.

My macho guy friends will, with every other redeemed person, happily transcend the time warp to be a part of that "great multitude that no one could count, from every nation, tribe, people and language, standing before the throne and in front of the Lamb. They were wearing white robes and were holding palm branches in their hands. And they cried out in a loud voice: 'Salvation belongs to our God, who sits on the throne, and to the Lamb'" (Revelation 7:9–10).

Who can find words for such worship? What thesaurus has the nouns or adjectives to convey "eating" life like fruit from a tree or "tasting" the Bread of Heaven? I want to lift up my hands and whisper, "Oh, the depth of the riches of the wisdom and knowledge of God! How unsearchable his judgments, and his paths beyond tracing out!... For from him and through him and to him are all things. To him be the glory forever! Amen" (Romans 11:33, 36).

Serving God by Reigning with Him

I have a confession. I'm more like my friends John and Mike than I've admitted. Just spend a few weeks with me and you'll understand. I love rolling up my sleeves down here on earth and pouring myself into serving God. I'm less of a human being, and more of a human *doing*. Visiting hospitals, advocating on issues, shopping for dinner, traveling in ministry, relating in marriage, painting at my easel, writing at my computer, working on radio programs, counseling on the phone, helping with Sunday school, and ad infinitum.

I'm also a perfectionist. If a painting is not up to par, it's shoved aside. If an article is not up to snuff, it's dumped in the trash. If a friendship is injured, it's painstakingly repaired. If my marriage is hurting, everything else gets canceled and Ken gets priority. If I feel a speech I give falls flat, I berate myself endlessly, thinking, *Why did I say that?... Why didn't I say this?* There have been days when I've thrown up my hands and sighed, "What's the use. I've blown it again!"

A lot of this pressure, because it is self-imposed, is unnecessary. However, some of it is real and needed. That's because God imposes pressure when He knows I've approached service to Him with a lazy, nonchalant attitude.

But in heaven, there will be no failure in service. No disappointment in doing. We will never struggle with failing to do the task God puts before us, as in a failed marriage or mission. We will never fall short of meeting our responsibilities.

And, boy, will we *do!* John and Mike will be on cloud nine, but only for a short time, because they will be busier than they ever were on earth. No idling away eternity strolling streets of gold. No passing time while plucking harps by the glassy sea. We will have jobs to do. I can hardly hold back the tears thinking of my friend, Cornelius, who has been bedridden for fifteen years, unable to lift a finger to do an ounce of work. I can just see this man now in his glorified body leaving John and Mike in the dust as he tackles all the labor he missed out on those many years on earth. We will serve God through worship and work—exciting work of which we never grow tired.

For me, this will be heaven. I love serving God. And if we've been faithful in earthly service, our responsibility in heaven will increase proportionately. No, I take that back. It won't be increased in proportion. God's too generous for that. Our service will increase completely out of proportion. It doesn't take a rocket scientist to read the formula Jesus gives in His heaven parable in Luke 19:17: "'Well done, my good servant!' his master replied. 'Because you have been trustworthy in a very small matter, take charge of ten cities.'"

Stop and read that again. Ten cities? In exchange for faithfulness in a very small matter? Whoa! When it comes to blessing us, Jesus goes beyond basic math and gets into calculus. Those who are faithful in a few minor things will be put in charge over multitudinous things.

Were you faithful in your marriage or a mission? Even if only in a small way? God is already thinking exponentially, as in His "ten cities" equation. He generously raises your capacity for service to the "nth" degree. The more faithful you are in this life, the more responsibility you will be given in the life to come.

Please note Jesus doesn't say, "Because you've been successful in a very small matter," He says, "Because you've been *trustworthy*." God is not scrutinizing the success of your marriage or judging the results of your mission. You could have spent forty-five years in marriage, forty of which you were hanging in there by a promise and a prayer. You could have invested twenty-five years sharing the gospel in the outback of Mozambique with only a handful of converts to show for it. When it comes to the judgment seat, God won't pull out the return-on-investment charts and do a cost-effectiveness analysis on your earthly service. Every Christian is on the same playing field. Success isn't the key. Faithfulness is. Being bigger and better is not the point. It's being obedient.

The more trustworthy you've been, the greater your service in eternity. Here's where our two buddies will shine!

Here's where we get to serve and be busier than we ever were on earth. For we not only get to praise Him forever, but we get to reign with Him forever. "To him who overcomes, I will give the right to sit with me on my throne, just as I overcame and sat down with my Father on his throne" (Revelation 3:21). Can you believe it? We will sit with Christ on His throne and reign with Him. We will be given a sphere of authority and oversight of God's eternal kingdom.

We get to reign with Him, plus more.

We are more than kings? Yes, we're sons and heirs. Romans 8:17 elevates us to an incredible position, saying, "Now if we are children, then we are heirs—heirs of God and co-heirs with Christ." Just imagine, we will sit with Christ on His throne, and we will join Him in overseeing His and our inheritance. We inherit what our elder Brother inherits. And Psalm 2:8–9 reads like His title deed: "Ask of me, and I will make the nations your inheritance, the ends of the earth your possession. You will rule them with an iron scepter." We're not talking a few acres on the back of the farm. Our sphere of authority will be heaven and earth.

We get to reign over earth with Christ!

Ruling Over Earth

I wish I understood the specifics, but God hasn't revealed them all. A hint is whispered in Revelation chapter 20 where we are "priests of God and of Christ and will reign with him for a thousand years," and in Isaiah 11 where "with righteousness he will judge the needy, with justice he will give decisions for the poor of the earth."

Time and again, the words "inheritance," "earth," and "reign" appear together. Flip through the Old Testament and you see repeated references to God's Anointed personally administering justice, uplifting the oppressed, or ruling with a rod of iron. The particulars may not be laid out, but there's one hint we're supposed to get: We will reign with Christ over the earth.

It's not clear if it's this earth or what the Bible calls "the new earth." But I do know that the pièce de résistance of God's creation, this jewel of a planet, will not be abandoned. It will not be left to go spinning off in space. God doesn't waste things, He redeems them and Romans 8:20–21 reveals the Lord's intentions for this beautiful blue marble: "For the creation was subjected to frustration, not by its own choice, but by the will of the one who subjected it, in hope that *the creation itself will be liberated from its bondage to decay and brought into the glorious freedom of the children of God.*"

The whole creation, like us, "is groaning as in the pains of childbirth right up to the present time" (Romans 8:22). I sense this whenever I see smog, a junkyard, and dead raccoons in the road. When I drive the coastal mountains just a stone's throw from where I live and marvel at the jutted, jagged rocks and canyons, I'm vividly aware I'm in the middle of earthquake country (the Northridge quake of 1994 felt like one of those "pangs of childbirth"). Mud slides and fires happen all the time around here. These hills are restless. They're also scarred by the improbable palaces of Malibu movie stars who litter the landscape with satellite dishes. My heart breaks for these mountains and trees (and movie stars!) to be liberated from their bondage.

This is the earth that Christ will bring into His glorious freedom. Can you hear the sighing in the wind? Can you feel the heavy silence in the mountains? Can you sense the restless longing in the sea? Can you see it in the woeful eyes of an animal? Something's coming ... something better.

If you want to know exactly what this "something" is, study Revelation and Isaiah. Delve into the hermeneutics. Scrutinize the eschatology. I have to confess I've never had the benefit of going to seminary, and I can't cut as straight a theological line as I'd like, but I'm satisfied just to know that heaven involves earth, old or new. It intrigues me to think that after Christ comes back for us, we may inhabit this very planet again. The paths that I wheel over in my chair now may well be the same ones my glorified feet will walk on when Christ reigns.

If so, then the mountains of the Sierras will actually be the ones Thad and I will ski. And the rambling mountain paths behind the Rose Bowl will, in fact, be trod by the heavenly feet of my friend and me. That is, if Thad, Rana, or others want time-out from their thrilling escapades in far corners of the universe!

The possibilities are endless, as well as exhilarating. Maybe our reign on earth will include lifting up the poor and the needy of Kurdistan, reforesting the hills of Lebanon, helping to judge the wicked, or planting trees along the Amazon. How about clearing the courts of corruption and schooling judges on godly wisdom? How about clearing the slums of Rio de Janeiro or getting rid of nuclear waste? Maybe we'll teach the nations how to worship God, as well as a new definition of peace and how to beat their swords into plowshares. Shall we do a patch job on the ozone layer and make the Blue Danube absolute azure rather than mud-brown? Cut government fat, get rid of red tape, and show everyone that a theocracy is the only rule in town?

One thing's for sure. There will be no shelters for the homeless (no homeless men and women!). No orphanages or mental hospitals. No abortion clinics. And no nursing homes for old people.

In the midst of it all, the glittering capital city of heaven, the New Jerusalem, will be set like a gleaming pearl. Kings and princes will pour into the Holy City from the far corners of the earth to pay homage. The image blows my mind, but it's laid out as clear as crystal glass in Revelation 21.

I realize this raises more questions than answers. Like, who are all these people who have to be ruled with a rod of iron? After the return to earth of the Lord Jesus and His saints, what are all those other folks still doing on earth? People who are wicked and need to be judged or the poor who have to be lifted up? Why are they still hanging around if heaven has come to earth?

Theologians are the ones who tackle questions like these all the time. Some scholars say that after the dead in Christ are raised at His return to earth, we will reign with Him over the people of this planet for a thousand years. At the close of this period, the devil will incite one last rebellion, which will kick off Armageddon. God's armies will win, the devil will lose, wicked people will be resurrected, the Book of Life will be opened, and the Day of Judgment will have come. After the final destruction of that old serpent and his wicked hordes, earth will be consumed in fire, cleansed, and made new and fit for eternal habitation. Got that?

Other scholars assert that when the Lord Jesus comes to earth as King of Kings, time will end after an immediate Armageddon, the defeat of Satan, the judgment of the dead, and a fiery holocaust that incinerates all of the earth and space beyond. When the smokes clears, the Lord and His saints will set up the eternal kingdom in the new heavens and new earth.

Whew, I'm glad theologians study these things! How the earth, whether new or old, fits into God's heavenly scheme of things, I can't say for certain. I tend toward the view that we shall reign with Christ on this earth for a thousand years, this period being a kind of vestibule to heaven. But all I really need to know is "we are looking forward to a new heaven and a new earth, the home of righteousness" (2 Peter 3:13). Heaven will feel like home. I will be a co-heir with Christ.... I will help rule in the new heavens and the new earth ... and I will be busier and happier in service than I ever dreamed possible.

And you will be too.

It's More Real than We Can Imagine

You know what thrills me most about reigning with Christ on earth? It's concrete. Heaven is not some never-neverland of thin, ghostly shapes and clouds. It's not a place where you can poke your finger through people only to discover that they are spacy spirit beings you can't really hug or hold. No way!

Just writing the last few pages has invigorated my excitement over how like the Rock of Gibraltar heaven is. We shall touch and taste, rule and reign, move and run, laugh and never have reason to cry.

Maybe years ago I assumed heaven was a misty, nebulous home for angels and—gulp!—humans, but not now. I get tickled thinking about how rock-solid real heaven is, and how much of a home—much more so than earth—it will be. Every time I want to visualize just how dynamic and definite heaven is, I flip through the pages of C. S. Lewis' *The Great Divorce,* a fantasy in which unredeemed people take a day excursion by bus to the bright borders of heaven. Listen to their words when they take an amazing peek at heaven:

> It was the light, the grass, the trees that were different; made of some different substance, so much solider than things in our country...
>
> I saw people coming to meet us. Because they were bright I saw them while they were still very distant ... the earth shook under their tread as their strong feet sank into the wet turf. A tiny haze and a sweet smell went up where they had crushed the grass and scattered the dew ... the robes did not disguise the massive grandeur of muscle and the radiant smoothness of flesh ... no one struck me as being of any particular age. One gets glimpses even in our country of that which is ageless—heavy thought in the face of an infant, and frolic childhood in that of a very old man. Here it was all like that.[4]

A real reign on a real earth.
And our Savior, our King of Kings, leading the way.
But watch out, wait till you see what we do out beyond this planet!

Chapter 4

Where Is Heaven and What Is It Like?

---

*T*he shadows of night were deep. Dawn was hardly a hint on the horizon. Suddenly, the stillness of night was shattered as our bedroom window rattled from two thunderous jolts: "Boom! Boom!"

A relaxed smile spread across my face even though I was half asleep. I knew it meant the space shuttle had just reentered earth's atmosphere and the astronauts would soon land at Edwards Air Force Base on the edge of California's Mojave Desert.

I glanced out my window to see the night still ablaze with a parade of brilliant stars, messengers of light kindling bonfires of victory all across the sky. I laid there almost envious of the astronauts who had touched the skirts of space that week. For a while, they had been friends of the stars, tickling the toes of the universe from earth's atmosphere. I yawned a prayer before I drifted back to sleep: "Soon, Jesus, I'll be up there ... so far beyond ... and even spacemen won't be able to catch me."

The universe fascinates me. If there's a program about stars or space exploration on The Discovery Channel, I'm tuned in. Whenever the space shuttle is in orbit, you can find me fixated to the NASA video feed on cable television—I lie in bed and pray over the nations of the world as a little icon of the shuttle moves slowly across a map of the planet.

I watched CNN when the *Endeavor* astronauts walked in space to make repairs on the Hubble space telescope. Beneath their floating figures lay the earth like a gigantic blue marble. I shook my head in breathless wonder to observe a live picture of our planet slowly turning, with Africa, then the Middle East, then India all gradually rolling by. What was more amazing were the conversations radioed between the shuttle commander and his coworkers as they manipulated the cumbersome telescope.

"Hold this wrench here and put—hey, look over your shoulder. That's Venus behind you." He gave a long, slow whistle. "Man, isn't that beautiful!"

"Watch that screw, it's floating away. Ah-h, would you look at that. There's New Orleans down there."

"Yep, and look, coming up fast, the west coast of Florida."

Like I said, amazing.

Then there were the call-in questions from viewers around the world. They fired question after question at the astronomers and scientists sitting behind the CNN desk. Average people like me, transfixed in front of their televisions, wondered the same thing: After the repairs, what would the Hubble telescope reveal?

One caller asked, "If Hubble is supposed to photograph the edge of the universe, what will they find on the other side?"

This is staggering, I thought. *Here we are, millions of people across the world, watching earth turn before our eyes and discussing what's beyond the universe.*

The astronomer replied, "People assume there's just empty space beyond the universe. But not so. There's another dimension we can't even dream of."

"Yeah," I said out loud to the television, "and it's called heaven."

Someone else asked, "I hear that this telescope is supposed to help scientists tell the age of the universe. How will they be able to do that?"

A scientist cleared her throat and answered, "The Hubble telescope will be able to photograph the distances between galaxies as they expand away from each other. When we determine the rate of expansion, we'll just 'run the movie backward' to show when the universe began."

I laughed at her answer. A few years ago Carl Sagan, the famous astronomer, was touting the universe as the only thing that was, is, and ever shall be. It had no beginning. It will have no end. That's passé now. With the snap of a finger and a few images from Hubble, astronomers are agreeing that the universe had a beginning. Just like that, Einstein's theory of relativity is proved. And if our complex, highly organized universe had a beginning, it stands to reason that Someone began it. They also agree the universe will have an ending—I wonder if scientists have thought to pick up the book of Revelation for a sneak preview.

I doubt it. That's not the way most of them do things. I began to lose interest in the program after one or two callers failed in their attempt to interject God into the discussion. The scientists sloughed them off. Experts would rather seek out Stephen Hawking or other theoretical physicists to enlighten them on dark and mysterious data. They would rather turn to the cool, rational world of scientific debate for answers. Forget that the heavens hold the home of their hearts' longing. Stick to what is flat and factual, impersonal and rational. And so, newly discovered supernovas are assigned numbers in the galactic registry, and stars are given less-than-romantic names like M–31. Yawn.

I flicked off the television.

The Time of the End

Several days later, when *Endeavor's* astronauts held a news conference, I was glad they recounted their romantic experience of gazing at Venus over their shoulders and watching the west coast of Florida pass by. I identified more with them than those unimaginative scientists.

I also identified with my father who, in 1909, saw the first Model T Ford chug down Howard Street, and then, months later, the Wright Brothers fly their plane over the Baltimore harbor. He told me it was just too much for his brain. The world was simply going by too fast. My father should have lived to see this day. Because now, a little more than a generation later, the world *is* going by too fast. Millions of gallons of information are being poured into our one-ounce brains as we stare at our planet passing before our eyes.

I wish the prophet Daniel could have lived to see this day too. Then again, maybe he did. Perhaps he saw CNN in some prophetic vision and could only watch in wide-eyed wonder. Maybe his brain could only absorb so much, and he turned away just in time to hear God say, "But thou, O Daniel, shut up the words, and seal the book, even to the time of the end: many shall run to and fro, and knowledge shall be increased" (Daniel 12:4 KJV).

Knowledge about our universe is flying at us from right and left. We grasp something new, only to find it obsolete the next time we hear a headliner from some international science conference. Does this proliferation of knowledge mean we've arrived at the time of the end? I wonder if God is unsealing some grand book that has been shut up for centuries in order to reveal, page by page, facts about the heavens that confirm His handiwork.

Scientists used to believe that the universe was full of wandering comets and slow-wheeling galaxies that meandered through space with no rhyme or reason. Now most experts are beginning to acknowledge that a powerful order exists throughout the entire universe, as well as a delicate, yet exact, relationship between forces, fields, and matter. Some dare to call it "beautiful" and "an evidence of a divine mind," but these are largely castigated by the scientific community. Still, there are molecular physicists, like Dr. John Templeton, who are bold enough to say in print, "As science yields more and more data about the universe, we see that in fact God is revealing himself more and more to human inquiry."[1]

It is this delicate and orderly simplicity in the universe that is tugging on the hearts of experts like Dr. Templeton. He and a handful of others are beginning to turn down the chatter on the scientific debate long enough to hear that haunting echo from the skies.

It is that same song, so ancient and so new, whose notes resound in Psalm 19:1–4: "The heavens declare the glory of God; the skies proclaim the work of his hands. Day after day they pour forth speech; night after night they display knowledge. There is no speech or language where their voice is not heard. Their voice goes out into all the earth, their words to the ends of the world." When we gaze at a starry dome in a nighttime sky, scientists, along with you and me, aren't simply "hearing things." It is a haunting and mesmerizing melody. It is the heavens declaring the glory of God.

How Far Away Is Heaven?

As a child I wondered where God lived in outer space and how long it would take to get there. Had I been old enough to read an astronomy textbook, I would have discovered a few statistics which would have blown me out of the water. Our solar system has a diameter of about 700 light-minutes. That's eight billion miles. But the galaxy in which our solar system is contained has a diameter of 100,000 light-years. Not minutes, but *years*. Forget doing the math on that one. Our galaxy is humongous. But here's the kicker: Our little galaxy, which is 100,000 light-years wide, is just *one* of billions of other galaxies out in the cosmos.[2]

I can't comprehend such gargantuan distances nor the breathless enormity of space. Billions of stars and planets, all created by God, most of which the Hubble Space Telescope will never have time to scan. But it's up there on the edge of earth's atmosphere obediently and systematically doing just that—scanning the universe. Hubble has recently captured images close to the very border of our cosmos, and I think it would knock our socks off if it could photograph the actual edge!

What *is* on the other side?

Scientific Journal may be stymied by that question, but not the Bible. Far beyond intergalactic space with its billions of swirling nebulae and novas lies another dimension. Some speculate it's the fifth dimension. You could call it infinity, but wherever it is and however far out, the Bible calls it the highest of heavens. "To the Lord your God belong the heavens, even the highest heavens," it says in Deuteronomy 10:14. The outermost reaches of space are not as void and lonely as we think, because the highest part of heaven is the abode of God. It would seem this "third heaven," as Scripture calls it, spreads out into infinity and completely engulfs our expanding cosmos with all its celestial bodies. It is the dimension where "the Lord says: 'Heaven is my throne and the earth is my footstool'" (Isaiah 66:1).

The dwelling place of God exists in infinity. It is far, far away. That's why I'm amused when the apostle Paul writes so casually in 2 Corinthians 12:2, "I know a man in Christ who fourteen years ago was caught up to the third heaven. Whether it was in the body or out of the body I do not know—God knows. And I know that this man ... was caught up to paradise. He heard inexpressible things, things that man is not permitted to tell."

The third heaven? The highest of heavens? C'mon, Paul, how did you arrive there so fast?

Paul wasn't the only one to reach the throne of heaven in a flash. To the dying thief next to Him on the cross, Jesus said, "I tell you the truth, today you will be with me in paradise" (Luke 23:43).

Today? Jesus, Paul, and a dead criminal spanned billions of light-years in the snap of a finger?

How Close Is Heaven?

I've always sensed that heaven was a lot closer than we are led to believe. As any good child in Sunday school, I believed that heaven was "up." In later years I discovered the Bible says it plainly: Paul was caught *up* to the third heaven ... Jesus *ascended* into heaven ... the Lord will catch us *up* into heaven when He returns ... and, conversely, "God looks *down* from heaven on the sons of men" (Psalm 53:2).

This is the language the Bible invites us to use, much as it encourages us to use other earthbound words like "crowns" or "seas of glass." And it makes sense. Heaven certainly can't be "down" or we'd dig a hole to China.

Yet even though the dwelling place of God may be a long way up, distances like "up" and "down" lose their meaning when you realize that heaven—even the highest heavens—exist beyond our space-time continuum. Latitude and longitude, as well as directions and distances are related to time, and time is a part of the fourth dimension. And the fourth dimension is only a small part of infinity. Time there will be swallowed up. Step beyond the edge of outer space and you enter the fifth dimension where gargantuan distances light-years long are a snap of the finger to, well ... to the dying thief who, when he died, instantly appeared in paradise alongside Jesus.

Had I been the dying thief, I would have been dumbstruck to hear Jesus say, "Today, you will be with me in paradise." Today? This instant? Like Jesus taking my hand and walking with me through a wall, as He did in the Upper Room? Or appearing on a beach to cook breakfast for His friends? Or ambling along the road to Emmaus one instant and—flash—arriving in Jerusalem in no time flat? Like being changed in the twinkling of an eye?

Yes, and the Lord gives a clue as to how He does it in Revelation 1:8 when He laughs at time and distance: "'I am the Alpha and Omega,' says the Lord God, 'who is, and who was, and who is to come, the Almighty.'" Notice that Jesus does not follow the convention of our logic about the way time flows; we time-bound creatures want to change the order to read Jesus *was,* is, and is to come. It sounds more chronological. It's consistent with our sense of the past, present, and future. But Jesus is the great "I Am" who always lives in the present. He is the God of the *now.*

I think of this every time I read Revelation 22 when Jesus says three times to the waiting church, "I am coming soon!" (To which the church replies three times, "Come!") It's interesting He doesn't say, "I will come … like, sometime around, oh, a couple of thousand years from now." Jesus puts it in the present tense as though He were but a hairsbreadth away, all ready to part the veil of time and distance and step back into our world. It's as though He were on His way back now.

So the kingdom of heaven, over which Jesus *is* and was and ever shall be King, is a place, but more so, a dimension where time and distance are not obstacles. The dying thief wasn't transported at superhuman speed to heaven when he died. Rather, he slipped from one dimension to the next, much like Jesus slipped from one room to another, through walls or whatever.

You cannot be *transported* to heaven. You cannot go there in a rocket ship. You couldn't even go there in a time machine, if there were such a thing. That's because heaven exists beyond even speeded-up time. Traveling at a zillion miles per hour might catapult you instantly to the edge of our universe, but to take a step into the third heaven requires more. It requires something different, for our flesh and blood cannot enter heaven.

You must be born again or you cannot, as Jesus warned, "see the kingdom of God." When the dying thief was born of the Spirit, he was given the spiritual "genes," so to speak, of God Himself—Christ who *is,* was, and ever shall be. And we are too when we are Spirit-born. We, like the thief, are fit for eternity. Of course, the fine print in the contract says we must also follow the dying thief in another way and die first.

Where Is Heaven?

Heaven is close. Perhaps closer than we imagine.

It's a little like saying to an unborn infant in his mother's womb, "Do you realize that you are about to be born into a great big world full of mountains, rivers, and a sun and a moon? In fact, you exist in that wonderful world right now."

"Wait a minute," the unborn baby might say. "No way. My world is the one surrounding me. It's soft, warm, and dark. You'll never convince me that just a few hairbreadths outside this uterus exists this place of rivers, mountains, and a sun and moon, whatever that stuff is."

Dear baby! There he is, safe in his little world, ignorant of the fact that a more glorious world is enclosing and encasing his. A world for which he is being fashioned. Only when he is birthed into it will he comprehend that all along his warm dark world was within it. This other place of wonderful beauty was present all the time. Only inches away.

Even this earth in all its birth pangs is about to give one last grunt and find itself born as a "new earth" in heaven. Actually, this moment, less than a hairsbreadth separates this material world from the spiritual world that is embracing earth. And like an unborn baby, we are being fashioned for the greater world into which we are about to be born (by dying, of all things!). We have a hard time believing that heaven encompasses this world, and so the Bible has to keep prodding us to fix our eyes "not on what is seen, but what is unseen." It's a matter of "seeing." Using our eyes of faith.

Faith assures us that heaven is *transcendent*. It is beyond the limits of our experience; it exists apart from our material universe. Heaven is also *immanent* in that it envelopes all the celestial bodies, swirling galaxies, and the starry hosts. If we believe that God is omnipresent, then we can at least believe that what the Bible in Ephesians 2:6 calls the heavenly realms are omnipresent, as well. For where God is, the kingdom of heaven is.

As I said, heaven is closer than we imagine even though we can't see it. I can almost see God laughing at people's propensity to fix their eyes only on that which is seen, when in Jeremiah 23:23–24 He reminds us, "'Am I only a God nearby,' declares the Lord, 'and not a God far away? Can anyone hide in secret places so that I cannot see him?' declares the Lord. 'Do not I fill heaven and earth?' declares the Lord."

One day we will take the same trip as the dying thief. We will arrive in Paradise. In the meantime we can say we operate in the realm of our omnipresent and sovereign God. In some respects, we exist in the kingdom of heaven now.

We *have already come* to Mount Zion, to the heavenly Jerusalem.

We *have come* to myriad angels in joyful assembly.

We *have come* to God, the judge of all men. There's a significant part of us, the "new creature in Christ," which lives in the present tense. Very much like our great "I Am."

This fact makes the far and distant, near and oh so close. When we seize this reality, we understand that the air we breathe is celestial. The ground we tread is sacred. The light we enjoy is divine. Could the rustling in the trees even be the whisper of angel wings? That's touching on romanticism, but as the Bible itself says, "[We] have come to thousands upon thousands of angels in joyful assembly" (Hebrews 12:22).

Literally.

Angels, Dark and Light

This year I took part in a nationwide prayer rally across Canada, which linked together Christian audiences by live satellite television. My role was to lead the nation in a time of repentance. I took the responsibility very seriously and asked the organizers if I could please visit the auditorium the night before.

I wheeled into the cavernous sports arena and stopped at the edge of the railing on the mezzanine level. The place was echoing with the sounds of workmen hammering and ushers rehearsing. We all knew that the next morning thousands of intercessors would fill the arena to shake the heavenly realms with their prayers. But a different kind of work needed to be done that night.

When it came time for my sound check, I wheeled to the microphone on the wooden platform still under construction. "Testing, testing," I said as my voice boomed across the arena. Ushers, technicians, and workmen continued their routines as the sound man adjusted his volume knobs.

My eyes scanned the empty seats. I tilted my head back and squinted beyond the dark rafters. While the sound man continued his work, I began to pray into the microphone, "Lord, we know that this arena has been the scene of everything from ice hockey fights to drug deals during rock concerts. There are a lot of fallen angels ... a lot of demons hanging around here, I can sense it."

I paused in my prayer and looked over each level. I felt a keen awareness of the presence of spirit beings. It wasn't angels. I continued to pray, this time a little louder so my amplified voice would reach the rafters. And as I did, some of the workmen stopped their drilling, and most of the ushers took seats and bowed their heads.

"Jesus, You told us in Your Word that whatever we bind on earth would be bound in heaven, and whatever we loose on earth would be released in heaven. So in Your name, we ask You to clear this place of evil spirits, and we ask You to dispatch big, powerful angels with swords drawn and shields held high to stand guard over this place. Make this sports arena a house of prayer."

And with that, virtually everyone in the place said, "Amen!"

Some skeptics wave you off and say that such a prayer is a nice token, but merely conciliatory. They would say, "There really weren't demons hangin' around that place, no more than there were angels. Don't take this stuff about the spirit world so seriously."

Christians know better. We know that not only is heaven close, but another part of the spirit world is too. The "kingdom of the air" is heavily populated with spiritual beings; and although we only have a hint in Ephesians 2:2 or 6:12, where it describes the "spiritual forces of evil in the heavenly realms," we know that they are real, powerful, and present.

But not as powerful as angels. I wish our eyes could be opened to see the heavenly realms all around us. Perhaps the reality of heaven would spring to life for us if we could peel away this layer, which is only as thick as a thin veil, and take a peek.

That once actually happened to someone. The servant of the prophet Elisha went out for a casual stroll along the top of the walled city of Dothan one morning. When he paused to enjoy the tranquil sunrise, what he saw made his blood freeze. The morning sun gleamed and flashed from countless enemy shields, arrows, and spear tips. He was struck with terror at the sight of the massive Syrian force that had come by night to surround the city. Filled with dismay, he scampered back to Elisha's chambers and reported that the enemy army was about to launch an early morning assault.

Elisha's reply was calm: "Do not fear, for those who are with us are more than those who are with them." And then Elisha prayed that his servant's eyes might be opened to see the heavenly realities all around him. The Lord answered his request and the servant saw that "the mountain was full of horses and chariots of fire all around Elisha" (2 Kings 6:16–17).

What was true for Elisha is true for any believer. When we sing in church, "Open my eyes that I may see / Glimpses of truth Thou hast for me," we wouldn't believe our eyes if God answered our request. Our eyes would pop at all the hosts of angels, chariots of fire, archangels and cherubim, living creatures, and ministering spirits. A few of which are most likely within a hairsbreadth next to you now.

How Will We Relate to Angels?

The more heavenly minded I become, the more convinced I am of the presence of angels in my life, whether it's acknowledging their whereabouts in a sports arena or calling them forth to surround the bedside of someone who is sick. Their job description has included bringing messages, as they did to the seven churches in the book of Revelation.

They aid in answering prayer, as they did with Daniel. God gets all the credit and glory, but angels mysteriously assist in the process—a case in point being Peter's miraculous deliverance from jail.

Angels bring with them something of the presence of God, as well as help the Lord shape history. They really shine when it comes to protecting or delivering us.

Suffice to say, they're busy.

I'm aware of this every time I drive my handicap-equipped van. Its steering and braking controls are sensitively torqued to accommodate my weak muscles in my shoulders (it doesn't have a steering wheel, but that's another story). When I cruise the Ventura freeway at fifty-five miles per hour, I am keenly conscious of a host of angels surrounding my van, sitting on the bumper, and holding onto the radio antenna. Maybe God has dispatched an extra few because I'm disabled, and He knows I need extra protection. How many accidents have I avoided because of those angels? When I get to heaven, I'll find out; and I'll thank them for all the times they "lost a few feathers" in near-misses on my behalf.

One of the best parts of heaven may be getting to know and fellowshiping with angels. They love God and they enjoy us. In a parable about sinners gaining entrance into the kingdom of heaven, Jesus said, "I tell you, there is rejoicing in the presence of the angels of God over one sinner who repents" (Luke 15:10). If angels rejoiced so happily over our conversion, how much more will they rejoice over us when we arrive at the foot of God's throne. To the angels, we will be a source of eternal joy. They will see our redemption completed, from beginning to end.

I actually saw an angel once. It was 2:00 A.M. on a pitch-black night. I was wide awake, propped up in bed, and straining my ears to hear the muffled voices of my family in the bedroom directly above me. They were surrounding the bed of my five-year-old niece, Kelly, who was dying of cancer. We knew her passing into heaven could happen at any moment, but I was unable to get up the narrow stairs to say good-bye with the others. Suddenly, a brilliant golden shape that glowed whisked by the large bay window I was facing—it didn't move from left to right, but from bottom to top. I screamed. I then searched to see if there were cars on the street outside. Nothing was there. In the next second, my sister Jay called down the steps, "Kelly's gone!"

A few of the family came downstairs to find out why I screamed. I told them exactly what I saw. My sisters sank on the edge of my bed in amazement. We knew I had seen a large spiritual being, probably sent from heaven to escort Kelly's soul into eternity.

We will also worship with the angels. They've had a lot of practice at worshiping, as well as access to heaven's throne. They've seen it all. Yet when we arrive in heaven, it will be *their* privilege to worship with us. Just think what our worship will sound like. In Revelation 5:11–13, angels crowd before the throne, "numbering thousands upon thousands, and ten thousand times ten thousand.... In a loud voice they sang: 'Worthy is the Lamb, who was slain, to receive power and wealth and wisdom and strength and honor and glory and praise!'"

Every time I read that verse, I recall a marvelous experience at the Moody Pastor's Conference. I was told that the singing would be out of this world. And it was. When I wheeled onto the platform and parked near Dr. Joe Stowell and the other speakers, I scanned the auditorium of 1,800 men and got the jolt of my life. Somehow, it escaped me that I would be amongst so many, many men.

The song leader had the men stand up, spread out into the aisles, and fill the stage. When they held hymnbooks high and broke into a rousing chorus, a jet blast of sound hit me head-on. A pastor held a hymnal close so I could sing along, but I only managed half the first verse. Something forced me to stop, close my eyes, and just listen.

Never had I been so utterly surrounded by sound. It was pure and powerful, clear and deep, enveloping me, resonating through my bones, and shaking the chair in which I sat. A thunderous waterfall of perfect bass and baritone, so passionate it made my heart break.

Through tears I tried to join in the second verse, but my wispy soprano voice sounded thin and frail. I was a tiny leaf carried helplessly along a surging current, spilling over and splashing with joy, all joy and music. It was a moment of ecstasy, so serendipitous and God-anointed, that I had to step outside myself and be carried heavenward. I could do nothing but laugh through my tears and enjoy the ride. If this earthly choir moved me, how much more when our voices blend with the angels!

Angels will also serve us in heaven. Their job description in Hebrews 1:14 extends beyond just earth. Angels will be subject to us in eternity. We will reign with Jesus; and if He has been given authority over all the heavenly hosts, then we will reign over angels too. Will we govern a few legions or many? What shall we command them to do in faraway galaxies? How will they aid us on earth to help carry out the kingdom rule? I can't say, but it's thrilling to imagine. And since I never took ROTC in college or engaged in military service, I'm sure glad I'll have a glorified mind to handle it. Strategic leadership will be a cinch for us and we'll be able to rally angelic legions, as well as lead the way in doing God's work in heaven and on earth.

One more thing. When it comes to fallen angels—demons—we will judge them. If 1 Corinthians 6:2–3 didn't spell it out in black and white, I'd laugh at the improbability of it all; for it says, "Do you not know that the saints will judge the world? And if you are to judge the world, are you not competent to judge trivial cases? Do you not know that we will judge angels? How much more the things of this life!"

Incredible!

A verse like this makes me want to settle my differences with my husband, Ken, real fast. I'm not joking. This short but powerful Scripture is another one of those exponential statements that smack of an almost unbelievable increase in our capacity to serve, as well as our responsibility in ruling. Once again, God will blow out all formulas on proportions and put us in charge of judging fallen angels. I cringe at the idea, because on earth I'm having a tough enough time deciding who's right in a friendly spat or who ought to get the last piece of pie or whether or not justice was served in a local court case.

Me? Judging angels? Again, I breathe a sigh of relief to know that I will have all of God's wisdom at my disposal; otherwise, the job would send me cowering. It's just another way we will rule with Christ in heaven.

Frankly, the idea intrigues me. There are a couple of evil spirits I can't wait to nail. On earth, I have been so harassed by troublesome demons of temptation or evil forces who keep trying to trip me up. I'm not saying "the devil made me do it" on earth; I take full responsibility for my choices and actions. But demons sure haven't helped. I could easily throw the book at them!

Then there are the more heinous powers and principalities of darkness who have incited wicked men to wreck havoc. These are the gruesome chief demons under Satan who for centuries have pushed evil men further into rebellion, murder, torture, and grisly massacres. The Nazi holocaust. The Armenian genocide. Stalin's pogroms. The Spanish inquisition. And especially those forces of evil who instigated the treason and injustice behind the crucifixion of God's own Son, even the demons who urged those drunken soldiers to slap and spit on the Second Person of the Trinity.

When I see news magazine photos of mutilated children in Rwanda, old women beaten in Bosnia, or twisted bodies in a bombed-out building in Oklahoma City, I naturally get mad at people who do such things. But when you consider who's behind it all, I don't vent anger at God, I get furious with the devil and his cohorts. The psalmist was speaking of evil men in Psalm 139:22, but I'll throw in fallen angels and say, "I have nothing but hatred for them; I count them my enemies."

These demons have had a heyday on earth for too long. I see their trademark on everything from pornography spewed from magazines to the humanism spouted from elementary school textbooks. Satan's legions have left a dark trace on this earth, which has been gutted and denuded of its resources, leaving ugly scars on mountains and smoky trails in the air. Most of all, it hurts when I see men and women gripped in the claws of spiritism and the occult; Satan has blinded their eyes. And unless the Sovereign Lord opens the eyes of wicked men and women through our prayers and witness, they will be crushed and tormented like grapes under His wrath.

This humbles me before God.

And yes, I hate the devil.

I'm one hundred percent behind virtually every sermon Jonathan Edwards preached about hellfire and brimstone, the place God created for the devil and his followers. I can hardly wait for that glorious—yes, glorious—day when Satan and his legions will be punished and eternally tormented for their procuring the fall of mankind. One day we shall have the pleasure of demonstrating "perfect hatred," as Scripture puts it, against the rulers, powers, and principalities of darkness.

Will There Be Envy in Heaven?

I'm speechless. To think that in addition to giving us the blessings of salvation and eternal life, God should reward us with such superior opportunities to serve Him beyond all reasonable proportion. If we think God is generous with His grace to us on earth, wait until we see Him pull out all the stops spreading far and wide His glory in heaven!

That's why I can't get out of my heart or head this thing about crowns. I am awed and inspired by the fact that what I do on earth will have a direct bearing on how I will serve God in heaven. The apostle Peter echoes this in his second epistle: "If you do these things ... you will receive *a rich welcome* into the eternal kingdom of our Lord and Savior Jesus Christ" (2 Peter 1:11). Our present conduct has a bearing on our entrance into heaven and how rich our welcome will be.[3]

Sometimes I feel like I'm in the minor leagues, working hard to be ensured a berth somewhere in the major leagues in heaven; because what I do here affects everything there. I'm not talking about earning salvation, but about earning reward. It affects everything from how much heart will go into my eternal worship of God to the kind of job I'll be assigned on the new earth. It even affects the way I'll govern angels to my capacity for eternal joy and possibly the extent of my appreciation for all that Jesus has done for me and others here on earth.

I know what you're thinking. *Joni, if you are suggesting that there are degrees of responsibility or even joy in heaven, aren't you inviting a little ... envy? Won't people get jealous if some have bigger, fancier mansions?*

May I straighten out one thing? I didn't dream up the idea of some people becoming greater in the kingdom than others, Scripture did. One of the very last things Jesus says in the final chapter of Revelation is, "Behold, I am coming soon! My reward is with me, and I will give to everyone according to what he has done." If you're faithful in a few things, watch out, it's "ten cities" coming your way. If it's a couple of talents you invest, lo and behold, the Master more than doubles your investment. God's Word is replete with conditional statements like, "Blessed is the man who perseveres under trial, because *when* he has stood the test, he will receive the crown of life" (James 1:12).

As far as envy is concerned, don't worry. It won't happen in heaven. Remember, we will be totally transformed. Envy will be an impossibility. We won't drool over someone's three-story sprawling mansion, and think we only live in a shack with a tin roof. No competing and no comparison in heaven. Still, it makes perfect sense that God will exalt those whom He chooses to honor. It's His prerogative. And whatever He decides or whomever He chooses to lift up is fine with me. I'll be more than happy for the godly men and women whom Christ will elevate as the most celebrated pillars in His temple.

Once after a speaking engagement, a woman came up to me to tell me how much she enjoyed my message. In her enthusiasm, she exclaimed, "You're so wonderful. I wish I could be like you ... you'll get a great reward in heaven!"

I appreciated her accolades, but I see it differently. God is by no means impressed that I can paint with my mouth, have written books, traveled all over the world, or am on speaking terms with Billy Graham. When He sees my name on a bestseller's list, He doesn't get all effusive and say, "Boy, am I proud of her, chalk another one up for the lady in the wheelchair."

I'm not discounting my painting or books or the exciting places I've served; I just feel that I have received a lot of my reward here on earth. I've enjoyed the reward of seeing the gospel go forth because of this wheelchair and of watching believers become encouraged and inspired. It is sheer ecstasy to watch Him work through my life, and I'm humbled and honored.

It's just when it comes to heaven, I'm convinced the highest accolades will go—and should go—to godly people who have labored loyally yet received no recognition. The grand and glorious purposes for my suffering are clear to all, but some dear saints have suffered for no apparent reason. I have a Christian friend named Dorothy who has silently lived with excruciating pain for years, such incredible pain that she has nearly passed out on many occasions. It's been agony, but she has bravely endured. I long to see her suffering atoned for when Jesus hands her a crown of life with extra jewels reserved for the saint who "perseveres under trial."

Yes, some will be greater in the kingdom than others. What a wonderful thought! I can't wait for the Lord to greatly honor the missionary in the back jungles of Brazil who spent fifteen years translating Scripture and then quietly moved on to the next tribe to do the same.

I want to see the Lord richly reward small-town pastors who faithfully preached every Sunday morning despite meager numbers in the pews. Better yet, pastors in China who are still suffering persecution and haven't seen the light of day from their jail cells in years.

I hope the Lord takes highest delight in elderly grandmothers in nursing homes who didn't dwell on their plight, but rather prayed, without fanfare, for others. Godly teenagers who held fast to their virginity, saying "no" time and again to peer pressure, intimidation, and their hormones. And moms and dads of handicapped children who, in the name of Jesus, served the family faithfully despite the day-to-day routine, isolation, and financial setbacks.

These are the real heroes and heroines over whom we will be exceedingly glad to hear the Lord say, "Well done, good and faithful servant!" When they receive their reward, I'll stand happily on the sidelines, cheering, whistling, and applauding wildly. I may have stood up to the vicissitudes of human hardship, like pain and paralysis, but their strength of spirit more than matched, even way surpassed, mine. And do you know what will thrill me most? The obedience of these unsung heroes will raise the wattage on God's glory. He will shine brighter because of them.

I won't be jealous of others with brighter raiment than mine in heaven. Neither will they be envious of anyone, such as the two people picked to sit on the right or left hand of Jesus. You won't be either. And do you know why you will be satisfied with the reward Jesus gives you? First, you'll be pleased with whatever Jesus bestows simply because He's Lord. Second, your perfect sense of justice will be in complete accord with the Lord's judgment. Third, your capacity for joy will be filled to overflowing.

Your reward will be your capacity—your capacity for joy, service, and worship. Jonathan Edwards described these capacities this way: "The saints are like so many vessels of different sizes cast into a sea of happiness where every vessel is full: this is eternal life, for a man ever to have his capacity filled. But after all, 'tis left to God's sovereign pleasure, 'tis his prerogative to determine the largeness of the vessel."[4]

When I think of my vessel, I picture a gallon bucket into which the Lord will pour His joy until it gushes over the brim, bubbling up and effervescing. I'll laugh with delight for others who will have a joy-capacity the size of a big bath tub, or a tanker truck, or a silo. Like me, they will be filled to overflowing, and we all shall be as happy as cats with nine tails!

Whether a small vial or a large vase, we shall all be spilling and splashing over with the joy of the Lord; and even those whose capacity is only the size of a thimble won't know jealousy. We shall be fat, sassy, and satiated with joy. Constant brimming over. Happiness unspeakable in worship and service. Each of us will have complete contentment for the station our Master has allocated us in eternal life.

So, I'm fixing my eyes on Jesus and focusing on things unseen. I'm stretching my heart's capacity for God here on earth to insure my bucket for joy in heaven will be deep and wide. I'm searching high and low in my heart to choose the right building materials, whether it be gold, silver, precious stones, or platinum-plated service. I'm down here on earth to win as many crowns as possible.

Uh-oh, you may be thinking, *Joni, aren't you being self-serving here? Isn't focusing on gaining rewards a bit mercenary?*

No. I have a clear conscience in light of 1 Corinthians 9:24, which encourages missionaries, prisoners, teenagers, moms and dads, all of us in the contest to "run in such a way as to get the prize. Everyone who competes in the games goes into strict training. They do it to get a crown that will not last; but we do it to get a crown that will last forever. Therefore I do not run like a man running aimlessly."

I always run for the reward harder and faster whenever I read this encouragement from Jonathan Edwards: "Persons need not and ought not to set any bounds to their spiritual and gracious appetites. Do not sow sparingly. Seek the most ample rooms in the heavenly kingdom."[5]

Is it selfish to run hard in order to gain the prize? Is working toward rewards mercenary? Certainly not. Heavenly crowns are not just rewards for a job well done on earth; when your focus is on Jesus, they are the glorious fulfillment of the job itself. Just like marriage is the reward and the happy consummation of love, and a medal of honor is the reward given at the end of a victorious battle, so it will be with heaven's crowns. A reward is the cherry and whipped-cream topping of the pleasure of serving God down here on earth. It is the joy of sticking to the call He gave at the beginning.

Heaven is one big reward. Gift after gift after gift.

In the second and third chapters of Revelation, God unfolds the rewards He has reserved in heaven for you and me, His overcomers. My friend, Margaret Clarkson, takes a stab at describing each reward when she suggests:

> He will give us the fruit of the tree of life, the hidden manna— what food that will be for souls that hunger and thirst for God! The white stone, with the new and secret name known only to God and the soul that receives it—what infinite value He must set on individuality of personality to know each one of His overcomers so personally and so intimately!
>
> The white raiment, forever spotless—what a joy after this life of soiling and defeat! The pillar in God's temple eternally erect—what a strength after this pilgrimage of weakness and failure! To receive the Morning Star, sweet synonym for the Savior's own person; to be given the holy name of God Himself and the name of His city and the new name of the Lamb—only a God like ours could have designed rewards such as these!
>
> And only the Head that was crowned with thorns could fashion such crowns of life, righteousness, and glory ... what can we do but fall down before Him who sits upon the throne and worship Him forever and ever?[6]

I have an idea that when we step into eternity, I won't be the only one who, with new resurrected legs, will drop on grateful glorified knees. Tens of thousands will have the same idea. Our knees will kneel on jade and jasper. Our feet will walk on gold. Our hands will touch walls of sapphires and emeralds. We will feel utterly at home in the golden throne room of the King.

But wait. At home? In a glittering throne room? A mansion made of sardonyx and chrysolite doesn't sound very homey, let alone comfortable. Even after looking at these pictures of what heaven will be like and sensing how it will feel on that "great-gettin'-up-day" for all of us in the future, one thought may still be nagging: Will I fit? Will heaven really be like home?

Part 2

—

Will Heaven Be Home?

Chapter 5

Why Don't We
Fit on Earth?

*H*ey, lady, your suitcase is over there!" a baggage handler yelled.
"Get that cart out of the way, would ya!"

"Taxi! Hey, stop—I said, 'Taxi!'" someone hollered outside.

It was mayhem. My friend was steering me in my wheelchair through
thick crowds and piles of suitcases in the baggage claim area of the Los
Angeles airport. Angry passengers bemoaned lost luggage. A line of people
jostled through a turnstile. Outside, taxis honked. Policemen hollered. It
was a crazy ending to an even crazier day of bad weather and a late arrival.
We found our luggage carousel, and my friend parked my chair to go
retrieve our things.

While I waited in the midst of pandemonium, I did what I always do.
I waited and sat still. Very still.

It's a fact of life. Because I'm paralyzed from the shoulders down, a
large part of me never moves. I have instant stillness. I don't run, I sit. I
don't race, I wait. Even when rushing, I stay put in my wheelchair. I could
be scurrying through a jam-packed schedule, doing this and that, but a big
part of me—due to my paralysis—is always quiet.

That's why, if you had seen me in that busy airport, you would have
noticed a satisfied smile. Perhaps in an earlier time I would have felt
trapped, useless, and resentful that I could not grab my own suitcase,
elbow the guy who butted in line, or hail my own taxi. But faith, honed
and sharpened from years in my wheelchair, has changed that. And so, I
sat there thanking God for built-in quiet and stillness before Him.

I also thought about heaven. With eyes of faith I looked beyond the sight of bumper-to-bumper traffic, the smell of sweat, cigarettes, exhaust fumes, and the sounds of my harried co-travelers, and began humming quietly ...

> *This world is not my home, I'm just a passing through,*
> *My treasures are laid up somewhere beyond the blue;*
> *The angels beckon me from heaven's open door,*
> *And I can't feel at home in this world anymore.*[1]

For me, it was a moment of faith. Faith merely the size of a grain of mustard seed. Remember, that's all it takes to be sure of things hoped for—future divine fulfillments—and certain of things you do not see, that is, unseen divine realities.

Of what was I so sure and certain? Here, let me sing it again: "The angels beckon me from heaven's open door, / And I can't feel at home in this world anymore."

I hum that haunting tune in other places besides the Los Angeles airport. Sometimes I get that "can't feel at home" sensation ambling down the aisles of K-Mart, watching women grab for the blue-light specials. Sometimes it happens sitting with Ken watching Monday Night Football's fourth instant replay of a team's third-down conversion. And I definitely feel "this world is not my home" as I sit on the Ventura-Freeway-turned-parking-lot.

Don't think I'm strange. Christians have felt the same for centuries. Malcolm Muggeridge, a British journalist who spent most of his years battling Christianity, finally succumbed to Christ in his seventies. The intellectual world had always been home to him, but now, in the hallowed halls of university life, he found himself saying,

> I had a sense, sometimes enormously vivid, that I was a stranger in a strange land; a visitor, not a native ... a displaced person.... The feeling, I was surprised to find, gave me a great sense of satisfaction, almost of ecstasy.... Days or weeks or months might pass. Would it ever return—the lostness? I strain my ears to hear it, like distant music; my eyes to see it, a very bright light very far away. Has it gone forever? And then—ah! the relief. Like slipping away from a sleeping embrace, silently shutting a door behind one, tiptoeing off in the grey light of

dawn—a stranger again. The only ultimate disaster that can befall us, I have come to realize, is to feel ourselves to be at home here on earth. As long as we are aliens, we cannot forget our true homeland.[2]

His words could have been mine as I wheeled through the Thousand Oaks Mall yesterday. I was a stranger in a strange land between the video game parlor on the second floor and the first floor movie complex running the latest Arnold Schwartzenegger film. Actually, I felt like a blessed stranger. A displaced, but satisfied person. Everyone seemed absorbed by the fashion show going on in the center courtyard, but I found myself thinking, *Does anyone else here realize that there's more to life than the new fall designs?*

That's what blessed strangers and satisfied displaced persons feel. They see that heaven is *home*. It's where we belong. "We all have a homing instinct, a 'home detector,' and it doesn't ring for earth," says Peter Kreeft.[3]

I did not feel at home in that mall. I did not belong. I saw its world as trite and commonplace. Mind you, I didn't view the people as banal or boring; if anything, my heart went out to the kids hanging around the video parlor and the ladies watching the fashion show. The troubling part was the "world" in which they were engrossed: The lure of shoe store posters on which grungy looking kids scream "Demand What You Deserve!" The morbid attraction of noisy video games that decapitate the heads and sever the arms of cartoon losers, and everywhere, huge discounts if you open up a credit account and purchase three pairs of anything. My heart especially went out to a teenage girl in jeans and plaid shirt who was staring enviously at the gaunt figure of a female mannequin who stared back at her through lifeless eyes. That said it all.

I couldn't help but see something past this world; it was not unlike the moment of faith I experienced in the Los Angeles airport. How so? Because faith is double-sided. It not only verifies heaven as real, giving hard and fast reality to that which we do not see, but it also makes us look differently at visible things on earth. Through faith's eyes, heaven becomes a rock-solid home, and the concrete world in which we live becomes drained of substance and importance. When we look at life through eyes of faith, things around us no longer possess the glow of excitement. Everything from Rolex watches to the latest episode of *All My Children,* from the newest Liz Claiborne fashions to the latest filibuster in Congress.

Because faith makes invisible things real, and visible things unreal, earthly dissatisfaction becomes the road to heavenly satisfaction. One place, heaven, supplants the other, earth, as home.

Aliens, Strangers, and Misfits

Faith does another thing. The more homelike heaven becomes, the more you feel like an alien and stranger on earth. Maybe some people price top-of-the-line Porsches, but that only reveals that "their mind is on earthly things. But our citizenship is in heaven" (Philippians 3:19–20). I'm not talking spiritual snobbery here, and I have no beef against Lexus cars or knits by St. John's. It's simply a matter of focus: "For where your treasure is, there your heart will be also" (Matthew 6:21).

Please don't think I drive a clunker, wear my sister's hand-me-downs, hate the mall, and never turn on a television. I like nice stuff. Don't forget, I spent the first chapter describing all the present moments and past memories that, for me, make earth so rich. I'm the one who enjoys earth's good things like prime rib rare with Yorkshire pudding, a night of romance with my husband, Bridal Veil Falls at Yosemite, and the feel of raw silk on my face. There's nothing trite, banal, or boring about these pleasures. What's more, if I could be entrusted, I'm sure my conscience would be thrilled to permit me to don a beautiful Jones of New York suit. (It would probably go to my head, which is why some of my Christian friends can wear this garb with grace while I can't.)

This feeling of being an alien or stranger on earth has more to do with the song I told you about. The haunting echo. The longing and yearning I felt that hot afternoon by the Kansas wheat field, and many times since. The writer of Hebrews 11:13–16 definitely had me in mind when he said, "People who say such things show that they are looking for a country of their own. If they had been thinking of the country they had left, they would have had opportunity to return. Instead, they were longing for a better country—a heavenly one."

I'm a little like a refugee who is longing for my better country called heaven. My heart is in quasi-exile. In fact, 1 Kings 11:14–22 is just a brief story, but it's "me" all over. It seems that Hadad, an adversary of Solomon, had fled for safety to Egypt with some of his father's family. There he found great favor with Pharaoh, married into the king's family, and reared his son in the royal palace. But when he heard that David was dead, "Hadad said to Pharaoh, 'Let me go, that I may return to my own country.'"

"'What have you lacked here that you wamt to go back to your own country?' Pharaoh asked."

"'Nothing,' Hadad replied, 'but do let me go!'"

That's the part I identify with. Earth may be rich with past memories and present moments as it was with Hadad, but I'm hot on his heels: "Let me go, that I may return to my own country." It is always the exiles who remember home. The Israelites, captive in a foreign land, remembered their true country when they mourned in Psalm 137:1: "By the rivers of Babylon we sat and wept when we remembered Zion." Like Hadad, like the Israelites, I carry in my exiled heart a hunger for my heavenly country, my soul's true home.

A person who feels at home "fits" with his environment, like a fish in water, a bird in the sky, or a worm in the dirt. But we don't "fit" here. It's not our environment. There is no harmony, no "rightness," with our surroundings. Remember my experiences in the Los Angeles airport and the Thousand Oaks Mall? It wasn't as though the hustle and bustle of that world offended me; it's just that it didn't jibe, it didn't resonate with the peace and stillness in my heart, a peace that echoed, "You don't belong here."[4]

Feeling like an exile is simply feeling a fact.

> *O Lord,*
> *I live here as a fish in a vessel of water,*
> *only enough to keep me alive,*
> *but in heaven I shall swim in the ocean.*
> *Here I have a little air in me to keep me breathing,*
> *but there I shall have sweet and fresh gales;*
> *Here I have a beam of sun to lighten my darkness,*
> *a warm ray to keep me from freezing;*
> *yonder I shall live in light and warmth forever.*
>
> A Puritan prayer[5]

Why Don't We Fit?

As Christians, you and I are not made for this world.

Well, in one sense we are. Our hands, feet, eyes, and ears equip us for physical experiences on this planet made of water and dirt. Our ears process noise, our eyes register sights, our noses detect odors, and our stomachs digest food. But we are also spirit. This makes for incredible tension. Someone once said, "Through faith we understand that we are not physical beings having a spiritual experience, but spiritual beings having a physical experience." A friend, Peter Kreeft, writes about this tension and I borrow some of his ideas here....

As spiritual beings, you and I are not made for this world because the earth is temporal. There is something in us that is definitely *not* temporal. That's why we squirm and groan against the confines of time. The clock, for us, is an adversary. Every heavenly moment—whether it be gazing into the soft eyes and gentle smile of the one we love or relishing the ecstasy of some glorious pleasure—every moment like this we embrace so we might keep time at bay. But we can't. We would like to call these moments timeless, but they're not. Time snatches them from our grasp.

This is where the tension *really* kicks in. For in one sense, as Sheldon Vanauken writes, "Time is our natural environment. We live in time as we live in the air we breathe. And we love the air.... How strange that we cannot love time. It spoils our loveliest moments.... We wished to know, to savor, to sink in—into the heart of the experience—to possess it wholly. But there was never enough time."[6] I can't explain the tension any better than that. Time is our natural environment, yet time is *not* our natural environment.

It's not just Christians who kick against the traces of time. People who don't believe in God consider time an adversary. For them, the ticking of the second hand sounds like the stalking of an enemy. Each minute moves them toward death. And everyone, whether rich or poor, tries to grab the hour hand to shove it backward. "Slow down and live" is a slogan on everything from highway signs to health books. But we can't slow down time. Wrinkle cream won't do it. Pumping your brain and brawn with Vitamins E and A won't do it. And freezing your body in an iced hydrogen chamber won't stop time either. It's the honest person who would agree with C. S. Lewis when he says, "Time itself is one more name for death."[7]

All of humanity senses this, for, "He has also set eternity in the hearts of men; yet they cannot fathom what God has done from beginning to end" (Ecclesiastes 3:11). Yes, people in general just can't fathom God, let alone this thing about a timeless eternity. They don't know what to do with it except to buy Shirley MacLaine's latest New Age best-seller or apply more Oil of Olay. Their only real recourse against the onslaught of time is their memories. "Memory is our only dike against the waves of time in this world," says Peter Kreeft.[8]

Longing for Another Time

I know what it's like to grab hold of memories, like bricks, and build a dike against time. When I was first paralyzed in 1967—and still new to this eternity thing as a young Christian—heaven was in no way my home. I was less interested in looking forward to a glorified body and more interested in turning back the clock to days when my body worked. Time was also an enemy in that it kept putting more distance between the past on my feet and the present in my wheelchair. The only way I could slow down the weeks and months was to dive into my memories.

I couldn't do much but listen to the radio or records. I laid on the stryker frame in the intensive care unit and tuned into Diana Ross moaning about a lost love or Glen Campbell crooning about an old flame wandering on the back roads of his memory. The Beatles were also popular then. I would fight back the tears when they'd sing of a yesterday when troubles seemed so far away.

Then there was Joni Mitchell. Folk music still lingered in the late sixties, and I found refuge in her restless songs about the past. Her music evoked a more powerful and fundamental nostalgia than pining for a lost love or a trouble-free yesterday. You can hear it in the sixties anthem she penned for a lost and searching generation. It was a generation that came in droves to find itself on the hot, rainy hillsides of a farm in New York. Listen to the ache and the haunting longing in her song called "Woodstock":

> *Well can I walk beside you?*
> *I've come here to lose the smog*
> *And I feel as if I'm a cog*
> *In something turning 'round and 'round.*

Maybe it's the time of year
Or maybe it's the time of man,
But I don't know who I am,
Yet life is for the learning.

We are stardust, we are golden,
Caught up in the devil's bargain,
And we've got to get ourselves
Back to the Garden.
We've got to get ourselves
Back to a semblance of a God.[9]

Joni Mitchell and thousands like her are looking for something incalculably precious they've lost, something they've got to get back to. They may mistake it for the nostalgia of the sixties or the fifties; they may mistake it for a childhood memory, a lost love, or a yesterday when one's troubles seemed so far away, but it's much more than that. It's a nostalgia not for the innocence of youth, but for the innocence of humanity. "We've got to get ourselves back to the Garden," a lost world groans, because it's Eden where we lost not just our youth, but our identity.

We may not realize it, but the whole of humanity is exiled from the bliss of the intimate presence of God, "walking in the Garden in the cool of the evening." But being "dead in our trespasses," humanity doesn't realize this is what it longs for. Most people don't understand that to walk with God is to feel at home.

What's funny is I'm convinced even if people could reach back into the Garden, if Joni Mitchell could go back to the moment of the creation of the world, it wouldn't be enough. She'd stand there in the middle of a perfect environment and feel perfectly ill at ease, not realizing satisfaction could only be found by taking one more step off the edge of time itself and into the mind of God. For our nostalgia for Eden is not just for another time, but another *kind* of time. Those who do not believe still feel the tug. Even those who do not hope for heaven still wrestle with this vexing enigma of "eternity" set in their heart.

Most people have it backward.

Unlike those who don't believe in God, our road is not back to the Garden of Eden, but forward. One should never look over one's shoulder on the road of hope. In Genesis, God sent the seraphim with the flaming sword to bar Adam and Eve from returning to Eden once they had fallen. "The road to God lies ahead, 'east of Eden,' through the world of time and history, struggle and suffering and death. Ejected from Eden's eastern gate, we travel through and around the world, from west to east, forever seeking the rising sun (the Rising Son!) and find Him standing at the western gate ... saying, 'I am the door.'"[10]

Our True Identity

Our lost youth and lost identity are not to be recovered in the innocence of Eden. God conceived of us before Eden, "before the foundation of the world." Only in heaven—the birthplace of our identity—will we find out who we truly are. Actually, we won't find it so much as receive it. This is beautifully symbolized in Revelation 2:17: "To him who overcomes, I will give some of the hidden manna. I will also give him a white stone with a new name written on it, known only to him who receives it."

Did you get that part about our new name? George MacDonald explains the connection between our new name and our true identity this way: "God's name for a man must be the expression of his own idea of the man, that being whom he had in his thought when he began to make the child, and whom he kept in his thought through the long process of creation which went to realize the idea. To tell the name is to seal the success."[11]

Our true identity will unfold in the new name God will give us. And the name is a secret between God and you. Think about that, friend! In heaven, you will not only find what was irretrievably lost, but when you receive it—your new name, your true identity—you will be a thousand times more yourself than the sum total of all those nuances, gestures, and inside subtleties that defined the earthbound "you." On earth you may think you fully blossomed, but heaven will reveal that you barely budded.

What's more, you will be like none other in heaven. The fact that no one else has your name shows how utterly unique you are to God. You touch His heart in a way no one else can. You please Him like none other. It is a royal seal of His individual love on you.

This shouldn't surprise us. God hasn't carved out a gigantic celestial ballpark called heaven into which His entire family fits. Paradise is not a general commune for a lump sum of saints. God has chosen to save certain individuals, and you have a specific place niched in heaven—in God's heart—which fits you and you alone. In heaven you will reflect Him like a facet of a diamond, and people will say to you, "I *love* seeing that part of God in you ... in fact, you show off that trait of His better than anybody up here!"

Everyone else will receive their true identity too. They also will reflect God in unique and complete ways; so you will probably say to that friend, "Well, I *love* the way you reflect Him this way!" And together the two of you, as well as all the other saints, will praise God that He is "all and in all" with such variety and beauty.

C. H. Spurgeon suggested this is why redeemed people will number more than the grains of sand on the beach or the stars in the sky. An endless number of saints will be required to fully reflect the infinite facets of God's love. Everyone is necessary in heaven. Could it be that without you, some wonderful nuance of God's love, dare I say, might not get reflected were you not in heaven?

United in perfect praise and love, we will finally and fully discover who we are, where we belong, and what God destined us to do—and we will have all of eternity to be and do that very thing. For centuries, theologians have attempted to describe this scene; I think Jonathan Edwards does a good job when he writes, "Thus they shall eat and drink abundantly, and swim in the ocean of love, and be eternally swallowed up in the infinitely bright, and infinitely mild and sweet, beams of divine love; eternally receiving that light, eternally full of it, and eternally compassed round with it, and everlastingly reflecting it back again to its fountain."[12]

You will *recognize* the ones you love. On earth you only half-recognized them. But in heaven, you will discover rich, wonderful things about the true identity of your husband, wife, daughter, son, brother, sister, or special friends, things that were only hinted at on earth. What's more, you will *know* them like you never knew them on earth. After all, we won't be less smart in heaven, we will be more smart. My husband, Ken, will be a thousand times more "Ken" than he ever was in flesh and blood. You will exclaim to your loved one, "Wow, so *this* is what I loved in you for so long!" for you will see him or her as God intended all along.

Until we are there, doing what God purposed for us from the beginning, we will be the caterpillar writhing to be free of the cocoon, to breathe celestial air. We will feel very much like Moses cocooned away in the back side of a desert who cried, "I have become an alien in a foreign land" (Exodus 2:22). And just as Moses was becoming, in the desert, the leader he would eventually be, we are pilgrims becoming, in the here and now, who we shall be in the hereafter.

So onward we pilgrims tread through this world of time and death, forever seeking the Son. We don't go backward but, "Forgetting what is behind and straining toward what is ahead, [we] press on toward the goal to win the prize for which God has called [us] heavenward in Christ Jesus" (Philippians 3:13–14).

General humanity refuses to go in this direction. In an anxious search to fit, people take the world's sextant and try to locate their present position using all the wrong coordinates: memories of childhood, an old romance, carefree days, songs, power, religion, wealth, or Woodstock. But humanity keeps failing to recognize that it is "made in the image of God." Only believers who understand that the coordinates converge in eternity can sing, "This world is not my home."

Our Place in Time

Joni Mitchell won't make it back to the Garden. She would do better to sing of God's Son in her quest for not only identity, but for another time. Jesus is the only One who was ever comfortable with His identity, as well as comfortable in or out of time.

One second Jesus could be conversing with friends on the road to Emmaus, the next He could bypass the hours required to travel to Jerusalem and appear there in no time flat. He could materialize one morning on a beach, then start a fire and whip up breakfast for His friends. One minute He could eat a fish, the next, pass through a wall. Stone walls and unopened doors in the Upper Room presented no barriers. Time, space, and therefore distance were, for Him, a cinch. This is *very* interesting because His ability to move in and out of various dimensions clues us into where time fits in heaven. I don't think heaven will destroy time, so much as swallow it up.

Let me explain using a principle I learned from high school geometry. If you move a dot through time and space, it makes a line—the first dimension. Take that line, move it laterally through time and space, and it becomes a plane—the second dimension. Move a plane through time and space, and you get a cube or some other polyhedron—a cube is the third dimension and it's comprised of a stack of planes.

And you and I, who are three-dimensional figures, move through time and space—we might consider that a fourth dimension. Each new dimension enfolds the previous ones, plus something more. This means eternity—we might think of that as a fifth dimension—will comprise all the interesting elements of the other dimensions, including time.

Hey, if you get that, you get an A in geometry. You also get that time won't stop in heaven, but will be swallowed up. Time will be folded into eternity and lose its distinction much like egg whites when they are folded into cream. Or more to the point, like folding one egg white into an ocean of cream. That's how all-encompassing eternity is.

Why is this thing about time so important? Peter Kreeft explains, "God fell in love with us creatures of time, us passing gusts of wind, us passing guests, and invited us into the inner sanctum of the Master of the House forever—all of us, lock, stock and barrel full of time. How dare we deny Him His heart's desire? It is our heart's desire, too."[13] He's right. There's something inside of me that time helps define, and I'm not so sure I want to deny it, as much as discover all its hidden treasure.

Jesus, having both a divine and human nature, presented a kind of formula for our nature and destiny. The way our resurrected Lord was able to move through time and space is a prescription for our future heavenly experience. Jesus perfectly embodies physical things caught in time yet spiritual things that exist outside of time. We gusts of wind will one day feel as comfortable as Jesus when it comes to living with a physical *and* spiritual nature.

Bear with me on one more item regarding time, geometry, and dimensions, and we both may get an A+. All this stuff about third, fourth, and fifth dimensions proves just how *interesting* heaven will be.

Let me show you by asking a question: How long would staring at a dot on a piece of paper hold your interest? If you can say five seconds, I'm impressed. But what if you placed a pen on that dot and drew a line to create a two-dimensional stick figure? That's a bit more interesting, but certainly not as provocative as observing a three-dimensional sculpture of that figure, right? If it's a good sculpture, it might hold your attention for a long time.

Now, take it a step further. Because a sculpture is a far cry from being as fascinating as a real live human being who moves through time and space in the fourth dimension. In fact, you could spend a lifetime getting to know this captivating person. It's a fact that each dimension is more interesting than the previous.

Now carry this little formula through to the fifth dimension, heaven. All the wondrous things about the previous dimensions will be in heaven, plus a whole lot more. This means heaven will be *extremely* interesting. It will be irresistible, enravishing, intriguing, and at least ten more columns of adjectives. We think earth is enthralling with all its color, glory, and grandeur! The exotic peacock, the perfect hexagons in beehives, the aquamarine of a tropical lagoon, the orangutan who makes us giggle, and the inspiring snowcapped peaks of the Alps are all part of the fourth dimension. And—ta-dah—the fifth one is about to be revealed! Our little lesson about dimensions proves heaven will be far beyond all the beauty of earth combined. Can you now see why Paul says, "No eye has seen, no ear has heard, no mind has conceived what God has prepared for those who love him" (1 Corinthians 3:9)?

Who knows what wonders the fifth dimension, and probably many other dimensions, will contain. In eternity everything is just a beginning. No borders. No limits. A. W. Tozer said, "How completely satisfying to turn from our limitations to a God who has none. Eternal years lie in his heart. For him, time does not pass, it remains; and those who are in Christ share with him all the riches of limitless time and endless years."[14]

Our pilgrimage to heaven is not a journey toward the end of time, but to another kind of time. And time travelers we shall be until we arrive ... at the beginning.

Discovering Unseen Realities

This dusty little planet keeps spinning through time and deep dark space, not realizing that all the while it is swimming in the ocean of eternity and surrounded by a host of unseen divine realities and divine fulfillments. But we realize it because as pilgrims "we live by faith, not by sight"

(2 Corinthians 5:7). By faith we live on a different plane, in another dimension, at a higher level than the earthly one. By faith the rock-solid world becomes drained of substance and importance, and we see a heavenly meaning behind *everything*.

People who lack faith look at the front range of the Rocky Mountains and assume, in a mechanistic way, that a tectonic plate pushed this way and that, causing a quake and a shifting in the earth's crust then—voilà—there appeared Pikes Peak. But pilgrims heading for heaven realize that "by him all things were created: things in heaven and on earth, visible and invisible, whether thrones or powers or rulers or authorities; all things were created by him and for him" (Colossians 1:16). He has created invisible things that are just as real—no, *more* real—than the Rocky Mountains. No wonder we praise our Creator!

People who lack faith look at a beautiful cherry tree, shrug their shoulders, and suppose a seed fell, rain poured, roots sprouted, a sapling grew, and soon it shall be someone's firewood. God, they think, just wound nature up like a clock to let it ticktock on its way. People with heaven-inspired faith, look at the same tree and marvel that literally "in him all things hold together" (Colossians 1:17). That means *all* things. Right now. This instant. Even buds, bark, and branches. Elizabeth Barrett Browning once wrote:

> *Earth's crammed with heaven,*
> *And every common bush afire with God;*
> *But only he who sees takes off his shoes,*
> *The rest sit 'round it and pluck blackberries.*

Those with an earthly perspective assume that the waves of the sea are made up of plain old H_2O, but those with a heavenly point of view believe that every proton on the Periodic Table of the Elements is held together by God, for He is "sustaining all things by his powerful word" (Hebrews 1:3). Let that fact sink in. If God were to withdraw His command, the mountains, oceans, and trees wouldn't collapse into chaos, they would go poof and disappear! God's creation isn't static and inert, it's dynamic and actually in the process of being sustained this instant by His powerful word.

And when it comes to the marvel of the human body, those who have no faith claim we've risen out of slime to the status of *homo erectus,* and assume that humans draw breath under their own power. But pilgrims with a heart for heaven know differently, "for in him we live and move and have our being" (Acts 17:28). In heaven we will be more human than what our species only hinted of here. We will be more the man or the woman than what our gender only whispered of.

The faith of which I've been speaking imparts heavenly purpose to everything—absolutely everything—around us. This happens to me every Tuesday, Wednesday, and Thursday morning when my artist friend, Patti, helps get me out of bed. Before I get in the van and she sends me off to work, we pause at the the opened garage door and take a few moments to observe the day. We look at Mr. Aquilevech's white pine trees across the street—there's usually a cranky crow sitting in the branches. We enjoy the way the spiky tips of the cedar trees lining my side wall have such sharp points—each tip is a perfect vertical aiming above. We admire the way Mrs. Hollander's shrubs are starting to turn color from a silvery green to gold.

The other day Patti commented on a hibiscus bloom, reminding us, "God dreamed up that color! Perhaps just for the sheer fun of it." Pilgrims see His delight in giving us pleasure. Heavenly sojourners see God in everything; they see that every bush they pass on earth's wilderness is a burning bush, afire with God. And with such faith it is truly possible to please Him (Hebrews 11:6).

> *Heav'n above is softer blue,*
> *Earth around is sweeter green!*
> *Something lives in every hue,*
> *Christless eyes have never seen:*
> *Birds with gladder songs o'er-flow,*
> *Flow'rs with deeper beauties shine,*
> *Since I know, as now I know,*
> *I am His, and He is mine.*[15]

Madame Guyon, a seventeenth-century Christian noblewoman, wrote the following words from a French dungeon, having no hibiscus, cedar tree, sweet green earth, or soft blue heaven to cheer her on:

[The heaven-minded Christian] walks by a simple and pure faith, . . . and when this sojourner looks out of his own eyes, he sees things as though he were looking through the eyes of God. He sees his own life, he sees his surrounding circumstances, he sees other believers, he sees friends and enemies, he sees principalities and powers, he sees the whole course of the pageantry of history itself through the eyes of God ... and is content.[16]

Too Heavenly Minded?

Don't think such heavenly mindedness makes us pilgrims no earthly good. Don't pooh-pooh it as looking at the world through pie-in-the-sky, rose-colored glasses. Sojourners who think the most of the next world are usually those who are doing the highest good in this one. It is the person whose mind is only on earthly things who, when it comes to earth, does little good. C. S. Lewis expands on this, saying, "Aim at heaven and you get earth thrown in. Aim at earth and you get neither."[17]

When a Christian realizes his citizenship is in heaven, he begins acting as a responsible citizen of earth. He invests wisely in relationships because he knows they're eternal. His conversations, goals, and motives become pure and honest because he realizes these will have a bearing on everlasting reward. He gives generously of time, money, and talent because he's laying up treasures for eternity. He spreads the good news of Christ because he longs to fill heaven's ranks with his friends and neighbors. All this serves the pilgrim well not only in heaven, but on earth; for it serves everyone around him.

A few weeks ago I went to the Hair and Nail Shoppe to get a haircut. My secretary, Francie, met me at the salon to help me out of the van and get settled in front of the mirror at the hairdresser's station. As the stylist whipped the plastic cape over me, I glanced around at the other women. Ladies sat under hair dryers absorbed in *Vogue* magazines. A few women gabbed with their manicurists about the latest shades of red nail polish. Blow dryers whined over Neil Diamond on the radio. I looked on either side of me: a redhead in jeans was cracking gum and cutting the locks of the lady to my right, while a short Asian woman with long black hair worked to the left.

What does a pilgrim do in an average ordinary place like this? (At least average and ordinary for southern California.) Sojourners look for the unseen divine realities around them. I tried to put myself in the shoes of these women, looking for their "realities"—divorce, dieting, raising children, running for the school board, fighting off alcoholism, and planning the next party. A few professional types in their power suits in for a quick repair on a fingernail were dealing with different "realities"—promotions, payoffs, and executive stress.

Because faith helped me see each woman as precious in His sight, I knew God had His own divine realities in mind for each woman. I could pray, "Thy kingdom come, Thy will be done in the Hair and Nail Shoppe as it is in heaven."

So, sitting with my hair all wet, I interceded off and on for each person, setting in motion God's powerful workings in their lives. All because of faith. This is the way ordinary pilgrims make themselves of some earthly good.

And not only through prayer. As I wheeled from the station to wait for my hair to set, I noticed a little girl sitting two chairs down, swinging her legs and flipping through a tattered magazine. I asked her what she was reading and learned she was the ten-year-old daughter of the Asian woman. Within minutes we were engrossed in conversation, me telling her a Bible story, and her, explaining the games she enjoyed playing with her best friend. I told the little girl I liked her smile, her friendly manner, and the way she bypassed my wheelchair and looked into my eyes. I also told her about Jesus. For those twenty minutes I knew I was one heavenly minded person doing this child real and lasting earthly good.

My husband, Ken, lives like this. He's been fostering a relationship with two young gas-station attendants from Iran who work at the Shell station down the road. Most people are in and out for a quick fill-up, but Ken keeps his eyes open for the unseen divine realities at work in the lives of these two men. We're convinced that time, prayer, friendship, and a Bible in the Farsi language will make a difference. He's one heaven-minded person looking for ways to do earth some good.

Besides this, pilgrims do battle. The spiritual war raged hot and heavy earlier this year when Ken and I helped chaperone the prom of the public high school where he teaches. The early hours of the prom were a great time to connect with students, admire their tuxedos, and wish them well at college. After dinner, though, the lights went out, the music went up, and the ballroom reverted into a wild disco. Ken had to go supervise the bathrooms; I tried talking to my dinner partner, but we got tired of screaming at each other. Through the dark and deafening noise I spotted a senior girl in a skimpy white-sequined dress sitting on her boyfriend's knee. I decided to pray for her. As I stared at her, silently mouthing my prayer, it struck me that although the ballroom was shaking, my prayer was more powerful than the 600-amp Bose speakers angled over the dance floor. A simple intercession was shaking and sending repercussions across heaven, as well as scattering a few demons.

This is how heaven's citizens live while temporarily residing on earth. Heaven tells us every person, place, and thing has a purpose. This is why "we do not lose heart ... we fix our eyes not on what is seen, but what is unseen. For what is seen is temporary, but what is unseen is eternal" (2 Corinthians 5:16, 18).

Homesick for Heaven

We pilgrims walk the tightrope between earth and heaven, feeling trapped in time, yet with eternity beating in our hearts. Our unsatisfied sense of exile is not to be solved or fixed while here on earth. Our pain and longings make sure we will never be content, but that's good: it is to our benefit that we do not grow comfortable in a world destined for decay.

And so we squirm and writhe, knowing we don't quite fit; "we groan, longing to be clothed with our heavenly dwelling." But, oh, what a blessing are those groans! What a sweetness to feel homesick for heaven! What a glorious longing fills my heart to overflowing!

Wait a minute, Joni, perhaps you are thinking. *I'm not homesick for heaven. I rarely groan and long to be there ... I want to, but I don't know where to begin. It's not like I'm absorbed by the things of earth, it's just heaven doesn't feel like my home yet. Besides that, I don't have a real prayer burden for women at hair salons, girls at proms, or guys at gas stations.*

If this is you, don't panic. If, for you, heaven is still a glass house on some golden street rather than a warm and loving home, then hang in there. If you find it difficult to muster up longing for celestial mansions, if you aren't into this pilgrim thing, then perhaps we need to take the focus off heaven as a place.

It's more than that ... much, much more.

Chapter 6

Heaven Has Our Heart's Desire

—

*L*et your imagination run wild for a moment. Jesus has gone on to prepare a place for us, and each of us is to have a big mansion—no down payment or mortgage to worry about, thankfully—on a golden avenue overlooking acres of fields and flowers. Wow!

Or for you, not "wow."

Perhaps, "Well,... that's nice."

When it comes to a glass house on a golden street, you may be tempted to throw a stone through the glass—out of sheer gumption, to see if celestial plate glass cracks. Or maybe you're simply feeling awkward and uncomfortable in God's glittering, golden throne room. For that matter, you're still hung up in this tangle of earthly imagery whenever you picture heaven. You see yourself seated at the Wedding Feast of the Lamb where, presumably, there's no need for air-conditioning or central heating in the banquet hall. But where do you draw the line in dispensing with the paraphernalia of earth when picturing heaven? If the banquet is to be eaten decently, surely we will need knives and forks. Pots and pans to cook stuff in. Mixers must be somewhere in the background. And who does the dishes? People in hell?[1]

I can understand if these images don't make you yearn for your heavenly dwelling. It's not that you're absorbed by the things of earth; it's just that heaven doesn't *feel* like home. Yet the images painted in the Bible represent something designed to grip your heart, possess your soul, and call forth a powerful homesickness that makes you want to hurry up and unlock the front door of that mansion of yours.

Wouldn't it be nice to feel nostalgic for heaven that way?

Take a minute to consider a time when you were actually homesick. Not for heaven, but for your earthly home. Remember the aching? The sense of feeling like a stranger in your surroundings?

Boy, I remember it. I felt like my guts were being ripped out. I bawled when I was a little girl and had to stay at Aunt Dorothy's while my mother had a gallbladder operation. Then there was church camp. I was miserable. And that Thanksgiving when I first moved to California (of course, everyone first feels like a misfit in California).

My most recent bout with homesickness was in Bucharest, Romania. It was the middle of the night and I knew I was an alien as soon as I wheeled into the musty hotel lobby. A single dangling light bulb cast long shadows over dusty sofas and lamps leftover from the fifties. Prostitutes hid in a dark corner puffing cigarettes. From somewhere behind the desk, a radio featured Elvis Presley wailing "I Wanna Be Your Teddy Bear." There were bullet holes in the concrete wall. Moths and exhaust fumes filtered in through the open door, and somebody was screaming at a neighbor down the street.

I was tired, hungry, and dirty. There were no ramps for my wheelchair. I didn't fit in the bathroom. I didn't feel at home in the restaurant where they served tough meat swimming in oil and garlic. Everything about the place—the language, the culture, and especially the pillow on my mattress—made me long for Calabasas, California. It was awful. I know you've felt the same.

Why did Calabasas grip my heart? Was it the sidewalk ramps and curb-cuts? Radio stations playing better tunes than Elvis hits? Superior restaurants? Why do I feel I fit in California and not in Romania?

Because home is where your heart is.

This powerful truth needs to be elevated for a moment above the cross-stitched plaques on which we usually read it. Because if "home is where the heart is," then home must be more than the street address where you live. When you get homesick, your heart may tug for your own mattress and pillow, but this doesn't account for that gut-wrenching ache. What makes home is not a place, but who lives there. You feel at home when your heart is nestled near the one you love.

But sometimes, when you least expect it, even the people who make up home aren't enough. Sometimes when you're all tucked in with your own pillow and blanket, with the voice of the one you love close by, another kind of homesickness—a deeper kind—sneaks up on you.

Still Not Satisfied

Fragrant pine branches and the softness of falling snow. Cinnamon-spiced tea and vanilla candles. It was home at its 1957 best. Especially with a Christmas Eve visit from Uncle George and Aunt Kitty who, when she leaned down to give me a big hug, let me bury my nose in her fox stole scented with Evening in Paris perfume. Together, with the rest of the family in the candlelit living room, we sat on the couch and listened to Bing Crosby Christmas music on the radio. It was a quiet time. It was home.

Suddenly, out of nowhere, I was broadsided with homesickness. Good grief, there I was in the coziest of houses snug on the couch between people I loved, yet mantled with homesickness—a nostalgia for a bigger kind of home. I didn't catch on at first, but I was in the middle of another one of those heavenly longings. It may have been winter and far away from that Kansas wheat field we visited the summer before, but it was the same.

The next morning that sensitive longing retired in the presence of mundane things, and I became my ordinary self. It was Christmas Day. I shelved my fascination with the strange longing and rushed headlong into my pile of presents. I ripped open the paper of one gift and asked, "Is there more?" And then another gift, asking, "How many left?" and then after the final present, whined, "Is that all there is?" What was I looking for? Why wasn't I satisfied?

Throughout the day, I knew I was free to play with my toys, but occasionally I would leave my gifts, go upstairs to my room and lean on the windowsill to gaze outside. What was I pining after? What did I want?

What Do We Want?

When it comes to heaven, we are all children opening a thousand beautiful Christmas presents and asking after each one, "Is that all there is?"

In fact, when it comes to heaven, why don't you make a Christmas list—all the best joys, gifts, and presents that you imagine heaven will offer.

Ask your heart the question: What do you want? There's no restrictions on the list. The sky's the limit. Would it be beauty or wealth? Fame? Driving a Ferrari?

Now imagine getting it all. How soon do you think you would grow restless? How soon before you would say, "Is that all there is?"

Try another list, a deeper one. Endless talks with Beethoven about scoring music or long chats with Mary Cassatt discussing French Impressionism. Strategizing football plays with Tom Landry. How about a fit, healthy body for all you who have disabilities? Running? Dancing? Cooking with Julia Child? Playing guitar with Eric Clapton? A good conscience, freedom, peace of mind? It might be a few more thousand years before these would bore you, but eventually even they would become ho-hum.

Peggy Lee was on to something back in the seventies when she serenaded us, asking, "Is that all there is, my friend? Then let's keep dancing, let's break out the booze and have a ball, if that's all ... there is."[2] The song scared me then, and it scares me now. Is there *nothing* that will ultimately satisfy our hearts? Peter Kreeft suggests:

> Can you imagine any heaven that would not eventually be a bore? If not, does that mean that every good thing must come to an end, even heaven? After eighty or ninety years most people are ready to die; will we feel the same after eighty or ninety centuries of heaven? ... If we don't want boredom in heaven, what do we want? If heaven is real, what real desire does it satisfy? We want a heaven without death and without boredom. But we cannot imagine such a heaven. How can we desire something we cannot imagine?[3]

We cannot conjure up heaven in our minds because our desires go deeper than what our minds can imagine.

Thankfully, our hearts are always a beat ahead of our minds and bodies. Proverbs 4:23 is not off base when it says the heart goes deeper than the mind: "Above all else, guard your heart, for it is the wellspring of life." True, it also says the heart is desperately wicked, but that still demonstrates that it is the seat of deep passions. Important things happen in the heart. Out of it "flow the issues of life." We may have one foot here and the other in the hereafter, but our heart is often that part of us which tugs and pulls at that one foot stuck in the mud of earth, saying, "Get off of the earthly images, would you? Look, here's your other foot anyway. Up here is what you're longing for."

Really? Does our heart have the answer?

Does our heart have something to say in response to this haunting echo?

Can we trust our heart to *really* know what it wants?

When people approached Jesus with a need, it's curious that He often responded, "What do you want?" I've always thought this was an odd thing to say since, first, He could read their minds, and second, their need was often obvious—like Bartimaeus, the blind beggar, for one. But Jesus has His reasons for asking. He urges us to explore our heart's list of wants because He knows that we desire something deeper than getting a few surface needs satisfied.

And when it comes to heaven, He knows we desire something more fundamental than pleasure, prosperity, or power. Our heart thinks it's desperate to get back to the Garden, or, if not there, then someplace where our innocence and identity are sequestered. Says C. S. Lewis:

> Our lifelong nostalgia, our longing to be reunited with something in the universe from which we now feel cut off, to be on the inside of some door which we have always seen from the outside, is no mere neurotic fancy, but the truest index of our real situation...at last to be summoned inside would be both glory and honor and also the healing of that old ache.[4]

Healing That Old Ache

When it comes to attempting to heal that old ache, the human heart has had lots of experience. It is restless and raging, trying this and dabbling in that, hoping to find fulfillment, to possess something that will give us innocence, identity, and ... heaven. Our poor bruised heart, though, does not really want to possess heaven so much as to be possessed by it. It desires not so much pleasure, for pleasure can be exhausted. After we experience it, it's over. Our heart wants something glorious that lasts. For forever? Yes, if it were possible.

What the heart desires is ecstasy.

Ecstasy is that marvelous euphoria in which we totally forget ourselves, and yet find ourselves. The dictionary describes it as a state of being overpowered by joy, which causes you to step outside yourself, and a subscript explains that in Greek ecstasy means to "stand outside oneself." But a powerful experience like this can't be defined by a dictionary. To appreciate its meaning, ecstasy has to be experienced.

It is rapturous delight. Intense joy. Pure passion. When it comes to heaven, we want to be overpowered and caught up in something grand and wonderful outside ourselves. We want to be swept and wrapped up in a joy that weaves itself through every nerve and fiber. A joy that makes time stand still. We want to lose all sense of time and, therefore, disappointment. Like Elijah in his chariot, we want to be captured and carried away.

This is what our heart wants. This would be heaven without boredom.

I'm convinced the ecstasy of heaven is not to be found in the halls of a hallowed habitat tucked behind a galaxy where birds chirp and organs play with heavy tremolo and angels bounce from cloud to cloud. An earthly image like this falls flat. It's not even a biblical symbol; it's a syrupy, superficial image.

No, when I allow my Spirit-inspired heart to take over, I get a different picture. Last night I experienced a taste of heaven when I wheeled out to my backyard to look at the full moon. It shone perfectly round and pale white through a sheer curtain of high, thin clouds. A sprinkle of blue stars peeked through the haze, and someone down the street was playing a Chopin melody on a piano. A warm breeze touched me. A half-forgotten poem came to mind as I strained to see the stars: "They were tiny peepholes in a great black wall with the party lights of heaven streaming through."

For a split second I was in ecstasy. My heart broke for joy and then ... it was gone. Whenever we stumble upon ecstasy, our heart knows beyond a doubt that this is *it*. It's a glorious healing of that old ache, even if but for a short moment. Lovers who speak of being "in love" feel it most often. They stumble into love, lose themselves, and then find themselves overwhelmed by something gloriously larger that possesses them. And it's ecstatic.

You know what it's like. You know how it feels. Your heart grows faint and your breathing grows short just picturing the soft eyes and tender smile of the one you adore. Just being in the same room together is a thrill. You ply him with questions just to hear the sound of his voice. And the thought of a kiss? An embrace? You all but melt.

This kind of love, romantic love, is as close as many people get to the healing of that ache. Trouble is, most people forget that romantic love, like all the other loves—agape, phileo, or eros—is meant to point us to a greater, more fulfilling joy that enraptures. People cherish the glory they see in their lover, and they forget that the glory is not *in* the one they love, so much as shining *through* him or her. Most people are blind when it comes to this. They don't realize that all the glory comes from beyond the one being cherished, like a light reflecting in a mirror. They make the mistake of idolizing the one by whom they are smitten, rather than reading the cues that keep whispering, "It's not me ... it's not in my eyes ... I'm only a reminder of something, Someone else. Quick, who do I remind you of? Here's a hint: I'm made in the image of God."

Most people never take this broad and glorious hint. They forget that the human soul was made to enjoy some object never given, but only alluded to. They forget and so they place in the hands of the one they love the incredible burden of keeping the cup of joy overflowing; they heap on the lover's shoulders the weight of sustaining ecstasy that only God can carry. The result? They are bitterly crushed when romance fades and the one they adore fails to be God, falling short of keeping them enraptured. And so, on to the next lover. And the next god. And the next.[5]

With Christians it is different. We are rightfully coaxed in 1 Peter 1:22 and 4:8 and elsewhere to, "above all, love each other deeply ... from the heart." And for good reasons. In the first place, Christians get the hint, recognize the cues, and understand that the person we love is stamped with the image of God. We have the "homing detector," the flight instruments to help us see that the converging points in eternity *do not* meet in the face of the one we love, but pass through to meet in the face of God. To love each other deeply is to acknowledge that the divine glory that we see in the eyes of another *is* a reflection from beyond. This makes Christian love all the sweeter and each friend is an open invitation to see Jesus in him or her. As the song goes:

> *I see Jesus in your eyes and it makes me love Him,*
> *I feel Jesus in your touch and I know He cares,*
> *I hear Jesus in your voice and it makes me listen.*[6]

What's more, the love Christians share lasts much longer than any old romance. It lasts longer than a lifetime.

Second, we have a built-in warning system that sounds an alarm if we start to idolize the one we love. It blares, "Wrong coordinates! The points converge not in this face, but in God's! Get back on track!" God wants us to learn that human love is a signpost pointing to divine love. We are to learn where love's focus should be, and not be like a puppy dog who wags his tail and sniffs your finger when you are trying to point him to his food. Christians can and should properly read the signs. The one we love is a gift from God and, as a gift, points us to the Giver who is the One and only One who can provide an overflowing cup of joy, if not occasional ecstasy. This warning system keeps love, whether for our husband, wife, or friend, rightly focused and constantly refreshed.

Third, and most important, when we Christians love each other deeply, we catch a glimpse of that particular facet of God's love that is being cut, honed, and shaped in the life of the one we deeply love. We savor a foretaste of their true identity reserved in heaven, we inhale the fragrance of the heavenly person they are becoming. We see a particular aspect of heaven in them, we rejoice, and God receives glory—the mirror reflects His image back to Himself, and, once again, we are reminded that one day in eternity He shall indeed "be all and in all."

C. S. Lewis was intimately acquainted with the way humans mirror a higher, more heavenly glory when he wrote, "Remember that the dullest and most uninteresting person you talk to may one day be a creature which, if you saw it now, you would be strongly tempted to worship...."[7]

For me, this is one of those unseen divine realities. When I look into the eyes of a brother in Christ whom I love or a sister whom I cherish, I can almost see the spiritual being they are right behind their pupils. I also can't help but see their future divine fulfillment: "Christ in you the hope of glory." So you know what I do? In my mind, I get out my brush, mix some flesh tones, and I paint their face. I choose a certain color for the eyes, or I angle my brush for the slant of the cheek. Often I get so engrossed in the face, I forget what's being said. It's interesting that I don't pick the hands or the body. The face is where matter is subdued by the mind; it is where the eyes show up the lamp that's lit in the soul. And, my, is that person beautiful! I just have to paint him! I hear the heavenly echo in his voice, the haunting in his eyes, and I just have to portray it. As I said in the first chapter, it is painters who most often try to capture the echo of heavenly music. And when I see that timeless look in someone's eyes, I head for that art easel in my imagination.

Within our heart we find a shadow of heaven, especially as we "love one another deeply," for love is an unconscious desire for heaven. We now know what we want. We know the answer to our heart's longing.

In the Heart of God

What you do find in your heart and what you see reflected in the ones you love, is God. He and He alone provides the healing of that old ache. That's why heaven has to be more than a place.

Much, much more.

It must be a Person.

If you need a bit more convincing, then take this test St. Augustine gave his students centuries ago. Imagine God appeared to you and said, "You want heaven? I'll make a deal with you. I'll give you anything and everything you ask. Nothing will be a sin; nothing will be forbidden; and nothing will be impossible for you. You will never be bored and you will never die. Only ... you shall never see my face."[8]

Brrrr! Do you feel that chill in your soul? Your heart and mind recoil in unison on this one. Your primordial desire is that you want God more than anything else in the world. Like St. Augustine said, "Thou hast made us for thyself, and therefore our hearts are restless until they rest in thee."[9]

Yes, your heart's home is in the heart of God. He has placed within you a yearning for Himself, a desire to know Him and understand what He is like. Every soul feels the void and the emptiness until it connects with its Maker.

> *Like tides on a crescent sea-beach,*
> *When the moon is new and thin,*
> *Into our hearts high yearnings*
> *Come welling and surging in—*
> *Come from the mystic ocean,*
> *Whose rim no foot has trod—*
> *Some of us call it Longing,*
> *And others call it God.*[10]

Pleasures and treasures on earth may be sought after and not found, but only God comes with the guarantee that He *will* be found. "'You will seek me and find me when you seek me with all your heart. I will be found by you,' declares the Lord, 'and will bring you back from captivity'" (Jeremiah 29:13–14). Hurrah, no more exile! No more strangers in a strange land! God assures us "I will be found by you."

More specifically, He will be found in Jesus Christ. God illumines our heart and mind when we sincerely search for the Truth and reveals Jesus, the photo image of the Father who dwells in unapproachable light. Jesus is the source of the haunting echo and the heavenly song. Jesus is God wearing a human face. He is real and not abstract. He invites us to do what we cannot do with the Incomprehensible—He invites us to drink and eat of Him, and "taste and see that the Lord is good."

> *All my life long I had panted*
>   *For a drink, from some clear spring,*
> *That I hoped would quench the burning*
>   *Of the thirst I felt within.*
> *Hallelujah! I have found Him*
>   *Whom my soul so long has craved!*
> *Jesus satisfies my longings—*
>   *Through His blood I now am saved.*[11]

"That God can be known by the soul in tender personal experience while remaining infinitely aloof from the curious eyes of reason constitutes a paradox best described as 'Darkness to the intellect but sunshine to the heart.'"[12] Jesus is sunshine to our heart. Not just to our logic, but our heart. Praise God, we *know* the answer to our heart's longing. It's Jesus!

The disciples of Jesus, at first, weren't so sure that this Man in their midst would fulfill their deepest longings, so "Philip said, 'Lord, show us the Father and that will be enough for us.' Jesus answered: 'Don't you know me, Philip, even after I have been among you such a long time? Anyone who has seen me has seen the Father'" (John 14:8–9).

Our longings are satisfied in Him for "the Son is the radiance of God's glory and the exact representation of his being" (Hebrews 1:3). We can know God—our Father who art in heaven—if we know Jesus. And knowing Him, as we would desire to know a Lover, is ecstasy. His invitation to "enter into the joy of the Lord" is like stepping into a raft and being carried helplessly along a surging current, spilling over and splashing with joy. Please note that the joy of the Lord does not enter into us, but we, into it. We are enveloped by something larger, something greater than ourselves, a heavenly "in-loveness" in which we can do nothing but laugh and enjoy the ride. Jesus smiles, stretches out His hand and welcomes us into His raft with the invitation, "whoever loses his life for my sake will find it" (Matthew 10:39).

When you enter into the Lord's joy, ecstasy spills not only into laughter, but into song. A song, like poetry, is more the language of the heart than mere prose. This is why the old hymn writers who were ecstatic about God *always* sang about heaven. I bet Charles Wesley was enraptured when he penned the fourth stanza to "Love Divine, All Loves Excelling":

> *Finish then Thy new creation,*
> *Pure and spotless let us be;*
> *Let us see Thy great salvation*
> *Perfectly restored in Thee:*
> *Changed from glory into glory,*
> *Till in heav'n we take our place,*
> *Till we cast our crowns before Thee,*
> *Lost in wonder, love and praise!*

Tears have streamed down my cheeks in church when I've sung that last line: Heaven is a place, and also a Person in whom I am lost in wonder, love, and praise. My heart insists that I sing when heaven courses through my veins.

Face-to-Face

Remember when I shared that lovers always focus on the face of the one they adore? And in that face they find ecstasy, albeit fleeting? Here's a pop quiz for all you romantics: in whose face do we find ecstasy lasting? Take a broad and glorious hint from Psalm 27:4, 8: "One thing I ask of the Lord, this is what I seek: that I may dwell in the house of the Lord all the days of my life, to gaze upon the beauty of the Lord.... My heart says of you, 'Seek his face!' Your face, Lord, I will seek." And if you need another reminder, listen to Psalm 105:4: "Look to the Lord and his strength; seek his face always." The points of eternity converge in the face of our Savior. Little wonder I not only want to paint in my mind the faces of friends I love, but also the face of Jesus.

Since you got the answer to that question, this next one is easy: What are the correct coordinates for focusing your faith? The faith of which I have been speaking up until now is only the lens, the spectacles through which "the eyes of the heart may be enlightened" (Ephesians 1:18). The faith I've been describing is only a way of seeing and, therefore, believing something. But this isn't the whole story.

The correct coordinates on which to focus the eyes of the heart are Hebrews 12:2: "Let us fix our eyes on Jesus, the author and perfecter of our faith." Jesus is the Unseen Divine Reality. Everything shall find its future divine fulfillment in Him. "For no matter how many promises God has made, they are 'Yes' in Christ," says 2 Corinthians 1:20. This means *every* promise. The Author and Perfecter has conceived every unseen divine purpose and has planned its fulfillment to be a part of the wonder of heaven, "so that in everything he might have supremacy" (Colossians 1:18).

Everything from Pikes Peak to my backyard washed in the glow of a full moon—every bit of beauty here is but a shadow of something far more beautiful there, and "we know that the whole creation has been groaning as in the pains of childbirth right up to the present time" (Romans 8:22). The creation is groaning, longing to be clothed with the beauty its Designer originally intended.

Not only this dusty little planet will find fulfillment but, God willing, the teenager in the white-sequined dress will too. The Iranian gas station guys. And the little Asian girl in the Hair and Nail Shoppe, for "we ourselves, who have the firstfruits of the Spirit, groan inwardly as we wait eagerly for our adoption as sons" (Romans 8:23). He will give us much more than the innocence we were groping for back in the Garden; He has imputed to us His righteousness. Our future divine fulfillment is alluded to in 1 John, for one day "we shall see Him and be like Him." Completely.

To pursue heaven is to pursue Him. To pursue Him is to find heaven.

It's that simple. If you wholeheartedly pursue Jesus, you can't help but be heaven-minded and sigh with Psalm 73:25: "Whom have I in heaven but you? And being with you, I desire nothing on earth."

Some will say, though, "Wait a minute, there are a lot of other things on earth I desire. Besides, I already know Jesus, I'm saved—have been for fifteen years—but I'm still not gripped by heavenly glories above. I'm still not homesick for heaven."

Set Your Hearts on Things Above

There's a solution. It may take effort, it will require commitment, but it can be solved: "Since, then, you have been raised with Christ, set your hearts on things above, where Christ is seated at the right hand of God" (Colossians 3:1).

This verse is a command. We may think this command isn't as necessary as other mandates in Scripture, but it is. When you consider that the first and greatest commandment is to love the Lord with all your *heart and mind,* it follows that we should set our *entire being* (that's what it means when it says "heart and mind") on things above.

My heart is the seat of all kinds of appetites and affections. Isn't yours? Our heart is hungry, not for food, but for a whole range of wrong coordinates. Sometimes the hunger in our heart gets us into trouble, and we wish we could curb the appetites. You'll be surprised, though, to learn who gives us these desires: "Remember how the Lord your God led you all the way in the desert these forty years, to humble you and to test you in order to know what was in your heart, whether or not you would keep his commands. He humbled you, *causing you to hunger* and then feeding you with manna, which neither you nor your fathers had known, to teach you that man does not live on bread alone but on every word that comes from the mouth of the Lord" (Deuteronomy 8:2–3).

The Lord is the one who causes us to hunger. He is the one who has put within our heart those yearnings. At first, this seems odd. Doesn't God know the "hungries" often get us into trouble?

God has good reasons for placing within us a heart that has such burgeoning appetites. He does so in order to test us and humble us, to see what is in our innermost being, to see whether or not we would follow Him. According to Deuteronomy, He places in our sight a whole range of things that *could* get us off track, but His purpose is never to tempt, only to test to see if we will zero in on the right coordinates. Will you succumb to the handsome face of your best friend's husband or will you choose heaven? Will you covet that third Penn International 50W fishing reel or will you desire heaven? Will you max out four credit cards on new wallpaper, carpet, and furnishings or will you invest in heaven?

To hunger is to be human, but to satiate yourself on God is to send your heart ahead to heaven. Feed on Him in your heart, and you will be yanking that foot out of the mud of earth and stepping closer to eternity.

I admit it's a constant struggle to set your heart on things above. Always and always we want more. And where we place our citizenship, whether in heaven or on earth, is revealed by those things we passionately desire. If we desire dull, sensual things of earth, our souls reflect that dullness; if our desires rise to find fulfillment in the exalted, in the noble, pure, and praiseworthy, then and only then do we find satisfaction, rich and pleasurable.

The great in the kingdom of heaven will simply be those who set their heart on Christ and loved Him more. The great will be those who, having received a "You're off course!" warning from the heart's homing detector, simply got back on track.

That's the way I want to live. When I read, "Delight yourself in the Lord and he will give you the desires of your heart" (Psalm 37:4), I want to focus on Jesus, not my heart's list of desires. Yes, I realize that curbing the appetites of my heart will heighten my loneliness on earth, but I'm convinced I am destined for unlimited pleasure at the deepest level in heaven. I also know that nothing now quite meets the standards of my yearning heart and this quiet but throbbing ache drives me to anticipate heavenly glories above.

For me, true contentment on earth means asking less of this life because more is coming in the next.

Godly contentment is great gain. Heavenly gain. Because God has created the appetites in your heart, it stands to reason that He must be the consummation of that hunger. Yes, heaven will galvanize your heart if you focus your faith not on a place of glittery mansions, but on a Person, Jesus, who makes heaven a home.

Set Your Minds on Things Above

Colossians 3:1 is really a double command. We are not only to set our hearts on things above where Christ is seated, but "set [our] minds on things above," as well. That's hard. Our hearts hold a shadow of heaven, but not our minds. I can prove it.

Take last week. After Bible study a few of the girls hung around and started talking as we sipped coffee. You'd think we would have discussed the apostle's encouragement to set our hearts and minds on things above, right? Wrong. Instead, we discussed the advantages of the new clean-and-easy, stand-up toothpaste tube with the convenient cap that flips up or unscrews for ease of use and cleaning. We discussed the sale at the May Company, whether or not Excedrin PM is just a marketing ploy to get more people on sleeping pills, and the latest reports of what the First Lady has been up to.

There's nothing wrong or immoral with these thoughts, but it's no surprise God said to Isaiah, "For my thoughts are not your thoughts, neither are your ways my ways.... As the heavens are higher than the earth, so are my ways higher than your ways and my thoughts than your thoughts" (Isaiah 55:8–9). Somehow, I don't think God stays up at night wondering why they don't standardize electric plugs worldwide.

God's thoughts are higher than ours. And the gap needs to be bridged. My thoughts need to rise to the heavenlies where Christ is seated. This means more than just thinking nice Girl Scout thoughts that are clean and reverent. "Set your minds on things above" means just that: thinking about things above.

This struck me not long ago when, during a visit to Italy, we explored Rome's Basilica. At the front of the cavernous cathedral, resplendent in Italian marble, mosaics, and statuary, was not the altar I expected to see. Instead, there was a large throne. It was fashioned from dark gold wood and surrounded by gilded clouds and bolts of lightning. Sun streamed through the windows above, washing the entire area in warm and beautiful tones. It sounds gaudy, but actually, it was rather inspiring. It was a pleasant surprise, albeit a feeble representation of the real throne of glory in heaven.

After I returned home, I thought about the throne in the Basilica as I laid in bed one night. It was nothing like the throne depicted in Daniel 7:9: "The Ancient of Days took his seat.... His throne was flaming with fire, and ... thousands upon thousands attended him." I tried to picture the real thing and it became a wonderful exercise in setting my mind on things above. The earthly imagery of a throne engulfed in flames, to my mind, sounded a bit like *Star Wars,* so I focused on the verse that says, "He sits on the throne of our praises."

I decided to *think* about just that: A throne made of people's praises. Each joint and leg represented "Thou art worthy" or "You are holy" or "Your name is wonderful" and many more. I pictured God's delight in reclining on such praises. Not your garden-variety delight, but joy-filled laughter for "the One enthroned in heaven *laughs*" (Psalm 2:4). Before long, I found myself laughing too, lighthearted and raised with Christ in the heavenlies; then, falling prostrate and praising Him for granting me access to the inner sanctum as well as the honor of building Him a throne of praise.

Is this all too heavenly minded? No way. When my mind chews on Scripture, as well as its symbols of heaven, faith has something to grow on. That time of contemplation helped yank my foot further out of the mud of earth, making my heart airier and my mind purer.

To set our minds on Christ means not only the contemplation of the divine in heaven, but the divine on earth. Think about Jesus and Him alone. Contemplate Philippians 4:8 and think about "whatever is true, whatever is noble, whatever is right, whatever is pure, whatever is lovely, whatever is admirable" about Christ. Picture Jesus blessing the little children and remark to Him in prayer how gracious or kind you think He is, how tender of Him to take a baby out of the arms of its mother, rock it gently, and kiss its cheek. Think about Him tousling the hair of a little boy or taking in His hands the face of a child and blessing her. How noble, how lovely of Jesus. Think about Him reaching out to heal the bleeding hurt of a woman with a hemorrhage. How tender, how compassionate of Jesus. Think about Him turning a face of steel toward religious phonies and squaring off against sin. How holy and awesome of Jesus. And how changed you are after thinking such thoughts.

This is where love really builds between you and God. Because remember, He is also thinking about you. Psalm 139:17–18 says, "How precious to me are your thoughts, O God! How vast is the sum of them! Were I to count them, they would outnumber the grains of sand." The Son makes the Father's thoughts available by stooping to make Himself comprehensible to our pea-sized brains. In the Bible, Jesus has given us His thoughts and we have "the mind of Christ" when we lay hold of Him and His ideas. Then and only then can we be drawn up to heaven.

Heaven and God ... God and Heaven

To think about heaven is to think about Jesus. To pursue heaven with your heart is to pursue Him.

I'm not taking literary license. I'm not being lazy with Bible interpretations. Heaven and God are intimately entwined, and the pursuit of one is the pursuit of the other. Matthew 23:22 says, "He who swears by heaven swears by God's throne and by the one who sits on it." If you swear by heaven, you are swearing by God. Heaven is the place where God so much *is,* that you can refer to one or the other and virtually mean both.

Whenever Scripture refers to the kingdom of heaven, it means the kingdom of God. John MacArthur explains:

> It's just another way to express God. In the period between the Old and New Testament, the Jews never used the name of God ... because they thought it was too holy to come through their lips. One of the things they substituted for the name of God was heaven. Instead of saying, 'I worship God,' they would say, 'I worship heaven.' Instead of saying, 'Call upon the name of God,' they would say, 'Call upon the name of heaven.' To enter the kingdom of heaven is to enter the kingdom of God.[13]

The King of heaven wants us to see this tight connection between the Place and the Person. When our heart melts into God's and when our mind is thinking on Him, Place and Person no longer seem separated. "God [has] raised us up with Christ and seated us with him in the heavenly realms in Christ Jesus" (Ephesians 2:6). Amazing! When we understand our position in Christ, we begin to grasp our position in the heavenly realms. We are *already seated* with Christ in the heavenly realms. I'm not talking about astral projection or anything spooky. We're not actually in heaven the place, yet. But we *are* in the heavenly realms in that it's a sphere in which we live under God's rule and His Spirit's blessing. We are under the dominion of the King of heaven, and that places us in His realm. The King has come as well as His kingdom. The King is in our midst, and His kingdom is within us. All signs point to there *and* here. All signs lead to Him because all signs come from Him.

Use your eyes of faith here. This is another one of those unseen divine realities. "You have already come to Mount Zion, to the heavenly Jerusalem. You have come to thousands upon thousands of angels in joyful assembly, to the church of the firstborn, whose names are written in heaven" (Hebrews 12:22–23). Why all the verbs in the present tense? Well, as I said in an earlier chapter, it *may* have something to do with the different kind of time in which heaven exists, or the next and new dimension of mansions and golden streets. More likely, God simply wants to get your mind racing and your heart beating with a present-tense excitement, a right-around-the-corner anticipation of heaven. Isn't that the way strangers on foreign soil are supposed to feel about their homeland?

Live in the present tense of heaven and you will smell the heavenly fragrance of the person you will become. Your life will have intensity and depth. You will sit close to self-scrutiny, understanding that by your words and actions you are doing earth a world of good. Your heaven-inspired faith will give you joy and peace, without parade or noise.

Most of all, you will begin to feel at home. You will begin to see "our Father who art in heaven" not as the Incomprehensible, but as Jesus sees Him: Abba-Father. Daddy.

Home is where Daddy is.

Let's Go Home

I like earth. But my heart pumps for heaven.

Calabasas, California, is nice, but it pales in the light of the heavenly realms. Home is pretty good here, but my homing instincts often have me pulling up a chair on the front porch of my mansion to shade my eyes and scan "a land that stretches afar." I have a glorious homesickness for heaven, a penetrating and piercing ache. I'm a stranger in a strange land, a displaced person with a fervent and passionate pain that is, oh, so satisfying. The groans are a blessing. What a sweetness to feel homesick for heaven for "a longing fulfilled is sweet to the soul" (Proverbs 13:19).

Never was this symbolized more clearly than at one of our recent JAF Ministries' retreats I helped lead for families of disabled children. After a week of wheelchair hikes, Bible studies, and arts and crafts, I listened as the microphone was passed from family to family, each tearfully sharing how wonderful the time had been. Some talked of meeting new friends. Others, of the games, music, and hikes. A few said how they wished the week could go on and on.

Then little red-haired, freckle-faced Jeff raised his hand. He had Down syndrome and had won the hearts of many adults at the retreat. People had been captivated by his winsome smile and joyful spirit. Everyone leaned forward to hear his words. Jeff grabbed the mike and kept it short and sweet as he bellowed: "Let's go home!" He smiled, bowed, and handed back the microphone. All the families roared with laughter.

His mother told me later that, even though Jeff thoroughly immersed himself in the week's festivities, he missed his daddy back home.

I identify with Jeff. The good things in this world are pleasant enough, but would we *really* wish for it to go on as it is? I don't think so. The nice things in this life are merely omens of even greater, more glorious things yet to come. God would not have us mistake this world for a permanent dwelling. It was C. S. Lewis who said something about not mistaking pleasant inns for home on our journey to heaven. I'm with him and I'm with Jeff. It's a good life, but I am looking forward to going home.

I miss my home.

I miss God.

Chapter 7

Heaven:
The Home of Love

—

*W*hen you're in love, waiting is hard.

It's as true now as it was two thousand years ago. Just ask Judith, a young Jewish maid who lived in the hills beyond Jerusalem, and Nathaniel who grew up in the city.

For Judith, the romance began long before her betrothal to Nathaniel. She was just a little girl drawing water at a well outside the city walls of Jerusalem when they met, and the smiles between them caught the eyes of their parents. The years passed, their friendship grew, and it wasn't long before the families of both Judith and Nathaniel were happily contemplating a wedding. The parents made the decision, while Judith and Nathaniel freely consented. That was the custom. That was the Jewish way.

The wedding bells started ringing for the two of them when Nathaniel took the first step. Leaving his home in Jerusalem one morning, he traveled to Judith's village to speak with her father about a betrothal. As he approached her home, Nathaniel got sweaty palms—Jewish tradition treated the betrothal as more important than the wedding itself!

He knew there were two things to discuss regarding the establishment of a betrothal covenant. First, he would ask Judith's father for his daughter's hand in marriage. Then he would negotiate concerning the price to secure his bride, a dowry that showed Judith's family that he, Nathaniel, had the means to be able to properly care for her. He loved Judith so much he was ready and willing to commit a large sum—he and his dad had talked it over, and they both agreed Judith was worth whatever it took.

That morning Nathaniel was not disappointed. Judith's father was glad to give his daughter's hand in marriage and a dowry was agreed upon. Nathaniel happily purchased his new bride and the betrothal contract was sealed. That afternoon, in a formal ceremony, the bride and groom confirmed their covenant by drinking together from a cup of wine. It was a beautiful symbol of their marriage covenant, and Judith's family spread hugs, kisses, and tears all around. Nathaniel and Judith at that point were officially married, a union that could not be dissolved except by divorce. However, it would be a long time before they would actually live together.

Nathaniel, full of happy anticipation, excused himself late that afternoon and traveled back to his father's house. As Judith watched her groom leave, she realized both of them had a great deal of work to do to get ready. Nathaniel was returning to his father's house to prepare a place for them to live. She knew he would be constructing a nice, large addition onto the home where they would live under the same roof with Nathaniel's family. In all probability, it would be an entire year before her groom would return for Judith and take her into his own house. She could hardly wait!

Weeks and months dragged by for the bride-in-waiting, but Judith knew he'd be faithful to his promise. She busied herself by gathering items for her new house, learning all she could about being a good wife, and daydreaming with her bridesmaids about what married life would be like. In private moments, though, when she was alone in her room, she pined for Nathaniel. The separation between them seemed endless.

One morning Judith woke up and realized a full year had almost passed. She knew Nathaniel could be coming for her at any time. She also knew he and his groomsmen would come for her at night. That was another custom. Which night? She had no idea and that made it all the more exhilarating. Judith spread word to her bridesmaids to be ready at any moment.

One evening after dinner, as she was leaning on the window sill, Judith heard a faint voice in the distance, "The bridegroom is coming! He's coming!" This was it! She quickly jumped up and ran to her room to gather the things she had packed, hoping all the while that her girlfriends in the village also heard the shout. Meanwhile, Nathaniel was marching toward the village with his friends in a torchlight procession. As more bystanders recognized the wedding party, they took up the call of celebration and cried out the good news, passing the word from block to block. The bridegroom was on his way!

The bridesmaids caught wind of the warning and hurried to Judith's home to help her get dressed in her bridal garment. In a matter of moments, the torchlight processional halted outside her home. Judith peeked out her window. The oil lamps threw off flashes of light as they dangled at the end of their long wooden poles held aloft. Her bridesmaids heard laughter and singing in the street below and began singing a song of their own. She took one glance in the polished metal mirror before she and her family and friends rushed outside to meet Nathaniel and his groomsmen.

When the bride dressed in her gown stepped through the door and onto the street, the wedding party cheered. Amidst singing and laughter, Nathaniel took Judith's hand and together, with the party, they walked by torchlight back to the home of Nathaniel's father, where the wedding guests were already waiting. When they arrived at the house, Judith and Nathaniel greeted the guests and welcomed everyone to the wedding banquet. The time had finally come for them to consummate their marriage, so, after excusing themselves, they moved to the bridal chamber. While the groomsmen and bridesmaids waited outside, Nathaniel took the hand of his beloved, and they entered the chamber alone. In the privacy of the room, he took her in his arms, kissed her, and after a time, laid with her in their bed, fulfilling the covenant they had made the year before. For the two of them, it was ecstasy and the long waiting period only made their lovemaking sweeter and more pleasurable.

After a while, Nathaniel left the bridal chamber and announced the consummation of his marriage to the other members of the waiting wedding party. Word spread like wildfire to the other guests at the banquet table, and the real feasting and celebration began—there was dancing, music, and laughter up and down the street where Nathaniel lived. During all this time, though, Judith remained hidden in the bridal chamber. This was a Jewish custom, as well, known as "the days of hiding." But at the very end of the seventh day of the wedding feast, the groom brought his bride from the chamber with her veil removed. "Please greet the wife of the groom," Nathaniel's friends announced, and everyone wildly applauded the new couple.

The two of them had longed for this moment all their lives, and, from that day on, Nathaniel and Judith lived happily ever after.[1]

Behold the Bridegroom!

I brushed off the dust from this story depicting the ancient Jewish custom of betrothal not to give a history lesson, but a spiritual one. The romance between Judith and Nathaniel is jam-packed with glorious symbols for you and me as we wait for heaven. Symbols that explain why I long for and actually *miss* my Savior.

John 3:29 tells me that "the bride belongs to the bridegroom," and, unlike the situation in modern marriages, I'm His possession. My life is hid with Christ in God, and who I am won't appear until He appears. My life is wrapped up in the One who redeemed me. Redeemed me in *love*. So, naturally I'm going to pine for Him and feel homesick to be with Him, especially when I know where He is and what He's doing: "In my Father's house are many rooms; if it were not so, I would have told you. I am going there to prepare a place for you. And if I go and prepare a place for you, I will come back and take you to be with me that you also may be where I am" (John 14:2–3).

These are the words of a Lover. The Lover of my soul. Maybe at one time the meaning in this verse eluded me, but when placed in the context of Him as Bridegroom, and me as bride, it has me packing my trousseau and getting ready to go.

My love for heaven is energized because I know how He feels about me: "The Lord will take delight in you.... As a bridegroom rejoices over his bride, so will your God rejoice over you" (Isaiah 62:4–5). Ponder that for a moment. He *rejoices* over you, and don't say that word like a plaster-of-paris saint in a less-than-amazing tone of voice. It's a jump-up-and-down, clenched fist, throw-your-head-back, and yell out loud, "Rejoice!" Jesus is brimming with heartfelt love for you when He says in Song of Songs 2:14, "Show me your face, let me hear your voice; for your voice is sweet, and your face is lovely." This is a God in love.

It's not a matter of sweet words. No. He gave his life as His dowry, and the Cross shows me that He and His Father agreed on an exorbitant price. Every time I drink from the communion cup of wine, I remember the covenant between my Bridegroom and me. And I've promised Him I will drink from that cup in remembrance of Him until He comes.

Until He comes. That's the hard part.

Waiting is so hard. It's even harder when you love someone.

Like Judith in our story, I sometimes find myself leaning on the edge of time's windowsill, wondering when, oh, when will He return? It makes me wonder about the rest of the marriage symbols between Judith and Nathaniel. Do the shouts in the city street represent the shout of the archangel heralding the coming of Christ, the Bridegroom (1 Thessalonians 4:16)? Does the sudden arrival of the wedding party mean that He will surprise us and come like a thief in the night (Matthew 24:42–44 and 1 Thessalonians 5:2)? Jesus drops a hint in Revelation 16:15 when He says, "Behold, I come like a thief! Blessed is he who stays awake."

What about the bride and His groomsmen waiting in the street? Is this a symbol of the Lord rapturing us from our homes and meeting us in the clouds? For "the dead in Christ will rise first. After that, we who are still alive and are left will be caught up together with them in the clouds to meet the Lord in the air" (1 Thessalonians 4:16–17). There are some who say that the Wedding Feast of the Lamb will be celebrated during the seven years of tribulation, and, just as the groom brought out his bride after her seven "days of hiding," so, after the seven years of tribulation, Christ will return with His bride to crush His enemies and set up housekeeping on earth. Is this the meaning behind these symbols?

I don't know. And I don't need to know. My responsibility as the betrothed is to be prepared and wait.

Be Prepared ... the Pure and Spotless Bride

I want to see the face of my Savior.

You may not realize it, but you do too. We want to see. We find it hard to rest comfortably in a relationship—with God, with anyone—when we cannot see the face of the one we adore. This is why I paint in my head the faces of friends I care deeply about, especially when I'm away from them. The essence of who they are is held in the eyes, the mouth, the smile. The face is the focal point of personality.

When it comes to brides and bridegrooms, full intimacy comes between a man and a woman face-to-face. And when the Bible speaks of longing for God, it speaks in terms of wanting to see His face. The psalmist pleads with God, "Make your face shine upon us," and "Do not hide your face from us." Ultimately, "in righteousness I will see your face; when I awake, I will be satisfied with seeing your likeness" (Psalm 17:15).

To hold the gaze of God is to find love, acceptance, and satisfaction. Well, yes and no.

There is still a thick shield between God and us. We cannot see what our heart longs to because as 1 Timothy 6:16 says, "God lives in unapproachable light, whom no one has seen nor can see." When Moses pressed hard upon God to see His face, he would have been glad to use thick glass coated with UV block and grab a quick peek at God through his fingers. But, no. Moses was only permitted to glimpse the backside of God's glory, for the Lord warned, "My face must not be seen" (Exodus 33:23). God didn't say this because there was nothing for Moses to see; He said it because He knew His light would kill. No man can see God and live. The Lord's glorious radiance would have snuffed Moses out in a nanosecond.

Even when Isaiah "saw" the Lord high and exalted on a throne, he did not behold God's face. He only glimpsed the periphery of the radiance of God. The sight threw Isaiah so deeply into despair over his sin that he cried, "Woe to me! . . . I am ruined! For I am a man of unclean lips" (Isaiah 6:5).

Sin is the problem. Sin is more than a thick shield between God and us, and acknowledging our stockpile of iniquities won't make it go away. No amount of confessing our sin will help us see God. That's backward. We don't have a clue as to the heinous nature of our sin until first we glimpse God's radiance, and then the words come tumbling out, "Woe is me!" The closer the apostle Paul got to God, the more he cried, "I am the chief of sinners." I used to think this was a pompous, grandstanding thing for Paul to say, but not any more. It's the cry of the saint sensitized to sin.

Our longing to see God is a longing, whether we know it or not, to see our sins exposed and to be cleansed by God Himself. Just as guilt will cause a child to hide in shame from her daddy's face, our deepest desire is to be clean, be free, to be transparent before the Father. And it won't happen until we see His face.[2]

This is a living paradox. We desire to see the face of God, but we cringe at seeing the face of God. We are cleansed from our sin, but we're still unclean. We're justified before God, but we've got miles of sanctification to go before we sleep. We're in the household of God, but not home yet. Our eyes have been opened, but we can only see through a glass darkly. It's frustrating!

This is partly why it's so hard to muster strong feelings about heaven. You and I going to heaven for a wedding? Our wedding? "His bride has made herself ready. Fine linen, bright and clean" (Revelation 19:7–8, fine linen stands for the righteous acts of the saints). Righteous acts! We glance down and see stains and smudges all over our wedding gown, which, by the way, is tearing at the seams and missing a few pearls and fasteners. Little wonder we cower at seeing our Bridegroom.

It's one thing to have funny feelings about a heavenly wedding, but I actually felt this way at my earthly wedding.

On the morning of the big day, my girlfriends laid me on a couch in the church's bridal salon to dress me. They strained and grunted to shift my paralyzed body this way and that, fitting me into the huge, cumbersome wedding gown. When I got back in my chair, an usher brought word that the guests were seated, and it was time to line up. We reached the glass doors of the church, they swung open, and the blast from the organ gave us goose bumps.

Just before the wedding march, I glanced down at my gown. I had accidentally wheeled over the hem. It left a greasy tire mark. My bouquet of daisies were off-center on my lap since my paralyzed hand couldn't hold them. No amount of corseting and binding my body gave me a perfect shape. The dress just didn't fit. It was draped over a thin wire mesh covering my wheels, but it still hung clumped and uneven. My chair was spiffed up as much as possible, but it was still the big, clunky gray thing with belts, gears, and ball bearings that it always was. I was not the picture-perfect bride you see in magazines.

My last bridesmaid began her walk up the aisle, and I inched my chair closer to the last pew to catch a glimpse of Ken at the front. I saw him waiting at attention, looking tall and stately in his formal attire. He was craning his neck to look up the aisle. He was looking for me. My face grew hot and my heart began to pound. Suddenly, everything was different. I had seen my beloved. How I looked no longer mattered. All that mattered was getting up to the front of the church to be with him. I *could* have felt ugly and unworthy, except that the love in Ken's face washed it all away. I was the pure and perfect bride. That's what he saw, and that's what changed me.

Years later, somewhere around our tenth wedding anniversary, I asked him, "What were you thinking on our wedding day?"

His answer delighted me. He said, "I woke up so early that morning, excited that I would see you in your wedding gown. And even though I knew there would be hundreds of people in the church, I knew my eyes would be for you only. In fact, I'll never forget that wonderful feeling when I saw you wheeling down the aisle in your chair. You looked so beautiful."

"You mean, you didn't think much about my wheelchair? My paralysis?"

He thought for a minute, then shook his head. "No. Really, I just thought you were gorgeous."

Our entrance into heaven may be something like this. One look from God will change us. And earth is just the dress rehearsal.

True, we presently see stains and smudges all over us, and we cower, thinking, *He'll never see anything lovely in me.* But still, we ache to see Him. And so, like Judith in the story, we live in hope. God *will* find us and He will *not* always remain beyond our sight. Our Bridegroom desires that I long and look for Him "while we wait for the blessed hope." And "everyone who has this hope in him purifies himself, just as he is pure" (l John 3:3).

It's called "being prepared," all you saints in your torn bridal garments, and "it teaches us to say 'No' to ungodliness and worldly passions, and to live self-controlled, upright and godly lives in this present age, while we wait for the blessed hope—the glorious appearing of our great God and Savior, Jesus Christ, who gave himself for us to redeem us from all wickedness and to purify for himself a people that are his very own, eager to do what is good" (Titus 2:12–14).

One day He will come for us and look into our eyes. We will hold His gaze. And all the stains and smears of sin will be purified out of us just by one searching of those eyes. It will be more than we dreamed of, more than we longed for.

> *Here, O my Lord, I see Thee face to face,*
> *Here would I touch and handle things unseen;*
> *Here grasp with firmer hand eternal grace,*
> *And all my weariness upon Thee lean.*[3]

Waiting on the Groom

We may be separated from our Savior, but that's no reason to sit around killing time until He comes. Jesus explains what brides ought to be doing while they're waiting for their groom:

> At that time the kingdom of heaven will be like ten virgins who took their lamps and went out to meet the bridegroom. Five of them were foolish and five were wise. The foolish ones took their lamps but did not take any oil with them. The wise, however, took oil in jars along with their lamps. The bridegroom was a long time in coming, and they all became drowsy and fell asleep.
>
> At midnight the cry rang out: "Here's the bridegroom! Come out to meet him!"
>
> Then all the virgins woke up and trimmed their lamps. The foolish ones said to the wise, "Give us some of your oil; our lamps are going out."
>
> "No," they replied, "there may not be enough for both us and you. Instead, go to those who sell oil and buy some for yourselves."
>
> But while they were on their way to buy the oil, the bridegroom arrived. The virgins who were ready went in with him to the wedding banquet. And the door was shut. Later the others also came. "Sir! Sir!" they said. "Open the door for us!"
>
> But he replied, "I tell you the truth, I don't know you."
>
> Therefore keep watch, because you do not know the day or the hour." (Matthew 25:1–13)

Foolish virgins are those who think that the betrothal is just one big insurance policy guaranteeing them access to the Wedding without lifting a finger. Wise virgins understand that the betrothal carries with it big responsibilities. They recognize they are married, albeit separated from the groom, and so they act like they're married. They watch. They work. They stay awake. They see the kingdom of heaven as the "pearl of great price," as the treasure in the field that—quick—must be purchased and plowed. They don't sit around on their hands. They pour their heart into the marriage covenant. In short, they act like they are loved and in love.

Before you rush to assume this means *doing* something, remember it means *being* someone. To wait is an occupation of the heart. To wait on the

Lord is to love Him with spirited affection. With passionate delight. To wait on Him is to fix your eyes on those converging points in eternity: Jesus.

The Bridegroom invites us to know Him this intimately. Jesus presses home the point about this intimacy more dramatically in John 6:53–57: "I tell you the truth, unless you eat the flesh of the Son of Man and drink his blood, you have no life in you.... For my flesh is real food and my blood is real drink. Whoever eats my flesh and drinks my blood remains in me, and I in him. Just as the living Father sent me and I live because of the Father, so the one who feeds on me will live because of me."

It's no wonder language like that sent the disciples scattering! But remember, He's talking about a spiritual intimacy.

Now, I'm not one to pipe up and call myself a wise virgin. But, thankfully, I've got some help with this thing about spiritual intimacy. My wheelchair. I get exhausted after a long day of sitting in my chair, and so most evenings I have to lie down at around 7:30. Lying in bed paralyzed, I have all the time in the world to wait on Jesus, to focus the eyes of my heart on those heavenly coordinates. My bedroom is a quiet place and softly lit. No music. No TV. The clock ticks. If there's a breeze outside, the wind chimes tinkle. Our dog, Scrappy, may curl up at the edge of the bed and softly snore. It's a place where I cannot *do* anything,... I can only *be*. And I choose to be the wise virgin who pours my love into the marriage contract.

I press my heart heavenward, maybe singing to the Lord a song just for His listening pleasure. Perhaps this one ...

> *Loved with everlasting love,*
>   *Led by grace that love to know;*
> *Gracious Spirit from above,*
>   *Thou hast taught me it is so!*
>
> *O, this full and perfect peace!*
>   *O, this transport all divine!*
> *In a love which cannot cease,*
>   *I am His, and He is mine.*
>
> *Things that once were wild alarms*
>   *Cannot now disturb my rest;*
> *Closed in everlasting arms,*
>   *Pillowed on the loving breast.*

> *O, to lie forever here,*
> *Doubt and care and self resign,*
> *While He whispers in my ear,*
> *I am His, and He is mine.*[4]

After an hour or so, Ken will amble in from the living room to check on me. Sometimes he gets concerned that I'm alone, or I should say, choose to be alone. But he doesn't need to worry. He finds me "boasting all the more gladly about my weakness" and "glorying in my infirmity," grateful that the paralysis affords me such a luxury: most women I know are doing the second load of laundry at 7:30 P.M. or putting the third child to bed. Their healthy bodies are at work, while my paralyzed one is forced to rest. What else is there for me to do but ... wait?

Lying there, looking at the ceiling, I squint my eyes of faith to focus on unseen divine realities and their future fulfillments. I set my heart and mind on heavenly glories above. And in the face-to-face intimacy I enjoy with my betrothed, I take Him at His word and "eat the flesh of the Son of Man and drink his blood."

Feeding on Him? I "taste and see that the Lord is good" as I ingest favorite Scriptures (Psalm 34:8).

Drinking His blood? "[His] love is more delightful than wine" in praying and singing hymns (Song of Songs 1:2).

Within a short time, I'm in the heavenlies, picturing myself kneeling on the throne room floor where Jesus is seated. Maybe one evening I'll imagine I'm His handmaiden, at the foot of His throne to serve. Another evening, His fellow intercessor kneeling next to Him against the rock in the Garden of Gethsemane. On another night, His sister. Sometimes His child. If I'm under spiritual attack, I go to Him as the Captain of the heavenly hosts.

When I relate to Him as the Lover of my soul, I'll quote out loud to the Lord a few verses from the Song of Songs. I'll tell Him He's the Rose of Sharon, the Lily of the Valley, the Fairest of Ten Thousand. "This is my lover, this is my friend, O daughters of Jerusalem.... He has taken me to the banquet hall and his banner over me is love ... his left arm is under my head, and his right arm embraces me ... strengthens me ... refreshes me ... for I am faint with love" (Song of Songs 2, 5). And then, maybe I'll sing another hymn of love ...

O Love that will not let me go,
    I rest my weary soul in Thee;
I give Thee back the life I owe,
    That in Thine ocean depths its flow
        May richer, fuller be.

O Light that foll'west all my way,
    I yield my flick'ring torch to Thee;
My heart restores its borrowed ray,
    That in Thy sunshine's blaze its day
        May brighter, fairer be.[5]

This intimate spiritual union is a two-way street. Occasionally, I'll picture Jesus whispering something to me that the Father said to Him in Isaiah 42:1: "Here is my servant, whom I uphold, my chosen one in whom I delight." Earth is one big premarital session for heaven, and although Jesus wants us to love Him passionately and single-heartedly, He more than matches it with love, pure and fervent.

On some evenings, He's the father running down the trail to embrace me, the prodigal, before I can speak a word of contrition. At other times, He is the mad farmer showering on me a full day's wage when I've hardly worked. On other evenings, He is the Master forgiving me, the sinful woman, before I realize I've done anything wrong. He's the king lavishing on me a banquet when I'm not even aware I'm malnourished. This is a God whose love for us is so active and so strong that most would say He was mad.[6]

While the Groom Is Absent

It is "heaven" to know Jesus this way. And I mean that literally. Because "this is eternal life: that they may know you, the only true God, and Jesus Christ, whom you have sent" (John 17:3). Eternal life *is* knowledge of God. When we deepen our relationship with Jesus, we get a head start on our eternal life here on earth. Heaven is already happening to us.

However, there are two kinds of knowledge. Just ask the wise and foolish virgins. If you asked a foolish virgin, "Do you know Jesus?" she would probably say, "Yes, I gave my heart to Him at a retreat in 1962, so

I'm saved and going to heaven." She's reading a statement right off her insurance policy.

What would the wise virgin reply? "Yes, I know Jesus. I've given my life to Him, and I enjoy such wonderful intimacy with Him in prayer and studying His Word. Let me tell you about some of the experiences we've shared together ... what kind of Person He is. Honestly, spending time with Him is the highlight of my day."

The apostle Paul knew Jesus and *knew* Jesus. He wrote in Philippians 3:8–9 of "the surpassing greatness of *knowing* Christ Jesus my Lord, for whose sake I have lost all things. I consider them rubbish, that I may gain Christ and be found in him, not having a righteousness of my own that comes from the law, but that which is through faith in Christ—the righteousness that comes from God and is by faith." Here Paul is talking about his position with God. He's talking about God doing something for him on His ledger, pronouncing, "You are forgiven." It's wonderful to have this kind of right standing (that's what righteousness means), but there's more to knowing Christ than this.

There's the bride/bridegroom thing. It's a different kind of knowledge. Paul touches on this deeper knowledge in the next verse when he yearns, "I want to know Christ and the power of his resurrection and the fellowship of sharing in his sufferings, becoming like him in his death, and so, somehow, to attain to the resurrection from the dead" (Philippians 3:10–11).

I love those words "to know." Scholars explain that in this passage "to know" implies learning about someone through a deep, personal experience. It's the same sort of intimacy alluded to in the book of Genesis where it says that Adam "knew" his wife, Eve. Theirs was a deep, personal experience. A level of relationship beyond head knowledge. It is also a physical illustration of the level of spiritual intimacy that God desires with us, something even more deep and personal.

God covers His end of the relationship when He positions us in Christ. Positioning is His responsibility in factoring us into heaven. We cover our end of the relationship on earth as we experience the depths of knowing God. Experiencing is our responsibility in fitting ourselves for heaven. It's what wise virgins do while they wait.

Right now, the bridegroom is absent. But, oh, I can hardly wait for the day when I break through to see the face of Jesus and once and for all *know* Him: To pass through Him, be united with and receive Him, "to share in the divine nature." To be overpowered, enraptured, and caught up in Someone grand and glorious beyond myself. To be swept and wrapped up in His joy. To no longer be hid with Christ in God, but be turned inside out, and appear face-forward with Him. For time to stand still in a heavenly ecstasy in which I forget myself and yet find myself. Like Elijah's chariot carrying me away to the wedding banquet!

"As the deer pants for streams of water, so my soul pants for you, O God. My soul thirsts for God, for the living God. When can I go and meet with God?" (Psalm 42:1–2).

The Wedding Gift

It's common practice for newlyweds to give gifts to each other. I suppose when I finally see my Savior, my gift to Him shall be whatever bits and pieces of earthly obedience I've done as evidence of my love. He said, "If anyone loves me, he will obey my teaching" (John 14:23), and I'm sure these bits and pieces will sparkle and shine like diamonds.

But what shall He give to us?

He will give the joy of heaven. Isaiah 35:10 is a peek at the gift: "They will enter Zion with singing; everlasting joy will crown their heads. Gladness and joy will overtake them, and sorrow and sighing will flee away." To have my head crowned with everlasting joy is one of those earthly images that looks askew, but I don't mind. People caught up in ecstasy don't worry about such things. Suffice to say, it's a gift. A crowning gift.

Look at the gift with me for a moment. Joy is a fruit of the Spirit and that means it has in it the essence of eternity. When joy grips us, it always appears new, like a surprise. At the same moment, it seems ancient, as though it had always been there. Joy always has in it a timeless, eternal element. Pleasure and happiness may come and go, but joy seems to remain. Happy feelings have nothing of that air of eternity about them that joy has. That's because joy, in its essence, is of God. He is "the Lord of joy."

Whether experienced in shadow here or in light, there, joy is dynamic. It cannot stay stagnant or bottled up. Joy flows. Actually, it overflows. It floods back to God in gratitude, out to others like a fountain, and rushes through our own hearts in a torrent. This is why people weep for joy. We human beings, all finite and compacted, cannot contain the overflow. We are too small for how big joy is, and so we must weep. This also explains why joy breaks our heart. For like love, joy cannot be contained. Remember when I said that lovers "in love" find themselves enveloped by something gloriously larger than themselves? Joy is the same. It will *overtake* us, Isaiah 35:10 says. This will be heavenly ecstasy.[7]

As an artist, I see something else about joy. It happens whenever I look at a certain painting that hangs on the office wall opposite my desk. It is a rendering of Mary, the mother of Jesus, and Gabriel, the angel. Whenever my mind is at rest and my desk is clear of work, I find myself drawn into that painting. I lose myself in it.

This may happen to you, if not with a painting, then with a great symphony. You're sitting in the symphony hall, your eyes closed, the music swells and surrounds you, and before you know it, you are lost. You're gone. You have become one with the sounds of the orchestra. There are times when I have listened to Schumann's *Romanze* that I would say I've "become one" with the music. A friend once discovered me crying in my art studio as I was listening to *Romanze*. I looked up with wet eyes and said, "This music is me." Have you experienced this? A Brahms melody that breaks your heart? A Mendelssohn waltz that fills your eyes with tears?

Or if you're a left-brained person who isn't into art or music, how about that exhilarating moment when, during the 1982 Winter Olympics, the U.S. hockey team pulverized the Russians? Whether in front of the television, in the stands, or on the ice, we all became "one" in the euphoria of victory. My strong, he-man father once told me about a time he was standing on the edge of a cliff overlooking Yellowstone Falls—with tears in his eyes, he described how he became one with the deafening roar of the water.

If you have experienced any of this, it's an inkling of the joy that will overtake us when we take just one glance at the Lord of joy. We will lose ourselves in Him. We will become one with Him. We will be "in Christ," we will have "put on Christ" at the deepest, most profound and exhilarating level. The Lord's wedding gift to us will be the joy of sharing totally in His nature without us losing our identity; no, we shall receive our identity. Thanks be to God for His indescribable gift!

This is why heaven is more than just a place of pleasure and happiness. If that were so, heaven would be boring. Pleasure is always seeking satisfaction. Happiness is finding satisfaction. But whether reached through pleasure or happiness, there is still something inert about satisfaction. It's a little too "still." That's why joy is satisfaction that is always moving. It bursts beyond pleasure and happiness; it calls for rejoicing out of sheer generosity. It is the real energy of praise. If we are to be praising God for all of eternity, which we shall be, then joy will be the dynamic.

Peter Kreeft writes:

> This state of mind is like light: traveling faster than matter, yet making no sound, no perturbation. Pleasure is the restless mind moving along a line, never reaching the end. Happiness is the mind resting at the end. Joy is the mind eternally moving *at* the end, motion at a point: the cosmic dance. Pleasure is moving; happiness is still; joy is moving while still. Pleasure is like work, happiness is like sleep, joy is like play. Pleasure is like action, happiness is like rest, joy is like contemplation. Pleasure is a river running to the sea; happiness is the full, calm sea; joy is a great and glorious storm on the sea.[8]

I like Kreeft's comment that "joy is like play." It happened to me earlier this year at another one of our JAF Ministries' family retreats.

One night, during the evening ice cream social, I powered my chair over to little red-haired Nicole in her wheelchair, Tiffany, her friend, and Rachel, standing next to her in her leg braces. After a couple of comments about the ice cream, we were soon playing a game of tag. Wheelchair tag. Before long, a kid in a walker joined us with his sister. And then a child with Down syndrome and her brother. Weaving in and out around the legs of the adults, we giggled and screamed as our foot pedals clunked together, bumping and bouncing like Dodge'm cars.

After the ice cream began to melt, John, our retreat director, looked at his watch and tried to herd the families back to their cabins. But we kept playing. We were so caught up in the game that I lost all track of time. Only after we waved goodnight to each other, exhausted, did I realize it was like heaven. It was heaven because of the play and the joy and the sense of timelessness. Right before I entered my cabin, I looked up to the stars and thanked Jesus for the sneak preview of heaven's joy. I had to smile at His answer from Matthew 19:14: "Let the little children come to me ... for the kingdom of heaven belongs to such as these."

As I laid in bed that night, the entire experience of joyful play kept echoing. *The kingdom of heaven belongs to giggling, happy, carefree children.* I kept thinking and straining my ears—or was I trying to open the eyes of my heart—to hear or see more. I *knew* there was much more than just play in that experience. I had touched a moment of great happiness and wisdom. I didn't realize it then, but I had touched eternity in time. Months later I came across another quote by Peter Kreeft that nailed it:

> When we touch eternity in time, it's like an echo. We smell the salt air of the sea, even here, far upstream in the river of time. Whenever we touch wisdom or love, we swim in salt water. Earth is God's beach and when we are wise and loving, we are infants splashing happily in the wavelets of 'that immortal sea.' But when we are spiritually full grown, we will buoyantly plow its breakers of wisdom and be borne up by its bottomless depths of love. Boredom, like pain, will be remembered only as a joke when we are drenched in joy.[9]

The Bridegroom Cometh!

And so now, we wait. We wait for our bridegroom. "I wait for the Lord, my soul waits, and in his word I put my hope. My soul waits for the Lord more than watchmen wait for the morning, more than watchmen wait for the morning" (Psalm 130:6). We lean on the windowsill of eternity, look to the sky, and whisper, "Come quickly, Lord Jesus, come quickly."

Oh, *when* will He come?

And every once in a while, when our heart grows weary of waiting, the Lord revives us with snatches of joy, such as the kind I experienced at that retreat. It is a preview of the joy that will overtake us when, finally, "the Lord himself will come down from heaven, with a loud command, with the voice of the archangel and with the trumpet call of God, and the dead in Christ will rise first. After that, we who are still alive and are left will be caught up together with them in the clouds to meet the Lord in the air. And so we will be with the Lord forever" (1 Thessalonians 4:16–17).

And it will all happen in the twinkling of an eye.

Before we realize it, if we are blessed to be living at the time of His return, we shall find ourselves in the embrace of our Savior at the Wedding

Supper of the Lamb. Heaven will have arrived. The Lord's overcoming of the world will be a lifting of the curtain of our five senses, and we shall see the whole universe in plain sight. Life and immortality will no longer be dim thoughts, but vivid and strikingly real. At first, the shock of joy may burn with the brilliant newness of being glorified, but in the next instant we will be at peace and feel at home, as though it were always this way, that we were born for such a place. At that moment, earth will seem like a half-forgotten dream, pleasant enough, but only a dream.[10]

I imagine great multitudes of people rushing from jungles of roses, down banks of violets, pulsing with light and songs of birds and the voices of angels.

"Are all here?" someone will shout.

There will echo, "Yes, we are all here!"

Now, enjoy an unseen divine reality. Rev up your heart and picture yourself taking a seat at the Wedding Supper. Open the eyes of your heart and marvel at the crystal-clear glory, the dazzle of light that just *is*. A holy city, the New Jerusalem sparkling like a prism. And a banquet hall resplendent with banners, color, stunning with jewels and light-and-joy-filled music. The celebration will kick off with a loud and resounding "Hallelujah! For our Lord God Almighty reigns. Let us rejoice and be glad and give him glory! For the wedding of the Lamb has come, and his bride has made herself ready" (Revelation 19:6–7).

As you pull up a chair to the banquet table, take a look at what's on the menu from Isaiah 25:6–8: "On this mountain the Lord Almighty will prepare a feast of rich food for all peoples, a banquet of aged wine—the best of meats and the finest of wines. On this mountain he will destroy the shroud that enfolds all peoples, the sheet that covers all nations; he will swallow up death forever. The Sovereign Lord will wipe away the tears from all faces; he will remove the disgrace of his people from all the earth. The Lord has spoken."

There's no mistaking. This is a real banquet. And a specific one too. They won't be serving bologna or Spam. It won't be USDA-approved meat; it will be "the best of meats." And the beverage selection will not be Kool-Aid or cheap wine, but "aged wine ... the finest of wines."

I get a charge just thinking about it! I wonder who will sit next to me, or across from me. I glance down the table and there's my friend, Verna

Estes, mother of seven, swapping baby stories with Susanna Wesley, mother of seventeen. There's her pastor-husband, Steve, getting the low-down on Romans 6 from the apostle Paul. There's Moses toasting Martin Luther. Billy Graham doing a do-si-do with a junior-high Sunday school teacher. My husband, Ken (whose lifelong ambition it was to fly an F–14 fighter), cornering astronaut James Irwin. St. Augustine giving a bear hug to that jungle missionary who labored long and hard, unknown and unnoticed. At the other end of the table, Fanny Crosby is doing harmony on one of her hymns with the widow who faithfully played the rickety piano at the nursing home every Sunday. As for me, as soon as I see my friends who spent years getting me up in the morning—Carolyn, Francie, Judy, Jay, Bev, and Irene—I jump up and grab a platter of meat. I just can't wait to serve them something.

Then I'll look up and walking toward me will be Dad. And Mother. He'll give me his ol' thumbs-up and a wink, my mother will start giggling, and before you know it, we'll break up into uncontrollable laughter. We will laugh and cry with a kind of tears that never flowed on earth. We will wipe our eyes and try to stop, then break up again, crying and laughing and pointing at everybody. "Look at this! Can you believe this? We're here! They are here! I knew it was true, but not this true!"

Since we always sang together as a family on earth, I'm sure we'll break into song right there around the table, harmonizing through our tears...

> When we shall say good-bye to earth
> We'll gather with the family 'round the throne,
> We will burst with joy at our Father's welcome
>   "Glad to be at home!"
>
> We'll praise the Father, praise the Son,
> We'll praise the Spirit three-in-one,
> We will celebrate that on this date
>   "Forever" has begun![11]

Now stop the music. Stop the moving picture and let's retrace an earlier question. Will there be plates, knives, and forks at the Wedding Banquet? Will someone be back in the kitchen shuffling pots and pans to cook stuff in? Will there be mixers and trash compactors? And what about the meat? Certainly there won't be slaughterhouses in heaven! Will Arabs eat with their fingers? Will Asians use chopsticks? Will people in hell do cleanup duty?

These questions seem ridiculous now. In light of the glorious celebration, who cares? I'm sure it'll be made plain. All I care about is that it is real.

A real streamers-and-confetti celebration that death has died.

A real ticker-tape parade announcing victory over sin.

The whole earth will join in the party, and "you will go out in joy and be led forth in peace; the mountains and hills will burst into song before you, and all the trees of the field will clap their hands" (Isaiah 55:12). Christ will open our eyes to the great fountain of love in His heart for us, beyond all that we ever saw before. It will hit us that we, the church, are His bride. Not just individually, but together. United. One with each other, and one with Him. Suddenly, our joy is multiplied a millionfold.

Most poignantly, when we're finally able to stop laughing and crying, the Lord Jesus will really wipe away all our tears. And then, we join hands around the banquet table, and "in that day [we] will say, 'Surely this is our God; we trusted in him, and he saved us. This is the Lord, we trusted in him; let us rejoice and be glad in his salvation'" (Isaiah 25:9).

And the party is just beginning!

Chapter 8

At Home with Our King

—

Holy, Holy, Holy! All the saints adore Thee,
Casting down their golden crowns around the glassy sea;
Cherubim and Seraphim falling down before Thee,
Which wert and art and evermore shall be.[1]

Above all, it will be Christ's coronation day.

I'm thrilled that we will enjoy the Marriage Supper of the Lamb with its feast of rich foods and the finest of wines, and we will delight in our reunion with loved ones, and, yes, it will be exhilarating to reign over angels and rule the earth with new bodies to boot. But I have to keep remembering it will not be *our* celebration. It will be *His*.

I could never dare keep those crowns for myself. Could you?

We shall press in line with the great procession of the redeemed passing before the throne, an infinite cavalcade of nations and empires, age following age, Europe, Asia, Africa, North and South America, all standing shoulder to shoulder, the people of the islands of the seas in one happy parade, generations of the redeemed before the Cross and after, all bearing their diadems before God Almighty.

Then as Jesus rises from His throne before this great host, all crowns are lifted, all chimes ringing, and all hallelujahs hailing until the vocabulary of heavenly praise is exhausted. We will press our crowns against our breasts, look at one another, and say, "Now?"

"Now!" all will shout. Together we will raise our voices, not in four-part harmony, but perhaps in twelve-part, with the twenty-four elders as "they lay their crowns before the throne" (Revelation 4:10–11) and sing:

> Crown Him with many crowns, the Lamb upon His throne:
> Hark! How the heavenly anthem drowns all music but its own!
> Awake, my soul and sing of Him who died for thee,
> And hail Him as thy matchless King through all eternity.[2]

If, indeed, we are given literal crowns, make no mistake about it—the diadems will be His. The judgment seat of Christ may have been center stage where Jesus showered praise on the believer, but all of heaven will turn the spotlight on the Lord to give Him back the glory. The universe will bow its knee and hail Jesus as King of Kings and Lord of Lords when He raises His sword in victory over death, the devil, disease, and destruction.

In a breathless moment—an infinite moment—we will comprehend that the whole plan of redemption was merely the Father's way of securing for His Son ...

A Bride.

A Family.

An Army.

An Inheritance.

But the crowning purpose of His plan will be to secure for the Son a grand chorus of Eternal Worshipers.

This is what I was made for. This is the answer to all the times I asked on earth, "Why has God chosen me? Why not someone else?" The response is simply, *I am the Father's gift to the Son.* Ephesians 1:11–12 will then make perfect sense for "in him we were chosen ... in order that we ... might be for the praise of his glory." I will be the flashing and iridescent gift for the Son who Zechariah admired, "They will sparkle in his land like jewels in a crown. How attractive and beautiful they will be!" (Zechariah 9:16–17).

This explains why I feel so beautiful when I sing that old Sunday school song. I *like* the idea of being a jeweled gift for Jesus:

> When He cometh, when He cometh to make up His jewels,
> All His jewels, precious jewels, His loved and His own:
> Like the stars of the morning,

His bright crown adorning,
They shall shine in their beauty—Bright gems for His crown.[3]

Earth was one big diamond mine in which I was chiseled from the dirt, cleaned, polished, and fitted for a King's crown. Can you now understand why I want to win as many crowns as possible while on earth? True, greater rewards will enhance my service in heaven, but they will also magnify the glory Jesus will receive. The more crowns, the merrier God's praise. My motive in gathering a truckload of diadems is not to hoard them, but to have more to cast at Jesus' feet.

You and I were chosen to praise Him. It's that simple. What a shame that on earth we made it so complicated.

In the early days of my paralysis when I first learned about heaven, I zeroed in on it because it was the place where I would receive new hands and feet. Heaven was the place I'd be freed from the pain, and so, it became an escape from reality. A psychological crutch. At times, heaven was so me-centered that I felt as though the whole point of it was to get back all it owed me, all I had lost. And so, heaven became a death wish.

Time passed, and with it I gained a little more spiritual maturity. It gradually dawned on me that the Day of Christ would be just that ... the Day of Christ, not the day of Joni. Glorified hands and feet, as well as reunions with loved ones, began to look more like fringe benefits to the honor of simply being on the invitation list to the coronation party.

You'll agree. The privilege of casting your crowns at the feet of Jesus will be enough of an honor. Ruling the earth and reigning over angels, becoming pillars in God's temple and co-heirs of heaven and earth are almost incidental. What we become, receive, and do in heaven won't be the highlight of heaven. To be there and to *be to the praise of His glory* will be enough.

It will be Jesus' Day.

Christ's Coronation Day

We should have known it all along. But it never sunk in. Oh, we understood it on paper, but how often did we live—really live—with the focus off ourselves and fixed on Christ as King of Kings? It takes heaven to force us to fully comprehend what should have been plain on earth all along. If only we had stopped and read—really read—that "the God who made the world and everything in it is the Lord of heaven and earth" (Acts 17:24).

Jesus is the Lord of heaven and earth.

We said it in our prayers, we sang it in our songs, and we would have sworn we believed it with a capital *B*. But it never really clicked for us. That's because "us" kept getting in the way. All those years when earthly trials hit hard, we burnt rubber in our brains trying to figure out what it meant to us. How problems fit into God's plan for us. How Jesus could be conformed in us. Everything was always "for us." Even Sunday worship service focused on how we felt, what we learned, and if the hymns were to our liking.

Why, oh why, didn't we take the hint from Acts 17:24 and switch our attention off us and onto Him? Why didn't we appreciate that God gave every trial, heartache, and happiness to show us something about Himself?

That we might appreciate His grace?

That we were being polished for the praise of His glory?

That we might see that everything fit together in order that we might know Him?

We always marvel that God shows an interest in us, but in heaven it will be clear that every earthy thing happened so that we'd show an interest in Him. In every trial, happiness, and heartache, God wanted us to think about Him. We will finally be convinced that the One whom we lauded with our lips as King truly did have supremacy in all things.

His kingdom came.

His will was done on earth as it is in heaven.

His word went forth and accomplished His purposes.

He was sovereign Lord over all.

While on earth, you never could have convinced us. We acted more like His kingdom sort of came, but not really. We behaved like His will was done on-earth-as-it-is-in-heaven mainly to benefit our jobs and relationships. And whenever we talked about heaven, it was more along the lines of an eternal playground where we would receive lots of new toys while God, like a granddaddy, would nod and smile to see us enjoying ourselves.

What a shame that on earth we acted as though we did God a big favor by accepting Jesus as Savior. We pitied Jesus because His reputation could never quite be vindicated. We felt sorry for God because it seemed like His justice was never quite served; in fact, at times we were embarrassed for our "King" as we scrambled to defend Him over earthly holocausts and horrors. Jesus never appeared to flex his kingly muscles, and thus never got credit, much less glory.

We weren't the only shortsighted ones. Even the disciples had a small-minded view of God. They too failed to recognize the King in their midst. Occasionally the fog lifted from their thinking, and once, toward the end of Jesus' ministry, they rose to a heavenly perspective of their King and said, "Now we can see that you know all things." For a brief moment, their focus was off the kingdom on earth and fixed on the kingdom in heaven. It was a rare flash of revelation, and Jesus was moved enough to exclaim, "You believe at last!" (John 16:30–31).

Those words of Christ's rip at my heart. All Jesus wanted from us was, at last, to believe. So why were our times of drastic obedience and absolute trust only flashes, brief moments of illumination? Why did we always have such a hard time acting like Jesus was King?

The King Who Won Against All Odds

Perhaps because on earth, He never acted like a king.

Or at least not like one would think a king should act. Jesus, however, had a good reason for cloaking His majesty under the robe of weakness, shame, and humility. It has to do with His glory in heaven. When the Father designed the plan of salvation, He initiated a scheme that would ultimately bring the highest and brightest glory to His Son, the King of the Cosmos. It was a plot that almost reads like an adventure story.

The plan was put into effect when the evil villain, Lucifer, enslaved the citizens of the kingdom of earth through treachery and deceit. He usurped the authority of the rightful Ruler and set up his own rival government. The good Ruler sent His most skilled servants to try to recapture the occupied territory, but with few exceptions, the villain seduced and defeated them. Finally, the Ruler sent His only Son, the rightful Prince, to invade Lucifer's territory, free the captive subjects, and retake the kingdom under the family banner.

But the battle tactics of the Son were odd, to say the least. In fact, the manner in which He fought seemed to insure defeat. At one point, when

Lucifer had the Prince pinned, the Son merely yielded to the deathblow. All appeared lost and the people's hearts fainted in despair. Little did they realize the best and final part of the plan was just about to go into play. It was called the Resurrection, and it was the only battle tactic that could deliver the killing blow to the enemy and his hordes of evil rulers.

Now any struggle between a hero and the bad guys is interesting enough, but when the hero is disadvantaged, a new element is introduced. Now the hero is in far more danger and he appears to have less chance of winning. But if in his weakness he overcomes against all odds, he ends up twice as much the hero. When weak heroes outmaneuver strong villains, the victory is awe-inspiring.

And so, the Prince of Peace, the Lamb who let Himself be slain, will be glorified, not because He employed brute force against Satan, but because He didn't.

The King Who Won Through Weakness

There's another aspect of the Father's plan which positions His Son as less than kingly, yet guarantees Him greater glory. It involves defeating the strong villain by using his own dark power against him.

It's kind of like judo.

My husband Ken could tell you all about it. Every once in a while he gets into his martial arts mode and starts jumping around the living room like a cat on catnip, pouncing helter-skelter, punching the air with his fists, and kicking toward the ceiling with the side of his foot. I always watch with distracted feminine interest.

Ken tells me that judo has its uses. It's the art of using the power of your enemy to defeat him; and although Ken may appear passive and even weak in a judo match, the secret is simply to wait for that moment when the opponent's full strength can be used to defeat him. When my husband is attacked, he simply judos his assailant and sends the guy flying over his shoulder.

Jesus appeared passive and weak. People kept looking for His diadem. We kept hoping He would behave as a monarch should and make the lives of His subjects happy, healthy, and free from trouble. But Jesus had other plans for earth—plans that involved greater praise for the believer and glory for Himself.

He kept doing judo. Especially against the devil. And most specifically at the Cross. At the exact moment the devil thought he had Christ cornered and pinned down in defeat, he unleashed his full satanic fury to finish Him off. But it was Christ's weakness and vulnerability that enabled Him to judo Satan into slitting his own throat.

James Stewart, the Scottish theologian, put it this way:

> The very triumphs of His foes He used for their defeat. He compelled their dark achievements to subserve His ends, not theirs. They nailed Him to the tree, not knowing that by that very act they were bringing the world to His feet. They gave Him a cross, not guessing that He would make it a throne.
>
> They flung Him outside the gates to die, not knowing that at that very moment they were lifting up all the gates of the universe to let the King of Glory come in. They thought to root out His doctrines, not understanding that they were implanting imperishably in the hearts of men the very name they intended to destroy.
>
> They thought they had God with His back to the wall, pinned and helpless and defeated. They did not know it was God Himself who had dragged them down to that point. He did not conquer in spite of the dark mystery of evil, He conquered through it.[4]

Something glorious happened when the world's worst murder became the world's only salvation. When the cross, a symbol of torture, became a symbol of life and hope, it meant triple the glory.

Jesus ends up triple the hero in heaven because He won using weapons of warfare that were spiritual, and not carnal. His triumph was assured using divine judo. He won using perfect timing and patience. "At *just the right time,* when we were still powerless, Christ died for the ungodly" (Romans 5:6). He won through waiting, yielding, and submission. Philippians 2:7–9 reads like "The Basic Principles in Martial Arts" because the weaker Christ became, the greater was His victory, and the greater the victory, the more glorious the honors: "[He] made himself nothing, ... he humbled himself and became obedient to death—even death on a cross! Therefore God exalted him to the highest place and gave him the name that is above every name."

If we pitied Christ on earth or felt badly that His justice seemed aborted, we wasted our time. If we were embarrassed for His sake over so much senseless suffering, we would have done better to take a few lessons in the martial arts. Jesus *did* flex His muscles as King on earth; our unskilled eyes, hearts, and minds just weren't trained to see it. He wore a crown; it just wasn't the crown we expected. Not one of gold, but of thorns.

Up in heaven, we may be tempted to smack our foreheads and exclaim, "Oh bother! How did we miss it?" But there will be no room for remorse. We won't berate ourselves for not having seen it. No, our King of Kings will be too gracious to permit us such regrets. It will be obvious why His medals of monarchy were hidden. It was all engineered to help us exercise faith, develop trust, and demonstrate obedience, as well as to teach us timing and patience, waiting and yielding. The King overcame the Cross so that we might have power to parlay a bullying devil and thus accept our thorns, share our burdens, and carry our own crosses, while all the time turning tragedy into triumph and heartaches into victories.

With good grace, Jesus will not scold us for being so us-centered. He will assure us He knew our frame and remembered that we were but dust. We will realize that on earth we were worse than we thought, but the Lord's grace went deeper than we thought, and so in heaven we will do better than we thought.[5]

The Lord Jesus will be sloppy with His kindness, letting it spill and splash over everything. Even our regrets. And *that,* dear friends, will compel us to love, praise, and rejoice in Him all the more. At that point, God's glory in heaven will open up exponentially to the hundredth power.

I get so happy for Jesus when I picture this moment. For He will show Himself as He is, no longer the weak and suffering servant, but the mighty Sovereign of time and space. His reputation will be vindicated. He will receive all the credit due Him, plus triple the glory. Most of all, His justice will be served.

And it won't look very nice. At least to some.

The Great and Terrible Day of the Lord

All this stuff about weakness and humility grates on the nerves of some people. They don't buy a God who would let Himself be mocked, kicked, and spit upon, all for the sake of justice. Especially justice on their behalf. How dare this weak, powerless God assert they need to be saved—and from their sin, no less!

On earth, they pushed their own kind of justice. And first on their agenda was to defame and defrock Jesus. Setting themselves up at the center of their own moral universe, they thought they had the power to put God on trial. They arraigned and indicted Him, accused and banished Him as some impotent third-rate deity. They kicked Him out of school classrooms and erased His mark from the public square. Profaning His name, they neutered God and tamed Him so He would bless their lusts and passions.

But in heaven, the record will be set straight. God will vindicate His holy name and dispense His pure and perfect justice. For a great many people, it will be terrifying.

What a shock when they behold this Jesus whom they tried to shove back into a Sunday school room. Horror will strike their hearts as the scene in Revelation 19:11–16 unfolds, and they'll cry:

> I saw heaven standing open and there before me was a white horse, whose rider is called Faithful and True. With justice he judges and makes war. His eyes are like blazing fire, and on his head are many crowns. He has a name written on him that no one knows but he himself. He is dressed in a robe dipped in blood, and his name is the Word of God. The armies of heaven were following him, riding on white horses and dressed in fine linen, white and clean. Out of his mouth comes a sharp sword with which to strike down the nations. "He will rule them with an iron scepter." He treads the winepress of the fury of the wrath of God Almighty. On his robe and on his thigh he has this name written: KING OF KINGS AND LORD OF LORDS.

These symbols aren't clunky at all; they're frightening! As an artist, not only could I not paint it, I would never want to. Eyes like blazing fire? A robe dipped in blood? This is no senile Benevolence that drowsily wished human beings well while they were on earth, a God to be pitied or felt sorry for. This is the great and terrible Lord, the consuming fire Himself. "See, the Lord is coming with fire, and his chariots are like a whirlwind; he will bring down his anger with fury, and his rebuke with flames of fire. For with fire and with his sword the Lord will execute judgment upon all men, and many will be those slain by the Lord" (Isaiah 66:15–16).

This is not a pretty sight for "it is a dreadful thing to fall into the hands of the living God" (Hebrews 10:31). The same mouth that spoke peace and reconciliation will one day emit the sharp sword of judgment. The same eyes that glowed with compassion will one day blaze with fire. Is this the Rose of Sharon, the Lily of the Valley, my Bridegroom? Yes, this same Jesus, into whose loving hands I first fell, is the dreadful living God.

Lover and Avenger? He is perfectly one and the same. He is altogether loving in His justice, and just in His love. And because He is perfect, His justice is pure.

How Will It Feel on That Terrible Day?

Once in heaven, we will know in every fiber of our being, beyond a shadow of a doubt that whatever the Judge declares about us is true. As He says we are, so are we. No more, no less. Maybe we will even realize, in a dim, hazy way, this was our actual deep-down self on earth all along. If the Judge rules we were righteous in Christ, then "Hallelujah! I knew it all along." If He declares us unrighteous, wicked, and steeped in selfishness, then "curse me! I knew it all along." The self-evident truth about you or me will be clear to everyone.

This fact is especially humbling to believers. Remember when I said that Christians will not have their sinful past replayed before everyone like some awful R-rated movie? Don't worry, I'm not throwing you a curve. It's true we won't have to bear that shame because God has separated us from our sin as far as the east is from the west.

But if it were not so, let's say if our secret closet sins *were* exposed, I'm convinced there's not a righteous soul who would protest. You and I would wholeheartedly agree with the Judge and say, "Jesus, You are absolutely right, Your justice is perfect. I was a manipulator on earth, always fudging the truth and faking it with everybody around me. That was my true deep-down self all along!"

In fact, I can picture myself tugging at His robe and saying, "Wait, Jesus, I have some other ugly hidden things about me I want you to expose. I want everyone to know how vast and far-reaching Your grace was to me. I don't want to cover up my sins. I want everyone to see how rotten-to-the-core I was so they know how deep-cleansing was Your grace!"

Jonathan Edwards takes this thought a step further when he says that sinners "will have so much the more admiring and joyful sense of God's grace in pardoning them, that the remembrance of their sins will rather be an indirect occasion of joy."[6]

If—and I say if—our gruesome pasts are to be replayed, it would serve to bring God greater glory for such great grace.

That's why, as uncanny as it seems to us now, we won't cringe or cower on the great and terrible day of the Lord. Oddly, we will rejoice. This sounds insane because our human sense of compassion abhors the idea of justice being executed with unbridled sound and fury. On earth, justice is served as prisoners are quietly escorted from death row to chambers where hushed groups of people sit behind soundproofed windows and, without emotion, watch death happen.

But not in heaven.

There, judgment is full of emotion.

Smack-dab in the middle of the apocalypse, as bowls of wrath are being poured out with smoke and fire, we are found singing and rejoicing while watching the Judgment. This parenthesis of incredible praise is squeezed between the rage of God in Revelation 18 and what looks like Armageddon at the end of Revelation 19. In the mighty praise chorus of verses 1–10, we are numbered among the angels, the elders, and "the roar of a great multitude in heaven shouting: 'Hallelujah! Salvation and glory and power belong to our God, *for true and just are his judgments.*'"

Why will we happily agree with Jesus as He treads the winepress of the fury of the wrath of God Almighty? Will it be because the tables will finally turn on the bad guys? No. We will accompany the Judgment with choruses of praise because we will love purity and hate the perniciousness of evil. We will desire truth deeply and despise lies and wickedness. With perfect minds and devout hearts, we will joyfully accent all of God's judgments with a hearty "Yes!" And we'll do it as He's treading His grapes of wrath.

The Day of Christ will be a great and terrible day. Great for the righteous and terrible for the unrighteous. "In the end that Face which is the delight or the terror of the universe must be turned upon each of us either with one expression or with the other."[7]

I'm just grateful that Scripture speaks of that time as only "a day." It may mean the Great Judgment will be swift. After all, "there are only two kinds of people in the end: those who say to God, 'Thy will be done,' and those to whom God says, in the end, '*Thy* will be done.' All that are in Hell, choose it."[8]

For all the people who insisted "My will be done!" God will not dissuade. He will no longer strive with them, either by pointing to His glory in creation or by preaching to them from the Gospel. For those who turn their backs on Christ, there is no heaven.

All That Are in Hell, Choose It

Yes, there is a hell.

It's unthinkable to talk about heaven without at least mentioning hell. Please note I didn't refer to it as "heaven's counterpart." Heaven has no counterpart. It has no opposite. Just as Satan is not God's opposite (for the devil is merely a created being—and a fallen one, at that!), neither does heaven have an opposite. In the vastness of God's infinite, as well as cleansed and purified universe, hell may end up being only a speck. A trash heap. A garbage dump.

Outside of Jerusalem, the holy city, there was a junkyard where the Jews took their garbage to burn. In earlier times pagan tribes, and wayward Jews themselves, had used this area called *GeHinnom* for performing rituals and sacrifices; that's why God's people thought it only a place fit to set fire to their waste. They ended up calling it Gehenna, and that became the biblical term for hell.

The actual hell will be the trash compactor of the universe.

> God makes no garbage, but we do; and a good cosmos must eventually purify itself of spiritual garbage like egotism, hate, greed, cowardice, or lust.... We can even rejoice that it exists, for we should want our spiritual garbage burned away, if we do not identify ourselves with that garbage. If we do, we are burned eternally.... God cannot allow that garbage into heaven; and if we do not want to throw it away, if we clutch our garbage so close that we become garbage, there is only one place for us.[9]

Hell will not pollute the purified universe, nor will it be a festering boil in the side of the new heavens, an ugly sore spot that forever seeps and demands somebody's attention. It may well be too small for that. I don't mean hell will be smaller than heaven in terms of population statistics, but in terms of its importance in the new heavens and new earth. Nobody pays much attention to smoldering junk heaps.

Since I brought up the subject of numbers, however, I'm reminded of the record of Jesus' words in Matthew 7:13–14: "Enter through the narrow gate. For wide is the gate and broad is the road that leads to destruction, and many enter through it. But small is the gate and narrow the road that leads to life, and only a few find it." No doubt about it. The world, for the most part, chooses the path to hell. Not many choose Christ and His heaven.

But I wonder, will hell have greater numbers than the repentant residing in heaven? What about the redeemed numbering more than the sands on the beach or stars in the sky? Revelation 7:9 claims there is to be a multitude in heaven that no man can number.

There's no contradiction between Christ's words in Matthew and His words in Revelation. C. H. Spurgeon reconciles it this way:

> I believe there will be more in heaven than in hell. If you ask me why I think so, I answer, because Christ in everything is to have the preeminence (Colossians 1:18), and I cannot conceive how he could have the preeminence if there are to be more in the dominions of Satan than in paradise. Moreover, it is said there is to be a multitude that no man can number in heaven. I have never read that there is to be a multitude that no man can number in hell. *I rejoice to know that the souls of all infants, as soon as they die, speed their way to paradise. Think what a multitude there is of them!*[10]

Rather than debate the census figures of heaven and hell, it is simply sufficient to say that hell exists; it's horrible, you don't want to go there, and you want to do everything in your power to keep others from choosing it. Jesus' teaching about hell with its wormwood and gall is meant to strike terror in our hearts, warning us that if heaven is better than we could dream, so hell will be worse than we can imagine.

Hell warns us to seek heaven.

It is its own best deterrent.

I know this firsthand. At the time of my injury, doctors pumped me up with powerful drugs to get rid of the infection that was raging through my paralyzed limbs. My body was on fire with pain. When nurses turned me facedown on the Stryker frame, I could only see the floor and people's feet. Horrified, I saw the ugly cloven hooves of demons where there should have been shoes of nurses. The feet of friends were webbed with claws. I screamed at the nurses not to flip me face up, fearful that I would see ugly monsters. But when they turned me over, I was shocked to find everything normal.

What a hell. Looking back, I know my terror was drug-induced. But those frightening images remained with me even through subsequent years of backsliding and bitterness. In fact, during those years when I teetered on the brink of rejecting Christ entirely, scary cloven hooves would flash in my mind. For me, it was a warning.

My teenage years were full of warning. I recall reading Jonathan Edwards' sermon, "Sinners in the Hands of an Angry God," while studying American Literature in tenth-grade English. My hands trembled as I held the book! I wish public high school students still were required to read Edwards, one of America's greatest thinkers, but times have changed. Few read such cautions as,

> The same God whom the saints see as their supreme lover, sinners see as the enemy of their souls. The divine and supernatural light of the saint is the divine and supernatural darkness of the sinner. As the redeemed see God as the source of every blessing that heaven affords, the impenitent see God as the source of every curse of hell. For the saint, heaven is God. For the wicked, hell is God. Cursed are the impure in heart for they too shall see God![11]

Does this seem unfair? Does it seem cruel that unbelievers "will be thrown outside, into the darkness, where there will be weeping and gnashing of teeth" (Matthew 8:12)? Our human sense of justice may think so, but remember, God owes this utterly rebellious planet absolutely nothing. Were it not for God's quickening grace, we would all remain dead in our trespasses. Plus, were it not for His grace, this planet would have ripped itself apart at the seams long ago in hatred and violence. That the human race has survived this long is a demonstration of God's compassion. The question is not "How could God let so many people go to hell?" but should be "How could God be so generous and save as many as He does?"

Human fairness is not the point, the justice of God is. If there's no judgment and subsequent hell, then it makes more sense to eat, drink, and be merry for tomorrow we die and ... period. Nothingness. It's all over. But there *is* a hell. As well as a Judgment. "I saw the dead, great and small, standing before the throne, and books were opened. Another book was opened, which is the book of life. The dead were judged *according to what they had done.* ... If anyone's name was not found written in the book of life, he was thrown into the lake of fire" (Revelation 20:12, 15).

That's the one verse in the Bible that makes my hair stand on end. Apocalyptic verses about signs of the times, earthquakes, floods, and pestilence don't do it. Not even word pictures about snarling beasts and ten-horned creatures or the heavens rolling up as a scroll and the mountains fleeing into the ocean. The worst verse in the Bible is the one about dead people being judged. That's because some of those dead will be my neighbor down the street, my elementary school teacher, the lady at the dry cleaners, or even those Muslim young men who work at the Shell gas station near my house (not to mention millions of others worldwide).

When I pray, "Come quickly, Lord Jesus," I utter that word "quickly" with caution. Do I really want Jesus to return soon? Yes!

And no.

Holding Off the Day of God's Wrath

The day dawned quietly over Nazareth, except for the crowing of a rooster and barking from a few dogs. The hour was still early but the sun was high, the air dry and hot. Any other morning the streets of Nazareth would have been bustling with hawking vendors and women chatting on their way to the well. But this was no ordinary day. This was the Sabbath. And this was no ordinary Sabbath. Jesus had come home and He would be in the synagogue.

No one was sure how long He'd been gone. Two, maybe three months? Rumor had it that one morning Jesus just hung up His carpenter's apron and headed off to the Jordan River to find the Baptist. Then something strange happened. When Jesus was baptized there was a thunderous voice, followed by a dove. Next, He vanished. Some say Jesus headed off into the wilderness. Others reported His whereabouts later on in Capernaum. That's when rumors really got weird. Sick people getting healed? Something about water becoming wine?

And now He was back in Nazareth.

The air in the synagogue was hot and tight. The attendant handed Jesus the scroll of Isaiah. He quietly unrolled it, found the verse He was looking for, and began to speak with the voice of uncommon authority: "The Spirit of the Lord is on me, because he has anointed me to preach good news to the poor. He has sent me to proclaim freedom for the prisoners and recovery of sight for the blind, to release the oppressed, to proclaim the year of the Lord's favor" (Luke 4:18–19).

He stopped in the middle of the verse. Just like that, Jesus left it unfinished and sat down. The eyes of everyone were fastened on Him. Little wonder, they had never heard Isaiah 61 read in such a way, like the words were His own. Finally Jesus broke the silence, "Today this Scripture is fulfilled in your hearing."

The rest was a blur. The crowd started demanding tricks, a magic show, shouting, "Do here in your hometown what we have heard that you did in Capernaum!" Jesus reminded them that crowds demanded the same performance from Elijah and Elisha, but like the prophets of old, He would do no miracles among faithless, stiff-necked, prideful people. A scuffle broke out and then a town riot. They drove Jesus out of the village and took him to the brow of the hill to throw Him down the cliff. The story abruptly ends there, with Jesus escaping and going on His way.

This incident in Luke 4 records the formal announcement of Jesus' ministry. From the very moment He embarked on His earthly mission, He made clear His motives and intentions. He had come for heaven's sake. But why wasn't the crowd satisfied with His mission statement?

Perhaps it wasn't so much what He said, as what He didn't say. Jesus did not read the entire verse from Isaiah 61. He announced He had come to proclaim the year of the Lord's favor, but He failed to finish the sentence. He did not say what the people were hoping He would say: That He had come "to proclaim the day of vengeance of our God." It was obvious to the people gathered in that synagogue that Jesus had no intention of executing the wrath of God upon their Roman oppressors. And everybody thought that's what the Messiah was supposed to do—execute wrath and judgment.

He left off the most terrifying part of the second verse of Isaiah 61 because He did not come to condemn or destroy. He came to seek and save the lost.

This threw everybody into confusion. Especially John the Baptist who was poised for the judgment. John had been paving the way for Jesus, proclaiming, "Repent, for the day of the Lord is at hand." He preached the coming hellfire and warned that the vengeance of God was at hand. Little wonder the Baptist was stymied. He had risked his life saying angry things against Herod as well as pointing the finger at hypocritical religious leaders. When Jesus failed to crush evil and castigate sinners, John was confused and disappointed. He got himself thrown into prison for the sake of the coming judgment, yet Jesus didn't lift a finger to release him from jail.

Jesus made it clear that His agenda was not to execute the wrath of God, but to bear in His own body that same wrath. I'm heartbroken by that statement: Jesus, precious Savior, did not come to execute the wrath of God, but to *bear in His own body* God's fury. All of the Father's white-hot anger against my sin was poured out on the cross. Because of Jesus, the Father has no anger left for you and me.

Instead, He's storing up His anger for the day His Son will come back.

One day Jesus is going to return and finish the verse from Isaiah 61.

He will judge the living and the dead. He will crush the wicked. Punish rebellious, impudent evildoers. He will upset nations and overthrow kings and rulers. He will institute the day of vengeance of our God.

This is what tempers my pleas for the soon return of Christ. Yes, I pray, "Come quickly, Lord Jesus," but in the same breath, I remember the high school girl in the white-sequined dress whom I prayed for at the prom and the ten-year-old Asian girl at the Hair and Nail Shoppe, and a few aunts and uncles who, unless they come to profess Christ as Savior, will end up getting trampled in the grapes of God's wrath.

Please hold off a bit longer that great and dreadful day of the Lord!

Still, I need to remember that God's timing is perfect. You and I have a job to do, just as the disciples were reminded when they asked Jesus when He would come back. The Lord said to them, "It is not for you to know the times or dates the Father has set by his own authority. But you will receive power ... and you will be my witnesses in Jerusalem, and in all Judea and Samaria, and to the ends of the earth" (Acts 1:8).

I need not bother myself with God's timing. I simply need to be bothered enough to witness. While Christ is in heaven, He is proclaiming through us the year of the Lord's favor, He is carrying out His agenda of compassion and forgiveness through you and me. He is still the tender, merciful Shepherd looking for more people to rescue, searching for lost men and women on whom He can gladly bestow salvation.

So when I begin to lean on the windowsill of eternity and pine for my Savior to fulfill His promise to return, I bite my lip and recall 2 Peter 3:9: "The Lord is not slow in keeping his promise, as some understand slowness. He is patient with you, not wanting anyone to perish, but everyone to come to repentance." That's all the reminder I need to get away from that windowsill and go rescue the perishing.

How patient of the Lord to hold His breath for virtually two thousand years before bringing down His vengeance. I don't mind the slowness of God even if it means having to spend extra years in this wheelchair. God's slowness means more time and opportunity to increase heaven's numbers. More time for His Inheritance to be enriched, His Body to be made complete, His Bride to be more beautiful, His Army to be greater in rank, and the grand chorus of Eternal Worshipers to be louder and more thunderous in their praise. In short, it means more glory for Him.

I can sum up 2 Peter 3:9 with this paraphrase: "The Lord is not slow in finishing His sentences, as some understand slowness. He is holding off the last part of Isaiah 61:2 so that, heaven willing, my neighbor, my relatives, and the people who work in my community will come to repentance."

Oh, how gracious of Jesus, how patient. How kind of our God, how merciful. Until the King of Kings and Lord of Lords returns with eyes of blazing fire, robe of blood, and sword and fury, you and I better get out there and proclaim the year of the Lord's favor.

Crown Him with Many Crowns

Is your blood pressure a notch higher like mine right now? Maybe you are feeling like me—awash in delight, yet reverent in fear. Tingling with joy, yet trembling with holy respect. Our God is an awesome God. That's why I wish we were huddled together against the cold night air right now, listening to my neighbor's whistling pine trees, and gazing at a thin slice of moon making a smile on the horizon. I wish we were standing together underneath a starry dome, feeling small and swallowed up, and tuning into the faint and haunting melody of a hymn. A certain hymn striking a resonant chord in our souls.

It would be a moment of great happiness and wisdom. But this time, we wouldn't let it go. Nothing mundane or ordinary could drown it out, and we'd not only hold ourselves in that ecstatic state of listening to heaven's music, but we would lift our voices and sing along ...

> *Crown Him the Lord of love:*
>   *Behold His hands and side—*
> *Rich wounds, yet visible above,*
>   *In beauty glorified.*
> *No angel in the sky*
>   *Can fully bear that sight,*
> *But downward bends his wond'ring eye*
>   *At mysteries so bright.*
>
> *Crown Him the Lord of life:*
>   *Who triumphed o'er the grave,*
> *Who rose victorious to the strife*
>   *For those He came to save.*
> *His glories now we sing,*
>   *Who died and rose on high,*
> *Who died eternal life to bring*
>   *And lives that death may die.*
>
> *Crown Him the Lord of heav'n:*
>   *One with the Father known,*
> *One with the Spirit through Him giv'n*
>   *From yonder glorious throne.*
> *To Thee be endless praise,*
>   *For Thou for us hast died;*
> *Be Thou, O Lord, through endless days*
>   *Adored and magnified.*
> *Amen.*[12]

Part 3

The Journey Home

Chapter 9

Getting Ready for Heaven

—

ile this, Francie, and make copies of this letter, would you," I said to my secretary without looking up from my desk. "And, oh yes," I sighed, "would you please pull out the sofa bed one more time?"

"Are you serious? Again?"

"Again." With that, my face flushed and my eyes became damp. For the fourth time that day, I needed to be lifted out of my wheelchair and laid down. I had to undress to readjust my corset—shallow breathing, sweating, and a skyrocketing blood pressure were signaling that something was either pinching, bruising, or sticking my paralyzed body. My secretary tissued away my tears and unfolded my office sofa bed.

As she shifted my body, examining my legs and hips for any telltale pressure marks or red areas, I stared vacantly at the ceiling. "I want to quit this," I mumbled.

We couldn't find anything wrong. She put my clothes back on, hoisted me into my chair, and stepped back.

I looked sheepish. "Where do I go to resign from this stupid paralysis?"

Francie shook her head and grinned. She's heard me say it scores of times. It's nothing new. My disability is, at times, a pain.

As she gathered the pile of letters off my desk, and was about to leave, she paused and leaned against the door. "I bet you can't wait for heaven. You know, like Paul said, 'We groan, longing to be clothed with a heavenly dwelling.'"

My eyes dampened again, but this time they were tears of relief and hope. "Yeah, it'll be great." I couldn't return to my dictating. The verse kept sticking with me, and I whispered a prayer, "Yes, Lord, I do look forward to being whole, to having a body that will never know pain. But to be honest, what I really want is a new heart that doesn't want to resign or quit."

I sat and dreamed what I've dreamed of a thousand times: the hope of heaven. I jerked my will right side up, refocused my emotions, and realigned my thoughts. I mentally rehearsed a flood of other promises and fixed the eyes of my heart on unseen divine realities and future divine ful-fillments. I zeroed in on a few heavenly coordinates to lift my sights above my physical pain: *When we see Him we shall be like Him. . . . The perish-able shall put on the imperishable . . . the corruptible, that which is incor-ruptible. . . . That which is sown in weakness will be raised in power. . . . He has given us an inheritance that can never perish, spoil or fade. . . . If we suffer with Him, we shall reign with Him.*

It was all I needed. I opened my eyes and said out loud with a smile, "Come quickly, Lord Jesus."

The scene I described can sometimes happen two or three times a week. Physical affliction and emotional pain are, frankly, part of my daily routine. But I only stay me-centered long enough to release a few tears, blubber a few gripes, and that's it. I learned long ago that self-pity can be a deadly trap, and so I avoid it like the plague. I quickly move upward and onward.

Hardships are God's way of helping me to get my mind on the here-after. And I don't mean the hereafter as a death wish, psychological crutch, or escape from reality. I mean "hereafter" as the true reality. And nothing beats rehearsing a few time-honored, well-worn verses of Scripture if you want to put reality into perspective.

Every time my corset wears a wound in my side or I'm faced with a four-week stint in bed or I feel the stab of someone else's pity, I look beyond the negatives and see the positives. . . .

I recall that pilgrims aren't supposed to feel at home on earth.

I set my heart and mind on things above and wait on the Bridegroom.

I remember the promise of a new body, heart, and mind.

I dream about reigning on earth and ruling in heaven.

I think about crowns and rewards and casting them all at Jesus' feet.

When these Scriptures strike that resonant chord in my heart, I tune into the melody and hold myself in the state of listening to heaven's music. Before I know it, the song lifts me, and I'm soaring on Spirit wings, breathing celestial air. I'm in heaven. It's a glorious vantage point from which to look down on my pain and problems. The soul that mounts up to heaven's kingdom cannot fail to triumph.

It's odd that it took a wheelchair—something that bolts me to earth—to make me see the futility of fighting spiritual battles on the earthly plane. When I attempted to live on the same low level as my bolts, gears, wheels, and leather, I made blunder after blunder. I was powerless there until I shifted to a higher battleground and chose a different perspective.

Looking down on my problems from heaven's perspective, trials looked extraordinarily different. When viewed from its own level, my paralysis seemed like a huge, impassable wall; but when viewed from above, the wall appeared as a thin line, something that could be overcome. It was, I discovered with delight, a bird's-eye view. It was the view of Isaiah 40:31: "Those who hope in the Lord will renew their strength. They will soar on wings like eagles; they will run and not grow weary, they will walk and not be faint."

Eagles overcome the lower law of gravity by the higher law of flight, and what is true for birds is true for the soul. Souls that soar to heaven's heights on wings like eagles overcome the mud of earth that keeps us stuck to a temporal, limited perspective. If you want to see heaven's horizons, as well as place earth in your rearview mirror, all you need to do is stretch your wings (yes, you have wings, you don't need larger, better ones, you possess all that you need to gain a heavenly perspective on your trials) and consider your trials from heaven's realms. Like the wall that becomes a thin line, you are able to see the other side, the happier outcome.

That's what happened to me that day in my office. I was able to look beyond my "wall" to see where Jesus was taking me on my spiritual journey.

Although paralysis has aided me in my pilgrimage, it has not made me automatically holy. You could say the same about your own suffering. Pain and problems do not make one instantly obedient. For me, it has taken time. Time, in more ways than one.

The View from the End of Time

Scripture mainly presents us with a view of life from the eternal perspective. Some call it "the heavenly point of view." I like to refer to it as the "end-of-time view." This perspective separates what is transitory from what is lasting. What is transitory, such as physical pain, will not endure, but what is lasting, such as the eternal weight of glory accrued from that pain, will remain forever. Everything else—numbing heartache, deep disappointment, circumstances that seem topsy-turvy—everything else, no matter how real it seems to us on earth, is treated as inconsequential. Hardships are hardly worth noticing.

The apostle Paul had this perspective when he said, "For our light and momentary troubles are achieving for us an eternal glory that far outweighs them all" (2 Corinthians 4:17). And regarding his own problems, he added, "I consider them rubbish" (Philippians 3:7).

Wait a minute. Did he say, "Troubles, light"? "Hardships, rubbish"?

The apostle Peter had this perspective too when he wrote to Christian friends being flogged and beaten. "In this you greatly rejoice, though now for a little while you may have had to suffer grief in all kinds of trials" (1 Peter 1:6).

Rejoice? When you're being thrown to lions? The Christians to whom Peter was writing were suffering horribly under Nero, the Roman emperor. Peter expected them to view their problems as lasting ... *a little while?* What sort of wristwatch was he using?

This kind of nonchalance about gut-wrenching suffering used to drive me crazy. Stuck in a wheelchair and staring out the window over the fields of our farm, I wondered, *Lord, how in the world can You consider my troubles light and momentary? I will never walk or run again. I will never use my hands. I've got a leaky leg bag ... I smell like urine ... my back aches ... I'm trapped in front of this window. Maybe You see all of this achieving an eternal glory, but all I see is one awful day after the next of life in this stinking wheelchair!*

I did not buy the heavenly point of view. My pain screamed for my undivided attention, insisting, "Forget the future! What's God going to do *now?*" Time does that. It rivets your attention on temporal things and makes you live in the moment. And suffering doesn't make it any easier. It tightens the screw on the moment, making you anxious to find quick fix-its or escape hatches. That's what it was like as I pitied myself in my chair. When I read Romans 5:3, "rejoice in our sufferings," my first thought was, *Sure, God, I'll rejoice the day You get me out of this thing! And if You don't, what's going on? Are You poking fun at my paralysis? Trying to convince me I'm in spiritual denial? That my hurt and pain are imaginary?* When it came to my affliction being light and momentary, God was obviously using a different dictionary.

Years later the light dawned. The Lord hadn't used a different lexicon when He picked words like "light and momentary" to define earthly troubles. Even if it meant being sawn asunder, torn apart by lions, or plopped in a wheelchair for the rest of one's life. The Spirit-inspired writers of the Bible simply had a different perspective, an end-of-time view. Tim Stafford says, "This is why Scripture can seem at times so blithely and irritatingly out of touch with reality, brushing past huge philosophical problems and personal agony. But that is just how life is when you are looking from the end. Perspective changes everything. What seems so important at the time has no significance at all."[1]

It's a matter of perspective. "Therefore we do not lose heart," 2 Corinthians 4:16 says. "Though outwardly we are wasting away, yet inwardly we are being renewed day by day. For our light and momentary troubles are *achieving for us an eternal glory that far outweighs them all*" (v. 17). What could possibly outweigh the pain of permanent paralysis? The coordinates of the new perspective are found in the next verse, "So we fix our eyes not on what is seen, but on what is unseen. For what is seen is *temporary,* but what is unseen is *eternal*" (v. 18). The greater weight of eternal glory is clear:

The healing of that old ache.

Joy, eternal and ecstatic.

Being beautifully robed in righteousness.

Knowing Christ fully, my King and co-heir.

The final destruction of death, disease, and the devil. The vindication of His holy name. The restoration of all things under Christ.

These things outweigh thousands of afternoons of sweats and high blood pressure any day. They outweigh a lifetime of not feeling or moving. Mind you, I'm not saying that my paralysis is light in and of itself, it only *becomes* light in contrast to the far greater weight on the other side of the scale. And although I wouldn't normally call three decades in a wheelchair "momentary," it *is* when you realize that "you are a mist that appears for a little while and then vanishes" (James 4:14).

Scripture is constantly trying to get us to look at life this way. Our life is but a blip on the eternal screen. Pain will be erased by a greater understanding, it will be eclipsed by a glorious result. Something so superb, so grandiose is going to happen at the world's finale, that it will suffice for every hurt and atone for every heartache. It also helps to know that the state of suffering we are in here is necessary to reach the state we want (more accurately, God wants!) in heaven.

This is why Jesus spent so much energy emphasizing the end-of-time perspective. The Lord had come from heaven, and He knew how wonderful it was. Thus, He was always focusing on end results—the harvest of the crop, the fruit from the tree, the close of the day's labor, the profit from the investment, the house that stands the storm. He knew if we were to rejoice in our suffering, our fascination with the here and now would have to be subdued. How else could He say to those who mourn, "You are blessed"? How else could He tell the persecuted to be happy? How else could He remind His followers facing torture and death to "count it all joy"?

Nothing more radically altered the way I looked at my suffering than leapfrogging to this end-of-time vantage point. Heaven became my greatest hope. In fact, I wondered how other people could possibly face quadriplegia, cancer, or even a death in the family without the hope of heaven. It meant no more wallowing away hours by the farmhouse window, scorning Romans 8:28, and muttering, "How can it say all things fit together into a pattern for good in my life!" God's pattern for my earthly good may have smelled like urine and felt painful, but I knew the end result in heaven would exude a fragrant and glorious aroma: Christ in me, the hope of glory.

It's all a matter of time. "God makes all things beautiful in his time," says Ecclesiastes 3:11. And for many, they won't see the beauty until the end of time. Time solves the dilemma of Romans 8:28, as well as all the other problems of evil, suffering, and pain.

The Connection Between Hardship and Heaven

You may not be paralyzed with a broken neck, but you could be paralyzed by other limitations. A broken heart. A broken home. A broken reputation. These things that presently scream for your undivided attention may close the doors to earthly satisfaction, but they can swing windows wide-open to a spirited hope of heaven.

Mind you, the closed doors—many of which have slammed in your face and crunched your fingers—are no accident. God wishes to instill within you a deep desire for your inheritance that can never perish, spoil, or fade, but in order to grip your heart, He will take drastic measures. You may not appreciate His *modus operandi* at first, but later, with an end-of-time perspective, you can be grateful for it. Samuel Rutherford described the connection between heaven and hardships this way:

> If God had told me some time ago that He was about to make me as happy as I could be in this world, and then had told me that He should begin by crippling me in arm or limb, and removing me from all my usual sources of enjoyment, I should have thought it a very strange mode of accomplishing His purpose. And yet, how is His wisdom manifest even in this! For if you should see a man shut up in a closed room, idolizing a set of lamps and rejoicing in their light, and you wished to make him truly happy, you would begin by blowing out all his lamps; and then throw open the shutters to let in the light of heaven.[2]

That's exactly what God did for me when He sent a broken neck my way. He blew out the lamps in my life that lit up the here and now and made it so captivating. The dark despair of total and permanent paralysis that followed wasn't much fun, but it sure made heaven come alive. And one day, when our Bridegroom comes back—probably when I'm right in the middle of lying down on my office sofa for the umpteenth time—God is going to throw open heaven's shutters. There's not a doubt in my mind that I'll be fantastically more excited and ready for it than if I were on my feet.

Suffering is no failure of God's plan. True, it is part of the curse, along with death, disease, and destruction. But before God comes back to close the curtain on suffering, it is meant to be redeemed. As Dorothy Sayers said, "Only in Christianity do we see a good God reaching down into what otherwise would be awful evil and wrench out of it positive good for us, and glory for Himself."

So what is this connection between heaven and our hardships?

Suffering Moves Our Heart Toward Heaven

Suffering makes us want to go there. Broken homes and broken hearts crush our illusions that earth can keep its promises, that it can really satisfy. Only the hope of heaven can truly move our passions off this world—which God knows could never fulfill us anyway—and place them where they will find their glorious fulfillment.

When I was on my feet, it would have been nice had I focused on heaven purely for Christ's sake, but forget that. Altruistic, yes. But realistic? No. I was healthy, athletic, distracted, and not the type to get hyped about heaven for anyone's sake other than my own. Who wants to think about heaven when you've got things to do and places to go here? Besides, you have to die in order to get there. I did not want to think about that at the age of seventeen.

It's the nature of the human beast. At least this beast. Some people have to break their necks in order to get their hearts on heavenly glories above, and I happen to be one of them. It was only after the permanency of my paralysis sank in, that heaven interested me.

Thank heavens, you don't have to break your neck to get grabbed. When you come to *know* that the hopes you have cherished will never come true, that your loved one is gone from this life forever, that you will never be as pretty or successful or famous as you had once imagined, your sights are lifted. You long and look forward to the day when your hopes will be fulfilled and heartache will vanish. The glorious day when "we will be whole" becomes your passion as you realize that, once and for all, earth can never meet your deepest longings.

My hope of running through earthly meadows and splashing my feet in a stream will never come true—but it will in the new heavens and new earth. My dream of hugging a loved one and actually *feeling* his or her embrace will never come true—but it will when we stand together before Jesus.

You can appreciate this, especially if earth has broken your heart. You may be a mother who has lost her child in an accident, a son who has lost his father to cancer, or a husband whose wife has passed on to glory. These dear ones take with them a part of your heart that no one can replace. And since the pursuit of heaven is an occupation of the heart anyway, don't be surprised if you find yourself longing for heaven after you leave the graveside. If your heart is with your loved ones, and they are home with the Lord, then heaven is home for you too.

A broken heart leads to the true contentment of asking less of this life because more is coming in the next. The art of living with suffering is the art of readjusting your expectations in the here and now. There are simply some things I will *never have* because of this wheelchair. Such longings heighten my loneliness here on earth. The psalmist wrapped words around this loneliness in Psalm 73:25–26 when he said, "Whom have I in heaven but you? And being with you, I desire nothing on earth. My flesh and my heart may fail, but God is the strength of my heart and my portion forever."

Larry Crabb writes, "Godly people ... nobly endure hard things. An anorexic daughter, a layoff, betrayal by a friend. They know that their existence is meaningful and that they are destined for unlimited pleasure at the deepest level (in heaven). Because they keenly feel that nothing now quite meets the standards of their longing souls, the quiet but deeply throbbing ache within them drives them not to complaint, but to anticipation and further yieldedness."[3]

But asking less is not a loss, and readjusting expectations is not a negative. It's good. When I was on my feet, big boisterous pleasures provided only fleeting satisfaction. In a wheelchair, satisfaction settles in as I sit under an oak tree on a windy day and delight in the rustle of leaves or sit by a fire and enjoy the soothing strains of a symphony. These smaller, less noisy pleasures are rich because, unlike the fun on my feet, these things yield patience, endurance, and a spirit of gratitude, all of which fits me further for eternity.

It is this yieldedness that gains you the most here on earth. You enjoy "a sincere heart in full assurance of faith" as it says in Hebrews 10:22, which in turn gives conviction to unseen divine realities and future divine fulfillments. You enjoy a new degree, a new release of energy at every point in your life as the eye of your soul is strengthened and spiritual understanding is quickened. A greater assurance of faith shows you that all things are, indeed, working together for good, and you realize without a doubt that the smallest of kind deeds done in Christ's name will result in a greater capacity to serve God in glory.

Suffering hurries the heart homeward.

HEAVEN ... YOUR REAL HOME

Suffering Prepares Us to Meet God

Just think. *Suppose you had never in your life known physical pain.* No sore back, twisted ankle, or decayed molars. What if you never had to use those crutches or that walker? How could you appreciate the scarred hands with which Christ will greet you?

Yes, Jesus will be the only One in heaven who will bear the scars of life on earth, the print of nails in His hands. We know this because on His throne, the risen Christ appears "as a Lamb that had been slain." And when we touch His scars, God will give us at least a partial answer to the "Why?" questions about our suffering, commenting to us, "Why not?"

If Jesus went through so much suffering to secure for us that which we don't deserve, why did we complain when we endured on earth only a tiny fraction of what He went through on our behalf? But if, instead, we stifled complaints and rejoiced in the privilege of participating in the sufferings of Christ, we will be overjoyed when His glory bursts on the scene. For "we share in his sufferings in order that we may also share in his glory" (Romans 8:17).

In a way, I wish I could take to heaven my old, tattered Everest & Jennings wheelchair. I would point to the empty seat and say, "Lord, for decades I was paralyzed in this chair. But it showed me how paralyzed You must have felt to be nailed to Your Cross. My limitations taught me something about the limitations You endured when You laid aside Your robes of state and put on the indignity of human flesh."

At that point, with my strong and beautiful glorified body, I might sit in it, rub the armrests with my hands, look up at Jesus, and add, "The weaker I felt in this chair, the harder I leaned on You. And the harder I leaned, the more I discovered how strong You are. Thank You, Jesus, for learning obedience in Your suffering. . . . You gave me grace to learn obedience in mine."

Not only will I appreciate the scars of Christ, but also the scars of other believers. There I will see men and women that in the world were cut in pieces, burnt in flames, tortured and persecuted, eaten by beasts, and drowned in the seas—all for the love they had for the Lord. What a privilege it will be to stand near their ranks! But what a shame it would be if, in conversing with them, we could only shrug our shoulders and prattle, "Me? Suffer? Well, there was that time I had to endure the most insipid color of yellow on my living room walls . . . and, oh yes, my gallbladder surgery. Do you want to see my scars?"

Forgive me for being flippant, but perhaps we would bite our complaining tongues more often if we stopped to picture the scene in heaven. The examples of other suffering saints are meant to inspire us upward on our heavenly journey home. This is why I love reading the biographies of missionaries like Amy Carmichael or J. Hudson Taylor, people who considered it a privilege to bear their sufferings with grace so they might share in Christ's glory.

Suppose you had never in your life known emotional pain. No stained reputation. No bruised feelings. No pangs of guilt. What if no one had ever offended you deeply? How could you adequately express your gratitude when you approach the Man of Sorrows who was acquainted with grief?

If you were never embarrassed or felt ashamed, you could never grasp how much He loved you when He endured the spit from soldiers, the spinelessness of His disciples, the callousness of the crowd, and the jeers from the mob. All for the love of you.

He took your shameful sins and made them His. You will be able to say, "Lord, I'm grateful that I felt the piercing stab of guilt. . . . I can better appreciate how You were wounded by sin on the Cross!"

Lastly, suppose you had never in your life known the struggle against sin. There's a distinct connection between heaven and this struggle. The apostle John tightened the connection when he wrote in 1 John 3:2–3, "We know that when he appears, we shall be like him, for we shall see him as he is. Everyone who has this hope in him purifies himself."

It is rare to find believers who, for the sake of heaven, purify themselves. But I want to be one of them, don't you? I want to sweep my conscience clean and jerk open every closet in my heart that hides a skeleton. It's painful to sit this close to self-scrutiny and cut away every sin that entangles, and I don't like "gouging out the eye" or "cutting off the hand" any more than you do. But it's what the Lord requires if we are to possess a lively anticipation of seeing Him face-to-face. Everyone who purifies himself has a heavenly hope, and everyone who possesses this hope, purifies himself.[4]

I want to be as happy as possible in heaven; and Bishop Ryle is on target when he warns, "Heaven is a holy place. Its inhabitants are all holy. Its occupations are all holy. To be really happy in heaven, it stands to reason we must be somewhat prepared for it. Our hearts must be somewhat in tune, somewhat ready for it."5

Yes, you want to be happy in heaven. And, yes, you'd like to feel at home with King David and the apostles Paul and John. Then live a life in agreement with the things they spoke about. Could we enthusiastically greet the apostle Paul who said, "Submit to one another out of reverence for Christ" (Ephesians 5:21) if we made it a practice of stepping on others to get ahead?

Could we look forward to hours alone with the apostle John who said, "Whoever lives in love lives in God, and God in him" (1 John 4:16) if in truth we settled for a halfhearted, ho-hum devotion to our Lord Jesus? Would we really feel comfortable with David who said, "I cry out to God Most High, to God, who fulfills His purpose for me" (Psalm 57:2) if we opted to ignore God when troubles came?

How could we be thrilled to meet the Lord face-to-face after clinging on earth to the very sins for which He died? It is impossible to hold onto sinful habits while, at the same time, holding onto the desire to touch the nail-scarred hands of Christ. No one can hope for heaven while consciously clutching onto sins he knows to be offensive. True, holy living is rugged and demanding, but its heavenly rewards are precious. It is heavenly minded people who nail their sin to the cross; who desire, like John, to lean upon Christ; who abandon themselves, like Paul, to be caught up into a third heaven; who wish, like David, to sit at the feet of His Lord.

Yes, it's a struggle. And the entire chapter seven of Romans assures us holy living will always be a struggle. But think of it as the best way of showing your love to Christ! "Of all the things that will surprise us in the resurrection morning, this, I believe, will surprise us most: that we did not love Christ more before we died."6

I don't know about you, but that's one surprise I want to avoid. I want to cut away every sin that entangles.

A curious thing will happen if you view your suffering this way. Once you see your affliction as a preparation to meet God, you won't be quick to call it "suffering" again. Even though I have rough moments in my wheelchair, such as the one in my office with high blood pressure and pain, for the most part I consider my paralysis a gift. Just as Jesus exchanged the meaning of the Cross from a symbol of torture to one of hope and salvation, He gives me the grace to do the same with my chair. If a cross can become a blessing, so can a wheelchair.

I'm inspired by Madame Guyon who, although locked away in the depths of a French dungeon for many years, wrote, "I have no desire that my imprisonment should end before the right time; I love my chains." And Amy Carmichael, the missionary to India who wrote from her bed of affliction,

> *Before the winds that blow do cease,*
> *Teach me to dwell within Thy calm:*
> *Before the pain has passed in peace,*
> *Give me, my God, to sing a psalm.*[7]

Misses Guyon and Carmichael would say something else. They would expect me to never dare say I was "suffering" paralysis. Once a gift, always a gift. The wheelchair is, in a sense, behind me now. The despair is over. There are now other crosses to bear, other "wheelchairs" in my life to be exchanged into gifts.

When you meet Jesus face-to-face, your loyalty in your hardships will give you something tangible, something concrete to offer Him in return. For what proof could you bring of your love and faithfulness if this life left you totally unscarred?

When Suffering Seems Insurmountable

Over the phone, I could hear the puffing and wheezing of Lisa's respirator as she labored to speak between breaths. "Joni, I don't . . . see why God . . . is putting me through . . . all this suffering. . . . Why doesn't He just . . . take me home . . . now?"

I leaned my head against the receiver and wondered, for the thousandth time, what to say. Lisa was a twenty-one-year-old woman who became severely paralyzed as a result of an accident two and a half years earlier. In that time she had been shifted from one hospital to another. The doctors had done all they could, and now they were deliberating over where to send her next. Her parents couldn't take her in. Independent living centers for people her age were overcrowded with long waiting lists. The only option? A nursing home.

I'd had many years in a wheelchair. Lisa, only a few. How could I expect her to grasp the things that had taken me ages to understand? What could I give or say to help?

"I'm a Christian," Lisa continued, interrupting my thoughts. "Why do I . . . have to go through all . . . this?"

I used to ask myself that many times. *Okay, I'll accept this connection between hardship and heaven, but what if the hardship is insurmountable? Overwhelming? Unbearable?* I'm paralyzed from the shoulders down, but Lisa is paralyzed from the neck down. She can't even breathe on her own. How can one deal with so much frustration and affliction? Questions such as these lose their academic tone when couched around the struggles of someone like her. This young respirator-dependent quadriplegic is thrust out into a no-man's-land, way ahead of the frontline trenches where most of us suffer.

As we talked on the phone, I sensed that her questions were not the "why?" of the clenched fist sort, but the "why?" of a searching heart. Bitterness was not her nemesis. Lisa was actually wondering how to live, how to view her affliction as meaningful. I knew that if she could rise above her circumstances to see her suffering from a heavenly end, she'd be in the enviable position of gaining more than most.

"You mean I've got more to gain than you?" she breathed into the phone.

"Yes, I believe you do," I answered gently.

"I'm ready . . . I want to understand . . . I don't want to live . . . my life in vain."

For the next hour, I slowly tried to lift her sights beyond the impassable wall of her hospital room. I began with the basics (which are really not so basic) and shared how her paralysis could become the best place from which to know God. " 'Be still, and know that I am God,' it says in Psalm 46:10. Lisa, the hours you spend in that bed of yours are a way of being still before the Lord. A large part of you doesn't move. Literally. It is always quiet. This built-in stillness can help you understand things about the Lord that most people never grasp," I explained.

Perfect stillness is not always available to those who would appreciate it most, and often not appreciated by those who have it. Lisa had a long way to go before she could learn how to be comfortable in her enforced stillness, but the softness in her voice assured me she was on her way. She will learn that it's not merely an absence of noise and fidgety movement, but a spiritual alertness, a receptivity. Jim Elliot, the missionary who was speared to death by Auca Indians, wrote, "Wherever you are, *be all there. Live to the hilt every situation you believe to be the will of God.*"[8]

"Enough has been wasted in your life, Lisa," I said. "Don't waste anymore of it. And don't worry about finding answers. . . . I don't think they would satisfy you at this point anyway. Just use the time you've got, the stillness you're experiencing . . . use it to get to know God."

"But how?"

I smiled at her question because I knew the answer was going to sound so simple it would seem sophomoric. "Talk to Him in prayer, and let Him talk to you in His Word."

"That's it?"

"That's it."

Lisa told me she would start doing just that, especially when I told her that the faintest prayers of those who suffer reach more deeply into God's heart. At that point, I imagined angels in heaven kicking up their heels and rejoicing. This vent-dependent quadriplegic who will lie in bed and spend long moments in prayer may not realize it, but she will be doing the work of angels. After all, there are angels in heaven who do nothing but praise God, such as the seraphim who proclaim day and night before the Lord, "Holy, Holy, Holy!"

She has an arduous road ahead, but when hurting people like her give God an inch, He always takes a mile. He wants those who suffer greatly to receive even greater glory.

> *The clock has stopped. The universe has flashed*
> *and cracked. The flood has swept the dam.*
> *Bright angels sift like gold dust from the gash,*
> *heralding invitations of the lamb:*
> *"Arise ye hobbling, tattered, orphaned, blind,*
> *Ye maimed in spirit, measured without merit,*
> *by men cast off as useless. Rise and find*
> *the crown, the throne, the birthright to inherit.*
>
> —Douglas Kaine McKelvey[9]

The Greater the Suffering, the Greater the Glory

There is a direct relationship between earth's suffering and heaven's glory. I'm not glorifying suffering here. There's no inherent goodness in Lisa's spinal cord injury. There's nothing applaudable about the agony. Problems are real, and I'm not denying that suffering hurts. I'm just denying that it *matters* in the grander scheme of things. It is light and momentary *compared* with what our response is producing for us in heaven—yes, suffering is pivotal to future glory. This places Lisa in that enviable position I mentioned earlier.

Let me explain. The greatest suffering that ever occurred happened on the Cross. And the greatest glory ever given in response to suffering was the glory ascribed to Christ when He ascended. He suffered "death on a cross ... *therefore* God exalted him to the highest place" (Philippians 2:8–9). There is a direct correspondence between suffering and glory.

When the mother of James and John approached the Lord and asked if her sons could please enjoy a position of prominence in the kingdom of heaven, the Lord replied, "You don't know what you're asking." Then He said to her sons, "Can you drink the cup I am going to drink?"

"We can," they answered.

Jesus said to them, "You will indeed drink from my cup" (see Matthew 20:20–23).

The Lord inferred that if His followers were to share in His glory, they would also have to share in His sufferings. And the deeper the suffering, the higher the glory. This is why the apostle Peter could say that to the degree one suffers, keep on rejoicing, "*Rejoice* that you participate in the sufferings of Christ, *so that you may be overjoyed* when His glory is revealed" (1 Peter 4:13). We rejoice on earth ... so that we may be overjoyed in heaven.

Does this mean that those who suffer greatly, yet nobly, will have a bigger halo? A shinier face? No, but it does mean that they will enjoy a greater capacity to serve God in heaven. Those who suffer beyond comparison will, if they honor Christ with an uncomplaining spirit, be glorified beyond all comparison.

I'm sure there will be times when Lisa will smirk—like I did—as she reads Romans 8:18, "I consider that our present sufferings are not worth comparing with the glory that will be revealed in us." Like me, she will go through cycles, thinking, *Is the Bible being flippant about my lot in life?* But as long as she keeps focused on the basics—being still and knowing God through prayer and Scripture—she will remain on the high road home. She will be more devoted to the future than the present. More devoted to the spiritual than the physical. And more devoted to eternal realities than temporal ones.[10]

Don't Go to Heaven Yet!

There's another cycle Lisa will have to go through. I still deal with it and I bet you do too. The firmer my heart becomes anchored in heaven, the more I want to go there. Now.

It has nothing to do with being tired of sitting down or getting cricks in my neck from holding up my head all day. It's just that less of my heart is here, and more of it is there. I identify with the apostle Paul who said in Philippians 1:21, "For me to live is Christ, and to die is gain. Now if I am to go on living, this will mean fruitful labor for me. Yet what shall I choose? I don't know. I am torn between the two: I desire to depart and be with Christ which is better by far . . . but it is more necessary for you that I remain in the body."

Like Paul, I often debate the pros and cons of life. But also like him, my earthly life is meant to be one of discontentment. I am torn between the two. I desire to depart. Since my heart has already gone ahead, I long to follow it home. But it is more necessary that I—Lisa, and thousands like us—remain in the body. For others.

I touched on why at the close of my phone conversation with Lisa. "If you remain faithful, despite the odds, it helps people like me more than you'll ever know."

"But it's hard . . . to think of others . . . when you're hurting."

"I know." My voice was nearly a whisper. "But it is more necessary for you to remain in the body . . . it is more necessary for me and many more who know you better. A fellow with a disability once wrote, 'For just as the sufferings of Christ flow over into our lives, so also through Christ our comfort overflows. If we are distressed, it is for your comfort and salvation; if we are comforted, it is for your comfort, which produces in you patient endurance of the same sufferings we suffer' (2 Corinthians 1:5–6)."

There was a long pause at the other end.

"The fact that you hang in there ... does something for the rest of us Christians. I'm not talking about you being an inspiration. It's more than that ... it's a mystery. God somehow strengthens others by your faithfulness. You may feel like a burden to others, but God thinks the opposite. He thinks it's necessary that others take care of you. ... You will be doing more for their spiritual well-being than you can imagine. What's more, it's all being credited to your account. The apostle Paul said so in Philippians 1:25–26 when he told a bunch of guys his example inspired, 'I will continue with all of you ... so that through my being with you again your joy in Christ Jesus will overflow on account of me.' Did you get that part about 'on account of me?' If good things happen to others because of your example, God chalks it up on your record."

Lisa threw a curve, "But I don't ... see others anymore. ... Everyone ... has gone away ... I may help you ... but nobody else."

At that point, she raised another reason why God hasn't taken her to heaven yet. She must endure not only for the benefit of others, but for the purpose of teaching the unseen powers, the rulers, and authorities in the heavenly realms about her powerful and all-sustaining Lord.

"You see," I explained, "I had a friend named Denise when I was in the hospital. She laid in bed for eight years, blind and paralyzed. Much worse than you or me. She hung in there despite the odds."

There was another long silence on the other end, and I knew Lisa was listening intently.

"Denise died after eight years in that bed. My human logic said, 'God, You should have taken her home to heaven sooner ... what did all her striving accomplish for the handful of nurses who happened to know her?' But then I read a verse in Ephesians 3:10 that says God uses our lives like a blackboard upon which He teaches lessons about Himself. And He does it for the benefit of angels and demons ... maybe not people, but quadrillions of unseen beings."

Something dynamic is happening in heaven right now. Angels and demons are learning new things about God. It happens when believers allow their painful circumstances to be the platform from which their souls rise to heavenly heights. Every day that we go on living in these bodies means fruitful labor—for us, for others, for the glory of God, and for the heavenly hosts.

Onward and Upward

Suffering does this. It always drives us in deeper and up higher. Always onward and upward into the heart of heaven.

Lisa and I said good-bye and continued to keep in touch. She settled into a living situation with a friend and began to attend a local college. She got involved with her church and started going to Bible study. After five years, we lost contact. I wasn't worried about her, though, because she seemed to be on a steady path.

This year, however, I got the shock of my life when, after I finished speaking at a conference, a young woman hooked up to a ventilator wheeled up to me with a confident smile. I knew immediately who she was. The light in her eyes assured me this was the same young woman. She was happily heading for home and making the most of every day on the way.

Had Madame Guyon been able to reach across the centuries to Lisa (confined in her own set of bolts and bars), she would congratulate her with these words penned from her dark dungeon: "What gain has been made compared to the little that has been lost! You will have lost 'the creature' in order to gain 'the Creator.' You will have lost your nothingness in order to gain all things. You will be boundless, for you will have inherited God! Your capacity to experience His life will grow just a little more. Everything that you once had, and lost, will return to you in God."[11]

Lisa and I have seen the future, and the future is us. A glorious future for those who, for Christ's sake, suffer valiantly.

Yours is a glorious future too. God has placed suffering in your life to remind you that heaven is not only for the future; it is for now, for this present moment. Heaven is meant to bless your path and be a source of strength in your suffering today. Valiantly welcome it and greet it.

> No heaven can come to us unless our hearts find rest in it today. Take heaven. No peace lies in the future that is not hidden in this precious little instant. Take peace. The gloom of the world is but a shadow. Behind it, within our reach, is joy.... Life is so generous a giver, but we, judging its gifts by their coverings, cast them away as ugly or heavy or hard. Remove the covering and you will find beneath it a living splendor, woven of love and wisdom and power. Welcome it, greet it, and touch the angel's hand that brings it.

Everything we call a trial, a sorrow, a duty: believe me, that angel's hand is there, the gift is there, and the wonder of an overshadowing Presence. Our joys too: be not content with them as joys. They too conceal diviner gifts. Life is so full of meaning and purpose, so full of beauty beneath its covering, that you will find earth but cloaks your heaven. Courage, then, to claim it, that is all! But courage you have, and the knowledge that we are pilgrims wending through unknown country on our way home.

—Fra Angelico, 1387–1455[12]

Chapter 10

Homeward Bound

⎯

*T*he glowing sunset behind the coastal mountains stopped me in my tracks as I left the JAF Ministries office. I sat by my van in the parking lot and watched the hues shift and deepen from vivid lilac to pink and then a fiery red. A show-off sunset it was, a sassy kaleidoscope, teasing, inviting me to follow it over the horizon. It was another one of those heaven-inspired moments wooing me not only over the horizon, but home. I knew I couldn't follow. For now, I could only sit and enjoy.

"Good night, Joni," a couple of coworkers smiled as they headed toward their cars.

"'Night." I said dreamily. I roused and added, "Hey girls, wait ... can you believe that sunset?"

My friends paused, and together we stood, quietly, face-on into the color. It washed us in its glowing tone, touching us like the finger of Midas and making our group a single and silent statue of gold. We were bound together in a timeless moment that we knew was slipping away even as we tried to hold on to it. *Drink it all in,* we seemed to understand, *this won't last forever.*

As the colors peaked, golden rays shot up from behind the mountain just as the last vestige of sun slid beneath its crest. Then, it was gone. Finished.

We watched the sky darken and threaten as fog from the ocean crept up over the hills. I shivered, we said good-bye, and went our separate ways. Getting into my van, I remembered a favorite line from Amy Carmichael: "We will have all of eternity to celebrate the victories, and only a few hours before sunset in which to win them."

Miss Carmichael knew a lot about the Christian life—and a lot about sunsets. She knew the colors of the fading sun mesmerize us with their beauty, making us stand still and almost believe in timeless moments. Then, in the next second, the lingering pink and gold vanish.

Why am I always surprised at how *fast* sunsets disappear? How fast my days disappear?

Then again, I'm always amazed at how fast *life* disappears. I watch a sunset, get in the van, drive away, stop at the gas station, the market, help Ken fix dinner, and then collapse in bed long after dark. Next morning I'm up and at it again. My life will be gone in a flash, in the twinkling of an eye. Suddenly—just like that—it will be over. Finished. The fading beauty of all the good things in life will disappear.

Drink it all in ... this won't last forever. Soon, much sooner than I realize, I will follow that sunset over the horizon and step into the other side of eternity. And if I'm able to look over my shoulder at earth, I know I'll be stunned that life went by so rapidly. But in heaven, there will literally be no time to think about it.

So I must think about it now.

That's why God gives us timeless moments in the here and now, striking that resonant chord in our heart that echoes eternity. He woos us away from this world with that heavenly haunting, and it happens when we're enfolded in the arms of the one we love. Or watch a baby break into a giggle. Or savor a Scripture that springs to life in our heart. Cry when a choir sings a triumphant hymn. Watch a sunset or gaze at the stars.

Timeless moments are those that send our hearts on ahead to heaven. Moments when we demonstrate drastic obedience, choose patience over complaint, or honor God when it's hard. Amy Carmichael calls this "winning victories" in the few hours we have before sunset.

"Be very careful, then, how you live—not as unwise but as wise, making the most of every opportunity, because the days are evil," Ephesians 5:15 echoes. Days are fleeting, hours are fading, and before you know it, we will no longer have the chance to prove our love to Jesus with our obedience. We won't have the time to get back on track. To build with gold, silver, and precious stones.

The sun will have set.

Twilight: Approaching the Passage to Heaven

No one appreciates sunsets like my mother. Lindy, as her friends call her, is like me in that she will put everything on hold to watch a sassy sunset. During the summer, her early evening ritual includes pulling up a chair and sipping coffee on the back porch of her condominium to watch the sun disappear below Sinepuxent Bay on the eastern shore of Maryland. Then she will watch the twilight give way to a thousand twinkling stars that stretch from horizon to horizon. She loves looking up and always telephones me to remind me when there's a full moon.

Mother is aware of how short the days are. At eighty-one years of age, she has seen ten thousand sunsets and understands that even the brightest day is sure to have its twilight. For her, the shadows are falling longer, thicker, and faster, and the warmth is going out of the air. Her strongest hours of building with gold, silver, and precious stones are waning as the afternoon of her life is passing. Lindy knows she is approaching twilight. But even in her twilight, even though Mother seems grand and old, she is so ... *young!*

I'm convinced it's because she keeps looking up and focusing on something far beyond her many birthdays and blocked arteries. Heaven is literally nearer to her, and such a focus will always infuse youth into the heart. After all, to live in the heavenlies is to live in a kind of timelessness. People who look up and see beyond the encroaching years enlarge their souls with eternity. They have about them the air of something eternal, not temporal. They know every year draws them closer to heaven, which, in turn, instills more youth into their hearts.

You don't have to convince my mother, and you don't have to twist the arm of my friend, Alice McIntire. Although definitely in her twilight, she won't tell her age because, as she puts it, "Any woman who tells her age, will tell anything." Alice—who I can at least say is beyond my mother's years—enjoys looking up as the shadows fall longer and faster. For years her heart has beaten in rhythm with her Savior's, and every once in a while she seems to tilt her head as if catching the strains of heaven's celebration. It wouldn't surprise me if she did. She has an ear for things festive. She lives and looks the part, even after eight decades. Alice knows she will have all of eternity to celebrate the victories, so she's making the most of the moments in her sunset years. She still teaches a women's Bible study, and she does it in St. John's knits with silk blouses and bows, earrings, and jeweled pumps.

Her Bible studies wouldn't be complete without the best china and linens for coffee and cookies afterward. Her spunk, humor, and style amaze me, and I once said to Alice, "You must be really looking forward to heaven," to which she replied, "Oh, honey, yes, but I hope I stay around for Jesus' return. . . . I never like to miss a good party."

Alice keeps looking up. This is why she stays so young (as does my mother). Every Christian who keeps looking up stretches his heart's capacity for heaven. They don't seem old, they are young.

Dr. Sherwood Wirt, editor emeritus of *Decision* magazine, is closing the ranks behind Alice McIntire and, like her, carries about him the air of youth. "People speak of the 'transitions' that age brings, usually in terms of externals such as thinning hair and hearing aids. I am now eighty-three years old and wish to testify that inside, where I live, age means nothing. I am the same person that I was at twenty-one, or forty-six, or sixty-five."[1]

I'm not ninety or in my eighties, but I identify. I feel so young inside, somewhere around the age of twelve or thirteen. As though I were a little girl. A girl like my mother who still bundles up to run outside and gaze at the moon. Or Alice who selects the latest designs off the petite rack. And Dr. Wirt who disarms you every time with that twinkle in his blue eyes. We feel young when we forget the temporal and focus on the eternal—that's what children do who have no concept of time, and of such is the kingdom of heaven.

People such as these understand that time is not their natural environment. They realize they are spiritual beings having a short stint in a physical experience. Time, for them, doesn't seem quite so much a stalking enemy as a passage—albeit difficult—into a brighter, better eternity.

When the Passage Is Painful

It may be brighter at twilight, but not necessarily easier.

That final passage for my mother, Alice, or Dr. Wirt may be swift and sweet, but there's no guarantee. For many, the passage is ugly and painful.

It was this way for Billie Barrows, the wife of Cliff Barrows. For more than forty years they labored together with Dr. Graham, full of zest for life and zeal for the good fight. That zeal buoyed Billie during her last nine years as she wrestled courageously against breast cancer, which spread into her liver, bones, and finally, her brain. She chose the high road and kept a joyful outlook, building up her body with the medicine of a happy heart, as well as a regimen of vitamins, various teas, and beet and carrot juice. But even with five chemotherapy treatments, Billie could not stave off the disease.

Surrounded by a loving family, boosted by prayer, and bolstered by a fighting spirit, hers should have been the model passage—wonderfully serene with chariots swinging low as the angels quietly came to carry her home. It wasn't that way. It was a knock-down-drag-out fight in the center ring, with time bullying and battering and showing no mercy.

On five different occasions her sons and daughters flew from the far corners of the country to join their dad at Billie's bedside. *Surely this time God will take Mother home,* they reasoned. But it was not her appointed time. During the last two weeks Billie's joy, which had been such an inspiration to Cliff, friends, doctors, and the family was silenced by the ticking of each painful minute that failed to bring release.

The deathbed was not a place of blessing for Billie. But it did become a place of blessing for the family. Cliff and his sons and daughters, in-laws, and grandchildren discovered a deeper, richer blessing in being together. Not around a holiday table with laughter and lighthearted moments, but around a bed of affliction that poignantly offered moments of love and reconciliation. Although Billie couldn't communicate, the large tears that rolled down her cheeks right before she died, said it all. Finally, blessed release came. She left the land of the dying for the land of the living.

Not long after Billie's funeral, I called her daughter, Bonnie. We talked about the wrenching agony of those last days. "Joni, Christians shouldn't glamorize death. Death is Satan's last-ditch effort, and he's going to make it as awful as he can."

There was a long pause.

"But God has the last word. Resurrection. And at the graveside we were able to sing—actually, we kept singing it every day—

> 'Soar we now where Christ has led,
> Following our exalted Head,
> Made like Him, like Him we rise,
> Ours the cross, the grave, the skies.'"

I could hear the smile in Bonnie's voice, and it wasn't hard to imagine that same smile through tears as she and her family left the graveside singing that hymn of victory, "Christ the Lord Has Risen Today."

As I hung up, I thought of Corrie ten Boom, the Dutch woman who was sent to a Nazi concentration camp for hiding Jewish families. Years after Tante Corrie's release, her companion, Pam Rosewell, sat by her bedside when she was old and stroke-stricken. Watching Corrie's mind and body waste away to a thin shadow of her former self, she wondered—much like Billie's family—why the Lord didn't take Tante Corrie home sooner. But Pam observed after the funeral of her elderly friend, "Every day she lived was a victory over the devil . . . he would have had her die fifty years earlier in Ravensbruck, but just the act of living, without doing a thing, just breathing life in and out was a triumph. If her final years had not influenced any person on earth and if the only reason the Lord allowed her to remain on earth was to make a silent daily statement to the principalities in heavenly places that 'Jesus is victor,' then it was an important silence indeed."

Was something of eternal value actually being accrued to Billie's account just by her surviving a few extra months or weeks? Were unseen divine realities at work? Realities that the Barrows family were unable to detect through the blinding veil of suffering? Perhaps God's glory will ultimately be more golden because of family faith forged at her bedside—a victory that will be credited to Billie. The days of her dying may have been evil, but she labored on the best she could. Her body obeyed the impulse of God-given life. And perhaps that—no glamour intended—was a victory.

In all their suffering, neither Tante Corrie nor Billie were diminished.

I am standing upon the seashore. A ship at my side spreads
her white sails to the morning breeze and starts for the blue ocean.
She is an object of beauty and strength, and I stand and watch her
until at length she hangs like a speck of white cloud just where
the sea and sky come down to mingle with each other.
Then someone at my side says: "There! She's gone."
Gone where? Gone from my sight—that is all.
She is just as large in mast and hull and spar as she was
when she left my side, and just as able to bear her load
of living freight to the place of destination. Her diminished

size is in me, not in her; and just at the moment when
someone at my side says, "There! She's gone," there are
other eyes watching her coming, and other voices ready to
take up the glad shout, "There she comes!"
And that is Dying!

—Author Unknown

I look at my own degenerating body and wonder how I will approach that final passage. Will it be short and sweet? Or long and agonizing? Will my husband be able to take care of me? Or will my quadriplegia better suit me for a nursing home? It's not so much I'm afraid of death as dying.

Whether it's painfully prolonged or a peaceful passing in the night, I'm strangely comforted by the thought that the servant shouldn't expect to suffer less than his Master. There is no holy peace with death. Theologian Alexander Schmemann wrote in his classic *For the Life of the World,* "Only if Christ is life, is death what Christianity proclaims it to be, namely an enemy to be destroyed, not a 'mystery' to be explained."[2] Even earth will convulse in upheaval in its final birth pangs before the new heavens and new earth. All seeds—whether a plant, a person, or a planet—must die. But then, the harvest.

Between Death and the Resurrection

Until the harvest, Billie and Tante Corrie are not diminished while they are presently in heaven. They gained immeasurably the instant they crossed from the land of the dying to the land of the living. Second Corinthians 5:8 explains that "to be away from the body [is to be] at home with the Lord." Billie and Tante Corrie are not present with the Lord in some soul-sleep right now; they are "at home" with Him in the best sense of the word. They are alive, awake, aware, and full of the joy of having come home. Home where they fit, feel warm and welcomed, a place where they belong. Who can begin to measure the fullness of the meaning of that word "home"!

There's another way that departed saints are not diminished and the clue is given in Luke 16:19–31. Jesus relays not a parable, but an amazing real-life occurrence after the death of a beggar named Lazarus and a rich man. The rich man was very conscious of his hellish surroundings as well as the condition of his brothers who still remained on earth, and he wanted desperately to warn his family. He felt, saw, prayed, remembered, and desired. My point? If lost souls can feel and care, how much more can those who have died in the faith!

Tante Corrie and Billie presently reside with the Lord of Glory, the Lord of love. How deeply they must feel and pray and see. How fervent must be their love. Could it be that our loved ones in glory are able to love us now? Pray for us now? Love does not die; it cannot die because it cannot fail. Love is a part of a departed saint's being, not his body, but his person. I'm convinced that Billie now loves her husband Cliff with a purer, holier, and more intense love than ever known on earth. And even if she is able to observe the mistakes, blunders, and tears of her loved ones on earth, she has the benefit of an end-of-time view, she is able to see the bigger, better picture.

In heaven, we do not lose, for "to die is gain." We aren't less, we're more. When we die, we're not in some soul-sleep of a stupor, not purgatory, and we're certainly not unconscious. We are at home with the Lord. Home!

Then, the Resurrection and Rest

Then one day, the Resurrection. "But your dead will live; their bodies will rise. You who dwell in the dust, wake up and shout for joy. Your dew is like the dew of the morning; the earth will give birth to her dead" (Isaiah 26:19).

The veil over this unseen divine reality was pulled back for me one peculiar Sunday afternoon. My mother-in-law recently purchased a family grave plot at a cemetery called Forest Lawn. She would not sign the papers, however, until Ken and I looked at the lot and gave our approval. "Do I have to?" I whined at Ken. I could think of better things to do with our Sunday afternoon.

Playing the submissive wife, I trekked to Forest Lawn with Ken, looked at my grave site located in a section called "Murmuring Pines," and listened to the realtor (that's what she was actually called) remind me that what with my head "here," and my feet "there," I would have a grand view of the valley and distant mountains. That's important, I told her. I also told her I did not have plans to stay there very long.

While the realtor and my mother-in-law conferred over the papers, I looked around at the hundreds of tombstones. It suddenly struck me that

I was sitting on the exact spot where my body will rise, should I die before Christ comes. Resting on that grassy hillside did more to ignite the reality of the Resurrection than hearing sermons or reading essays on the subject. One day actual beings will return to actual graves and reunite to rise.

And then, heaven.

Then, rest.

Not the rest of inactivity, but rest from the pain, the weariness, and the disappointment. I may only be cresting middle age, but like many of my friends who have toiled for years, I'm ready for a rest. No more wrestling against sin. No more prying the world's suction cups off my heart. No knock-down-drag-out fights with the devil. No collapsing in bed after an exhausting day only to snatch a few hours before you are up and at it again. "There remains ... a Sabbath-rest for the people of God" (Hebrews 4:9).

This thought alone makes the earthly toil not only bearable, but lighter. I can remember how, after hours of riding my horse to check gates and fences, my weary mount would be wet with sweat, her head hanging low. I had to urge her to put one tired hoof in front of another. Then as soon as she caught a whiff of home or recognized the fences of her own pasture, her ears would pick up and her pace would quicken. The nearer we came to the barn, the more eager her trot. After a quick unsaddling, she would joyfully roll in the dirt and take long deep drinks from the trough. How good it feels for a beast to be home, to be able to rest.

How good it will feel for us to rest, to be at home.

Maybe the writers of the Bible—some who had scars on their bodies from stonings, others whose joints were stiff from chains that chaffed— had this sweet rest in mind, a rest that perked them up and quickened their pace. They wrote vigorous encouragements like, "Let us, therefore, make every effort to enter that rest" and "Seeing that the days are short, make every effort..." and "Redeem the time for the days are evil." The weary labor for them seemed featherweight compared with the glorious rest into which they were about to enter.

Seize the Day!

The sun is setting. There are only a few hours left in which to gain heavenly victories.

I believe we are in the twilight of our hardships as well as the twilight of the world's history. I believe the days are short. My closing words for you are "Make the most of every opportunity" (Colossians 4:5). It is what Alice and my mother are doing, and it is what Billie and Tante Corrie did those last painful years of their lives. If we could hear it from the lips of Amy Carmichael herself, perhaps we would sense the urgency of winning triumphs for Christ in these last few hours before the sun disappears.

I tried to drive home this "end-of-time" perspective to Kim, a young Christian woman with Lou Gehrig's disease who was vacillating between going on a respirator or not. She wasn't sure if a respirator would be something that would sustain her life or just prolong her dying. We talked about how the impact of her decision would affect not just her but a wide circle of family and friends. We discussed the facts of her disease and whether or not she was, indeed, imminently dying. We talked about the difference between selfishness and selflessness.

I breathed a quick prayer, asking God to help me to be as sensitive as I could, and then I said to Kim, "If you can resolve these questions with a Spirit-controlled conscience, then I don't think you can make a wrong decision. But between the two, there may be a better choice. And to guide you, let me read one final and powerful verse from 2 Peter 3:8.

"It begins, 'But do not forget this one thing, dear friends.' You probably know from your days in Sunday school that what Peter is about to say is ultra-important, like Jesus saying, 'Verily, verily!' And he continues, 'With the Lord a day is like a thousand years, and a thousand years are like a day.'"

I explained to Kim why that verse is so key. We all recognize the old adage that God looks at the last two thousand years as only a couple of days gone by, but how many of us ever consider the next half of the verse? The part about seeing each day as like a thousand years? It's a little like divine geometry, a mathematical formula assuring us that each day is a chance to invest in a thousand years worth of eternity. God gives us a twenty-four-hour slice of time in which to make the most of every opportunity, opportunities that will have eternal repercussions.

The way we spend—the way Kim spends—the hours and moments counts. It counts far more than we realize. I suggested to Kim that she ought to smile and say "thanks" when her mother syringes liquid lunch into her G-tube. It's a way of making the most of an opportunity, and it could resound to 359 years of eternal benefit to her, her mother, and glory to God. Kim gave a little laugh when I told her this. "And when you bite your tongue from complaining about something, it could shake out to 500 years of eternal bliss, benefit, and glory!" What a way for this young woman to live out her remaining days. If Kim were to live only two more weeks with this heavenly perspective, it pans out to be fourteen thousand years in heaven. If she were to live a month, that figures out to thirty thousand years of eternal investment.

I'm not saying that every day here exactly equals one thousand years there. Remember, heaven has a different kind of time. Time just *is* in heaven. My purpose in using 2 Peter 3:8 was simply to give heavenly meaning to Kim's earthly hours.

Little wonder Psalm 90:12 says, "Teach us to number our days aright, that we may gain a heart of wisdom." *This* is the kind of wisdom God wants you to apply to your twenty-four-hour slices of time. This is the kind of wisdom that sends your heart on ahead to heaven.

Oh, if we could only realize how short life is. James 4:14 says, "What is your life? You are a mist that appears for a little while and then vanishes." And if we need another nudge, Isaiah 40:6–7 says, "All men are like grass.... the grass withers and the flowers fall, because the breath of the Lord blows on them. Surely the people are grass." Therefore make every effort. The days are evil. Redeem the time.

Make the most of your moments.

Come Home!

Yes, the older I get, the younger I feel. The faster time flies, the more precious my hours become. On some days, I feel as though I might be called Home any moment.

I had this "let's go home" feeling when I used to play in the woods beyond our backyard. As soon as I got home from elementary school, and while Mom was preparing dinner, I would put my things in my room and race out the back door to play tag with Kathy and a few neighborhood kids. We would call to each other and our shouts would echo through the tall oak trees. Everything echoed—the chatter of birds, the distant clatter of an old lawnmower, the slamming of screen doors. Our play was so much fun that an hour would go by and I'd hardly realize it. I barely noticed the rays of the sinking sun cutting long shadows through the trees. Kathy and I knew that soon Mother would call us home.

Funny, I rarely took it upon myself to go home unless called. I rather enjoyed hearing the sound of Daddy's or Mom's voice through cupped hands, shouting my name. No sooner did I hope they'd call when I would hear the familiar ding-ding-a-ling-ding of the dinner bell by the back door.

"Supper's ready ... time to come home!"

It's odd how I can still hear Mother's voice. It almost makes me cry; it just about made me cry when I was a child. The echo of the bell ... the haunting sound through the woods ... the joy about to break open my heart for the love of home, the warmth of family ... not to mention fried chicken and mashed potatoes by a glowing fire in the dining room. And often during summer, after the table was cleared and dessert was over, we'd sit in the backyard and watch the sun go down.

"There it goes.... "

"It's almost gone ... just a little tip of light left."

Our family would vie for who'd be the last one to see the sun set.

And then, we'd wait until the stars came out, singing hymns and counting the constellations. It was all I could hope for as a kid. And here I am an adult still looking beyond Ursa Major, singing heaven's melodies, and winning victories until earth's twilight gives way to the dawn of eternity.

Most of the things that have deeply possessed my soul have been echoes that have died away as soon as they caught my ear. But the echo of that dinner bell, now, many years later, has not died but is swelling into the sound itself.

When that happens to any of us, when those tantalizing glimpses, those promises never quite fulfilled find broader, more complete fulfillment in our maturing years, then we know we've found what we've longed for. Beyond every possibility of a doubt, we would say, "Here at last is the thing I was made for ... this is the healing of the old ache."

That's why for me, the echoes are getting louder. They resonate with the rich, full, and deep tones of Someone calling just a short distance away.

Softly and tenderly Jesus is calling,
Calling for you and for me;

See, on the portals He's waiting and watching,
Watching for you and for me.
Come Home, come Home,
Ye who are weary, come Home;
Earnestly, tenderly, Jesus is calling,
Calling, O sinner, come Home![3]

Epilogue

Years ago when I became paralyzed in a diving accident, my world was reduced to the basics. Lying for two years in a hospital bed on starched sheets surrounded by starched hospital workers, I lived in a sterile vacuum, doing little more than eating, breathing, and sleeping. I had all the time in the world to ask questions of God.

Perhaps friends who visited me thought I was being too philosophical. But they weren't faced with the larger-than-life questions that were plaguing me: "What is the meaning to life?" and "Where are we all heading?" Haunted and hurting, I realized there had to be more to life than just existing.

That's when I came face-to-face with the God of the Bible. I decided it was better to throw my questions at Him rather than shrug my shoulders and turn away. Those two years in the hospital were like one long question-and-answer session.

Heaven ... Your Real Home is, in part, a result of that time of questioning. What is the meaning to life? To know and glorify God. Where are we all heading? To enjoy Him forever ... at least for those who know Him.

My heart's longing is that you know and enjoy Him forever too. And if your heart has been warmed by the things you've read on these pages, if you sense in them the ring of truth, then it is God who is saying to you, "Come home, come home ... ye who are weary, come home." The first step in the right direction Home begins with a prayer, honest and from the heart. If you wish to be certain that you're homeward bound to heaven, and not hell, then feel free to borrow the following words and make them your personal prayer ...

> *Lord Jesus, I realize I have lived my life far from You*
> *And I see now how my sin has separated me from You.*
> *Please come into my life—my heart, mind, and spirit—*
> *And make me the person You want me to be.*

Forgive me for living away from You all these years
And help me to turn from my old ways
To Your new and righteous ways.
I invite You to be Lord of my life
And thank You for the difference You will make.
Amen.

If this is your prayer, then the next step in the right direction is to find a church where you can share your newfound affection for the Lord Jesus with other like-hearted believers in Him who center their faith around the Bible as God's Word. Step-by-step, you will grow to know Him better and to enjoy Him more. I look forward to the day when our journey Home will end on the other side of those gates of pearl. When you get there, let's do heaven, and until then, let's do all we can to help other hearts get Homeward bound.

Joni Eareckson Tada
JAF Ministries
P.O. Box 3333
Agoura Hills, CA 91301

Notes

Epigraph

Nancy Honeytree, "Joni's Waltz." Used by permission.

Chapter 1
What's So Great About Heaven?

1. This idea is from A. W. Tozer's book *The Knowledge of the Holy.*
2. This idea is from the writings of Nathaniel Hawthorne.
3. C. S. Lewis, *Perelandra* (New York: Macmillan, 1965), 33.
4. C. S. Lewis, *The Inspirational Writings of C. S. Lewis* (New York: Inspirational Press, 1991), 358.
5. C. S. Lewis, *The Problem of Pain* (New York: Macmillan: New York, Inc., 1962).

Chapter 2
Who Are We in Heaven?

1. *The Book of Common Prayer* (Philadelphia: Reformed Episcopal Publication Society, 1932), 512.
2. Robert L. Sassone, *The Tiniest Humans* (Stafford, Va.: American Life League, 1995), viii.
3. C. S. Lewis, *Weight of Glory* (Grand Rapids: Eerdmans, 1949), 15.
4. *Book of Common Prayer,* 5.
5. This idea was suggested to me by my reading of C. H. Spurgeon.
6. C. S. Lewis, *The Four Loves* (New York: Harcourt, Brace, Jovanovich, 1960), 126.
7. A. A. Hodge, *Evangelical Theology* (Carlisle, Pa.: Banner of Truth, 1976), 400.

Chapter 3
What Will We Do in Heaven?

1. Lewis, *The Weight of Glory,* 10.
2. C. S. Lewis, *The Great Divorce* (New York: Macmillan, 1973), 42–44.

3. E. L. Maskell, *Grace and Glory* (New York: Morehouse-Barlow, 1961), 68–69.

4. Lewis, *The Great Divorce*, 29–30.

Chapter 4
Where Is Heaven and What Is It Like?

1. John M. Templeton, *The God Who Would Be Known* (San Francisco: Harper & Row Publishers, 1989), 25.

2. Robert Jastrow and Malcolm Thompson, *Astronomy: Fundamentals and Frontiers* (Santa Barbara: John Wiley, 1977), 4, 12.

3. This idea was suggested to me in a personal letter from David Parrish.

4. Dr. John H. Gerstner, *The Rational Biblical Theology of Jonathan Edwards* (Orlando: Berea Publications, Ligonier Ministries, 1993), 552.

5. Ibid., 554.

6. Margaret Clarkson, *Grace Grows Best in Winter* (Grand Rapids: Eerdmans, 1984), 187.

Chapter 5
Why Don't We Fit on Earth?

1. A. E. Brumley, "This World is Not My Home" (Glendale, Ca.: Praise Book Publications, 1951), 111. Used by permission.

2. Malcolm Muggeridge, *Jesus Rediscovered* (New York: Doubleday, 1979), 47–48.

3. Peter Kreeft, *Heaven* (San Francisco: Ignatius Press, 1989), 66.

4. This idea was suggested to me in Peter Kreeft's book *Heaven*, 69.

5. Arthur Bennet, *The Valley of Vision* (Carlisle, Pa.: The Banner of Truth Trust, 1975), 203.

6. Sheldon Vanauken, *A Severe Mercy* (San Francisco: Harper & Row, 1977), 200, 202.

7. C. S. Lewis, *A Grief Observed* (New York: Bantam Books, 1976), 16.

8. Kreeft, *Heaven*, 71.

9. "Woodstock" by Joni Mitchell. Copyright 1969 Siquomb Publishing Corp. Used by permission. All rights reserved.

10. Kreeft, *Heaven*, 83.

11. C. S. Lewis, *George MacDonald: An Anthology* (New York: Macmillan, 1978), 8.

12. John H. Gerstner, *The Rational Biblical Theology of Jonathan Edwards, Vol. 3* (Orlando, Berea Publications, Ligonier Ministries,1993), 543.

13. Kreeft, *Heaven*, 84.

14. A. W. Tozer, quoted in Edythe Draper, *Draper's Book of Quotations for the Christian World* (Wheaton, Ill.: Tyndale House, 1992), 180.

15. George W. Robinson, "I Am His, and He Is Mine," (public domain).

16. Madame Jeanne Guyon, *Spiritual Torrents* (Auburn, Me.: The Seed Sowers Christian Books Publishing House, 1980), 99.

17. Edythe Draper, *Edythe Draper's Book of Quotations* (Wheaton, Il.: Tyndale House, 1992), 305.

Chapter 6
Heaven Has Our Heart's Desire

1. This idea is from Harry Blamires, *Knowing the Truth about Heaven and Hell* (Ann Arbor, Mich.: Servant Books, 1988), 111.

2. Jerry Leiber and Mike Stoller, "Is That All There Is?" © 1966 Jerry Leiber and Mike Stoller Music. All rights reserved. Used by permission.

3. Kreeft, *Heaven*, 44.

4. Lewis, *Weight of Glory*, 12.

5. The ideas in these three paragraphs are derived from C. S. Lewis, *The Four Loves*.

6. Sharalee Lucas, "I See Jesus in You" (Nashville: Rambo-McGuire Music, 1986). Used by permission.

7. Lewis, *Weight of Glory*, 15.

8. Idea from Augustine, *Ennarationes in Psalmos* 127.9.

9. Augustine, *Confessions* I. I.

10. William Herbert Carruth, "Each in His Own Tongue" (public domain).

11. Clara T. Williams, "Satisfied" (public domain).

12. A. W. Tozer, *The Knowledge of the Holy* (San Francisco: HarperCollins, 1992), 15.

13. John MacArthur, *Heaven* tape series (Panorama City, Ca.: Grace to You, 1987).

Chapter 7
Heaven: The Home of Love

1. The original idea for this opening portion of chapter 7 is from the Rev. Louis Lapides, Beth Ariel Fellowship, Sherman Oaks, Ca. Sources: Maurice

Lamm, "The Jewish Marriage Ceremony" in *The Jewish Way in Love and Marriage* (San Francisco: Harper & Row, 1980), 145–168; and Alfred Edersheim, *Sketches of Jewish Social Life in the Days of Christ* (Grand Rapids: Eerdmans, 1974), 148.

    2. Idea from Tim Stafford, *Knowing the Face of God* (Grand Rapids: Zondervan, 1989), 182.

    3. Horatius Bonar, "Here, O My Lord, I See Thee Face to Face" (public domain).

    4. George W. Robinson, "I Am His, and He is Mine" (public domain).

    5. George Matheson, "O Love That Will Not Let Me Go" (public domain).

    6. Idea suggested by the writings of Andrew Greeley.

    7. Idea from Kreeft, *Heaven*, 124–161.

    8. Kreeft, *Heaven*, 143.

    9. Ibid., 96.

    10. These ideas were borrowed from C. S. Lewis's *Till We Have Faces*.

    11. Lynn Hodges and Joy MacKenzie, "Heavenly Praise" (SpiritQuest Music, 1994). Used by permission.

Chapter 8
At Home with Our King

    1. Reginald Heber, "Holy, Holy, Holy" (public domain).

    2. Matthew Bridges, "Crown Him with Many Crowns" (public domain).

    3. George F. Root, "When He Cometh" (public domain).

    4. Ravi Zacharias, *The Veritas Forum at Harvard University Tape Series* (Norcross, Ga., Ravi Zacharias International Ministries, 1992).

    5. This idea is from Dr. Jack Miller, Westminster Theological Seminary.

    6. Gerstner, *The Rational Biblical Theology of Jonathan Edwards*, 558.

    7. Lewis, *The Weight of Glory*, 10.

    8. Lewis, *The Inspirational Writings of C. S. Lewis*, 382.

    9. Kreeft, *Heaven* 121–122.

    10. C. H. Spurgeon, *Spurgeon at His Best* (Grand Rapids: Baker, 1988), 95.

    11. Gerstner, *The Rational and Biblical Theology of Jonathan Edwards*, 538.

    12. Matthew Bridges, "Crown Him with Many Crowns" (public domain).

Chapter 9
Getting Ready for Heaven

    1. Stafford, *Knowing the Face of God*, 221.

    2. Samuel Rutherford, *Letters*.

3. Larry Crabb, *Men and Women, Enjoying the Difference* (Grand Rapids: Zondervan, 1991), 92–93.

4. Idea from the writings of Bishop J. C. Ryle.

5. J. C. Ryle, *Holiness* (Cambridge: James Clarke), 43–45

6. *Ibid.*, 45.

7. Amy Carmichael, *A Rose from Brier* (Fort Washington, Penn.: Christian Literature Crusade), 49, 12. Used by permission.

8. "Stillness," *The Elisabeth Elliot Newsletter* (March/April, 1994), l.

9. Douglas Kaine McKelvey, *Cattail, Fishscale, and Snakeskin* (Chicago: Cornerstone, 1994), 38. Used by permission.

10. Source for these ideas: John MacArthur, Jr., "Secrets to Endurance" message (Panorama City, Ca.: Grace to You, 1994).

11. Madame Guyon, *Spiritual Torrents*, 80.

12. Clarkson, *Grace Grows Best in Winter*, 191–2.

Chapter 10
Homeward Bound

1. Sherwood Wirt, "Remembering the Joy," *Decision* (December, 1994).

2. David Chilton, "Where is thy sting?" *World* magazine, vol. 9, no. 30 (January 7, 1995), 28.

3. Will L. Thompson, "Softly and Tenderly" (public domain).